D1479066

PROTECTOR

PROTECTOR

THE
HARRY BELLUOMINI
STORY

BY MATT HADER

Books by Matt Hader

Protector: The Harry Belluomini Story
Bad Reputation: The Complete Collection
God Loves a Madman
Two-Seven Remainder
Amika Press

Confessions of a Rock Star
Famous Monsters Music

Hardcover First Edition   ISBN 13: 978-1-956872-25-5

AMIKA PRESS   466 Central AVE #23 Northfield IL 60093   847 920 8084
info@amikapress.com   Available for purchase on amikapress.com

Edited by John K. Manos. Cover illustration by Leo Feltman. Designed and typeset by Sarah Koz. Body in Maiola, designed by Veronika Burian in 2005. Titles in Modesto Condensed and Balboa Condensed, designed by Jim Parkinson in 2000 and 2001. Thanks to Nathan Matteson.

DEDICATED TO

ROY L. "BILL" FRAKES

& WENDY FRAKES

"COULD IT BE...that the hero is one who is willing to set out, take the first step, shoulder something? Perhaps the hero is one who puts his foot upon a path not knowing what he may expect from life but in some way feeling in his bones that life expects something of him."

—P.L. TRAVERS

IN JULY OF 1992, a reckoning was set into motion in the basement garage of the Dirksen Federal Building in downtown Chicago. The murderous escapee didn't realize it, but his end was near.

IT WOULD BE A FULL STOP.

PREFACE

IN THE summer of 1992, I was working as an emergency 9-1-1 Communications Officer at the Hamilton County Communications Center (Ohio). I was three years into the job after relocating from Chicago to the Cincinnati area, where my wife's family lived. Back home in Chicago, I also worked as a 9-1-1 Communications Officer for the Evanston, Illinois, Police Department.

Before we moved to Ohio, we made our home in Chicago's Edison Park neighborhood. The neighborhood is located on the far northwest side of the city. Many Chicago police officers and firefighters reside in the area. It's a tidy, cramped, and warm little neighborhood full of mom-and-pop shops and restaurants. My wife, first son, and I lived in a cozy two-bedroom apartment on busy Northwest Highway in that sliver of the city.

After working many a midnight shift at the Evanston PD, I'd drive my gray Dodge Omni westbound on Touhy Avenue from the lakefront and then head south on one of the several confined side streets that would lead me to Northwest Highway and home. Most days, as I traveled south from Touhy onto Oriole, Olcott, Oleander, or any of the other "O" streets that lattice the area, I'd see other men and women exiting their parked personal vehicles lined up along the curbs. These public servants would be wearing police and fire uniforms or white t-shirts over dark blue uniform pants—all of us just arriving home after exhausting midnight shifts. We would nod and wave to one another, although not personally knowing each other, realizing that we all existed in the same professional circumstances.

In July of 1992, while at home in Ohio watching the nightly network news, I was shocked and saddened to learn that 58-year-old Harry Belluomini, a retired Chicago Police Department detective, had been killed in a shootout in the basement of the Dirksen Federal Building in Chicago. I didn't personally know Harry, but he was one of Edison Park's own. A few days later, I tuned into Chicago-based WGN News and witnessed Harry's funeral, which was presided over by the priests at St. Juliana's Catholic church—located at the corner of Touhy Avenue and Oketo Avenue—one of the "O" streets that I knew so well.

The shootout took place when a federal prisoner, Jeffrey Erickson, a former police officer who was on trial for a series of bank robberies in the Chicago area, slipped his restraints, got his hands on a US Marshal's revolver, and tried to escape the courthouse building. The incident shocked the residents of the Chicago area and the nation, and my fellow 9-1-1 Communications Officers in suburban Cincinnati. I recall the other people at work talking about the incident days after, wondering how such a heinous episode could occur, especially in a protected Federal Building. Unfortunately, it was one of many "innocence lost" moments America would experience over the next decade, including the Oklahoma City Bombing and the terror attacks in September 2001.

The killing of Harry Belluomini and the lack of any meaningful media stories about his courage and bravery struck a sour chord. Even though I didn't know Harry or his family, we had been neighbors, and I took his death personally.

For years afterward, the focus seemed to be on the criminal. Written articles, a television film and documentary, and even a theatrical feature film about the former-cop-turned-bank-robber known as the "Bearded Bandit" were produced, and no one seemed to pay any real attention to Harry Belluomini. Yet Harry had quite literally placed his life on the line to single-handedly save countless others and put a stop to a murderer's rampage.

When I set about to writing Harry Belluomini's story, I knew that I was perhaps in for a few years of effort to complete the project—and that was before Covid-19 took hold around the world. As with many other tasks that were begun pre-pandemic, this project experienced delays. I researched Harry Belluomini for some time before I began to cement an approach to writing the book. Even that initial approach changed over time, especially once things were moving at an accelerated clip. There were months and months of scouring sources to build a foundation for where to originate this book. But that type of research will only go so far in creating a nonfiction piece about a human being who no longer walks the earth. First, I had to meet the people who knew Harry the best—his family.

In May of 2018, I mailed a letter to Harry's daughter Anne. At least I believed that I was sending the letter to the correct Anne Belluomini. I didn't want to cold-call Anne for fear that I'd frighten her off. I couldn't have her wondering who in the world was calling and asking about her father. So I took a nuanced approach and typed a one-page letter, introducing myself, filling Anne in on a bit of my background, and advising her that I was hoping to write a book about her father.

Months passed before I received a reply. Anne Belluomini phoned. She explained that I had, indeed, sent the letter to the correct family member and that she and her sister and brother, Karen and Michael, would be interested in meeting me for lunch to discuss the proposed book. Unfortunately, Anne's mother, Milly, lived in northern Wisconsin and wouldn't be available to attend our meeting.

We met on a weekday at Moretti's, a mainstay Edison Park eatery and pub. And from the moment we began speaking to one another, we fell into the familiar conversational rhythm of people raised within a particular geographical region and who have had a similar upbringing. For me, it seemed—instantly—as if I had known Harry Belluomini's children for a long, long time.

As we got to know one another, eldest sister, Karen, cleared her throat and said, "Well, just so you know, we had you checked out by a private investigator before we met with you." She seemed reluctant to let me in on that bit of information, but I felt relief, knowing that I must've passed the "sniff test." Karen continued, "We know a private investigator who used to be a detective for the Evanston PD. He said that he knew you and that you were okay."

Once the formalities of getting to know one another were out of the way, we began discussing their father. Two hours passed in what seemed like minutes. What emerged for me in that time was that Harry's own children didn't know much about what he had accomplished while on the Chicago Police Department. Belluomini had done an excellent job of separating his family and professional lives. In that moment, I decided to keep the chapters of the book separate as well, and not to layout the piece in a succinct chronological order. So here you'll find chapters about his police work accompanied by separate chapters about his family life.

At the end of our lunch meeting, the Belluomini children agreed to provide phone numbers and otherwise help me track down some of their family members and the former detectives their father worked alongside at the Chicago Police Department. And once that lunch was over, I got to work.

While employed as a 9-1-1 Communications Officer, I was also doing my best to become a professional writer. I had a lifelong appreciation and pursuit for creating fictional stories, and I found some success beginning in the mid-90s. But I didn't believe I had the talent to tackle an intensive true-life project about the retired hero cop. Even after writing and selling screenplays and having novels published, I still didn't feel that I could write a work that would properly honor the man. So I'm still not sure if I'm worthy of creating a suitable written account of Harry Belluomini's life. But I offer up this piece in the hope that the reader will learn more about Harry and what he meant to his immediate family and his friends and colleagues.

And I want to answer a question: Why write about Harry Belluomini, his family, and his legacy now, thirty years after the tragic events that took place in the Dirksen Federal Building garage? Because selfless service and heroism never fall from favor.

1

ON JANUARY 9, 1990, the First National Bank of Wilmette, Illinois, was robbed. Bank robberies in the well-heeled North Shore suburban area of Chicago are a rarity. The perpetrator that day was calm and professional—a tall Caucasian man armed with a pistol, wearing a fake beard, ball cap and leather driving gloves. He held a portable police scanner in his free hand. The Wilmette robbery, and the ones to follow from this same offender, seemed to be meticulously planned because the offender seemed to always get away without any trouble. The police had very little evidence to work with at the beginning of the robber's spree. Still, the FBI and local police authorities would later allege that Wilmette was first bank robbery committed by Jeffrey Erickson.

At the time, the 31-year-old Erickson was about to become the owner of a small used bookstore in the western Chicago suburb of Roselle. He was an ex-police officer, having once worked as an auxiliary police officer for the Rosemont Police Department and as a patrolman for the northwest suburban Hoffman Estates Police Department before being let go for reasons never officially revealed. Sources for this book have stated that Erickson, known to authorities as the "Bearded Bandit," was allegedly let go after being caught by a supervisor doing Western-style "quick draws" with his loaded service weapon in the police department's locker room. Other sources stated that the rookie cop was fired for being "too nice" and letting speeders go during traffic stops.

Erickson was a large and physically fit man, standing 6'4" and weighing 240 pounds. He trained in police procedures and tactics, which could come in handy when taking down a bank. He was also a combat-trained Marine, comfortable with firearms, and an accomplished marksman.

The Wilmette bank job was believed to be one of at least eight such robberies attributed to the Bearded Bandit in the next two years, a suspected crime spree that would garner an estimated $180,000 for the offender. However, some close to the investigation into the Bearded Bandit's crime spree and his subsequent trial believe the number of banks he robbed to be closer to 20—the amount of money taken, unknown. But these allegations have never been proved.

2

TWENTY-EIGHT-YEAR-OLD CHICAGO Police Department detective Harry Belluomini (bell-Wah-mini) stood at the corner of North Lamon Avenue and West Altgeld Street on the evening of July 6, 1962, studying closely the imposing brick structure that sat before him. His concentration was strangely forced, in a way, not much like his usual demeanor. Harry had a naturally gregarious personality, complete with a gravelly yet booming voice. He could easily "read a room" after entering almost any situation, determining who was sincere or who was bullshitting him in just a few seconds. But this July day was so hot. The hottest day of the year so far in Chicago, and Harry was feeling its effects. He was queasy, a bit dizzy, and quite nervous, but he was here to do his task.

Harry was not a tall man—a stocky 5'9", 180 pounds, with jet-black hair—but there would be pity for anyone who physically challenged the officer. He'd once gotten into a fight with a combative suspect in front of a drug store and launched the aggressive perp, a bigger man, through one of the business' plate glass windows when the man tried to get the better of him.

Harry began his duties as a patrolman with the CPD in 1957 and had only made it to the detective ranks a few months earlier. He'd found himself in challenging situations on the job over those past scarce years, like the time weeks earlier when the detective partner he was working with failed to watch Harry's back when they responded to a domestic violence call. The angry woman inside the home launched a heavy clay flowerpot at Harry's head when the officer turned away, striking him in the face and blackening his eye. The domestic call was terrible, but he was much more nervous about what he was getting into that July evening. He was both nervous and excited.

Moments after entering the large brick structure and approaching his objective, the harsh elements of the day finally took their toll, and Harry passed out. The heat and his nerves had gotten the best of him. The priest presiding over the wedding rehearsal at St. Genevieve's church that evening turned to Milly Cutich, Harry's soon-to-be bride, and asked, "Is he drunk, or what?"

Harry wasn't drunk, but his nerves and the weight of a huge wedding, with 350 guests arriving from all over the states and Canada, plus the heat, had done what many an aggressive perp hadn't, which was to drop Harry to his knees.

Enrico Alberto "Harry" Belluomini was born at St. Elizabeth Hospital in Chicago on Sunday, October 8, 1933. Harry's father, Francesco "Frank" Belluomini, was one of six children born to Alberto and Zita (Michelotti) Belluomini of Lucca, Italy. When Frank reached adulthood in the 1920s, he traveled to the United States to visit relatives who'd already arrived in the country. However, Frank also wanted to find work. So he stayed with his cousins, the Pellegrini family, in Tacoma, Washington, for a time, worked hard, saved his money, and then returned to Lucca.

Harry's mother, Rufina Checchi of Carrara, Italy, known as Ruth, had a widowed mother named Carlotta who worked in a convent, cooking and cleaning for the nuns. That's where Ruth learned to prepare excellent meals and how to expertly sew and repair clothing. Ruth was an only child and, from all accounts, quite shy.

Once back in Italy, Frank met Ruth, and they fell in love and married. Frank and Ruth lived with Frank's parents for a short time in Lucca. There, Ruth furthered her domestic education at the hip of Zita Belluomini.

In the late 1920s, Frank and Ruth permanently immigrated to Chicago, Illinois, and they purchased a tavern at 1418 w. Madison Street, across the street from the current CPD 9-1-1 communications center. Frank worked the bar, and Ruth ran the kitchen. Shortly after they moved to Chicago and purchased the tavern, Frank and Ruth welcomed a baby girl named Loretta to their family. Harry arrived five years later.

Harry Belluomini was raised in the Austin neighborhood on Chicago's west side, mainly in the apartment above his parent's tavern. Young Harry didn't appreciate the long hours his parents had to work to hold onto their business, but he helped out by sweeping the floors and keeping the coolers stocked with ice.

Harry's lifelong friend Bill Broderick recalls that their childhood was pretty all-American. The boys loved following the Bears and White Sox. "We were about ten years old when we met. We talked about who was a better baseball or football player, stuff like that. We went to the same schools. We went to the same Catholic Church."

Broderick, who retired as the treasurer of the American Farm Bureau, added, "We were both fairly friendly with each other's parents. I'd stop by to see his parents, and he'd stop by to see mine. Harry's parents were old-country Italians. Mr. Belluomini had his own business, but then the family moved a bit further west, and he became a waiter at the Italian Village restaurant." The restaurant is still in existence in Chicago's Loop. Broderick exudes a professional disposition as he towers over others in the room. His measured words about his childhood friend are carefully thought through. The word that Broderick used over and over again to describe Harry's mother was "nice."

During those childhood years, Harry Belluomini developed as a top-flight wiseass, a skill he held onto for his entire life. Broderick noted, "You could never get the best of him if we were trying to pick on one another. Generally, you just didn't want to pick on him."

Harry was also a peacekeeper from an early age. He watched out for his friends and neighbors when trouble arose. "Harry was very strict about rights and wrongs. And he was like that even as a kid. Harry was a buddy. If you needed something, you just asked Harry, and he could ask me," said Bill Broderick.

Harry and Broderick started high school together at Chicago's St. Ignatius High School on Roosevelt Road. After a year, each transferred—Broderick to St. Mel High School and Harry to Austin High School on West End Avenue.

Milly Cutich Belluomini, Harry's widow, says that there isn't much more known about Harry's initial upbringing or the precise reason he left St. Ignatius. However, Harry told her that he constantly got his knuckles whacked with rulers by the Jesuit priests, so he may simply have been fleeing their particular manner of discipline.

To his parents' dismay, Harry eventually dropped out of high school altogether and instead found employment at Nabisco, then Motorola, in the warehouse. Harry received his GED and was drafted into the Army in the early 1950s. His assignment in the Army was maintenance, specifically on light AAA artillery weaponry. He trained at Fort Bliss, Texas, and although he wanted to transfer overseas, he served entirely stateside. He was stationed at Fort Lewis near Tacoma, Washington. Luckily, the Pellegrini family—Harry's cousins—lived in Tacoma, and he spent a lot of time with his family away from family. For his service, Harry received the National Defense and Good Conduct Medals along with his honorable discharge.

His cousin Neena Pellegrini is a Seattle-based journalist. She remembers Harry visiting her home to have dinner when she was a child. "Harry was a unique character," Neena said. "He had a big voice and a big brain. He was street smart but had a big heart, too." When Neena was a journalism student at Northwestern University in Evanston, Illinois, she stayed with Harry and his family at their Edison Park home. Neena added, "He never talked about work at home. And I remember he loved watching *Barney Miller* and *The Honeymooners* on TV. Harry was the best Monopoly player. He'd have the board memorized and know who was where and what they owned. He always had to have the car game piece for himself."

Once he left the military, Harry returned to his old inventory clerk job back at Motorola. He also applied for and tested at both the Chicago Fire Department and the Chicago Police Department. The CPD called him first, which was Harry's first choice, anyway. After graduation from the police academy, he was assigned to the Wood Street Station.

Harry had always been a very social person, and the pattern continued in his early days at the CPD. The pay for rookies was meager in the late 1950s—around $5,000 annually—and his outgoing personality was a benefit to supplement his pay. He moved furniture and made deliveries for a liquor store. Belluomini took the liquor store job for more than an extra paycheck, though. He had a standing discount on any liquor he purchased from the store, which came in handy when he and his friends hosted their social gatherings.

His childhood friend Bill Broderick said, "Harry and another buddy named Bob Bernard formed the Young at Heart Club or YAH Club. Bob was a partner in a bowling alley. Everyone who wound up joining the group was bowling in one league or another, and we just got to know one another. It got so that even when we weren't bowling, we'd show up at that bowling alley—Lorraine Bowling Alley— and just all became friends. We'd meet once a month, informally. We had a wonderful time. We'd go to different programs," he explained, meaning movies, plays, and other outings, "and then we'd go out to dinner. The YAH Club lasted twenty years."

It was a close-knit group and very particular about maintaining memberships. Broderick added, "One fella's wife dropped out for years and tried to come back in, but that didn't work out."

Nearly 30 years after Harry Belluomini's death, Bill Broderick still has constant thoughts about his old friend. "Harry was very intelligent, and when he came out of the service, he had a thing about the police department. And he found his calling for police work. I remember him talking about that a lot. That was his chosen profession. He would sometimes moan about the police job after he was on the force, but that was nonsense. It's exactly what he wanted to do."

3

"I MET HARRY through my friend Millie Reever. She knew Harry from a bowling league they were in together at Lorraine Bowl at Chicago Avenue and Cicero Avenue," said Milly Cutich Belluomini, a tall and stately woman with short blonde hair and intelligent blue eyes. Milly's warm personality and welcoming smile exude a sincere and instant familiarity when you meet her for the first time. You feel as if you've known her your entire life. I met Milly in person, after speaking by phone many times, in the spring of 2019. I had arrived early at the Edison Park diner, and when Milly, Karen, and Michael Belluomini walked through the door, Milly took one look at me and said, "You must be Matt. You look exactly like you sound."

Still recollecting how she and Harry met, Milly continued, "Some of the people in the league worked at Motorola, and Harry met my friend Millie Reever and others through his own friend, Bill Broderick. Harry and Bill started their own club called Young at Heart, or the YAH Club." Millie Reever went out on a limb, attempting to get Harry Belluomini and Milly Cutich together. She's the one who believed they were perfect for one another. "And she sure was right, I tell ya," added Milly Cutich Belluomini. "My friend Millie Reever said, 'I want to fix you up with this guy Harry Belluomini. He's so funny, and I think you two would have fun together.' And I thought, who? I don't know. I'm having too much fun on my own.'" In her youth, Milly was quite tall, a striking blonde woman with incredibly welcoming eyes. Her open personality and intelligent wit served her well as she made her way into the world following high school.

Milly's career at Motorola was just beginning, and she was enjoying the exciting single life that a bustling 1950s-era Chicago could offer her. There were new restaurants opening and Chicago Blackhawks hockey games to see. Milly loved going to her Blackhawks games. But her friend Millie convinced her, in part because the "Motorola Sweetheart dance was coming up."

The Sweethearts of Motorola was a group of young, attractive female employees, initially selected by a popular vote of all local personnel. The Sweethearts represented the corporation at large functions, both private and public. It may seem anachronistic (at best) now, but in the 1950s, being elevated to represent Motorola as a Sweetheart was the height of a young woman's professional standing in the company. The Motorola Sweetheart crown winner represented the corporation at events for an entire year after receiving her crown. A grouping of ten finalists was chosen from the first ballots cast. And an individual winner was picked each year, always announced at a well-attended Motorola family dance. Milly Cutich was voted into that top Sweetheart spot the year before she met Harry Belluomini. She enjoyed a whirlwind of activity associated with the title, helping to preside over corporate events and dinners, and on the anniversary of her winning the crown, she would be passing it along to the newly chosen Sweetheart at the next family dance. It was scheduled for September, 1959.

Milly was less than enthused. "I didn't want to bring a date to this dance because I was giving up my Sweetheart crown. But I didn't want to hurt Millie Reever's feelings, so I said okay. And I found out that Harry didn't really want to go either, but he, too, didn't want to hurt Millie Reever's feelings."

So they agreed to meet ahead of time. Millie Reever set up a casual dinner where the two could become comfortable. "So Millie and I got to The Rex, a restaurant at Chicago Avenue and Austin Avenue. Harry wasn't there yet. Millie and I went ahead and ordered dinner.

Harry finally showed up, and he said, 'You know, I almost didn't come inside because there were no parking spots until this one car pulled out right in front of the restaurant, so I figured I better go in.'"

Milly was initially unimpressed. "He had this rough little voice, you know. He was wearing this raggedy flannel shirt, raggedy pants, and he had a hole in his shoe. He'd just come from working on a furniture moving truck. That was one of his side jobs. We talked, but we just didn't hit it off. I don't know why. Harry and I didn't like one another at first at all. He was rude, and so was I." Harry was built like a middleweight boxer, and he had the don't-mess-with-me expression and disposition to match. He never wanted to be surprised and lose control of a situation, so he was always carefully searching his horizons for threats. His threat evaluation skills may have seemed like he was being too tough on some individuals, but it was always done to protect those dear to him. Of course, Milly knew none of this at the time—she saw only the rough exterior.

To appease Millie, though, Milly Cutich decided to give Harry a second chance, albeit rather unenthusiastically. "Anyway... I ended up giving him my phone number, and I don't know why. He said, 'Would you like to go to the Sweetheart dance?' I said, 'Well, okay.' He picked me up the night of the dance. We got to the event, and I just avoided him the entire evening. I was going to go out with my friends afterward. When I told him that, he said, 'No, I brought you here. I'm taking you home.' We ended up going to a little restaurant on Madison Avenue, one of those places that are open all night long. We wound up staying there until three or four in the morning. We just talked and talked and talked."

After being introduced to Harry, Milly decided that she was now in a place where she could begin to expand her own Chicago horizons a bit further. "The second time Harry and I went out, we went to a Chicago White Sox game. I was a Cubs fan, and I had never gone to Comiskey Park. I thought, sure, I'll go to the game. At the game, we had a couple of beers, and he started to fall asleep. I thought, 'My God, what's wrong with this guy? Why would he ask me out and now he's falling asleep?'" Milly wound up driving them both home after the game.

The next day, however, Harry redeemed himself. "He sent flowers to Motorola and called me at work to apologize and explained that he worked midnights as a police officer, and then he had to work in the day on the moving truck. So he had worked a double shift, and he was really tired." Harry had finally found his way to Milly Cutich's heart. "I felt bad for him after that. I accepted his apology. He wanted to make it up to me by taking me to dinner. We went to a really nice place in Gurnee. So we just started dating. It was a lot of fun. I was seeing another guy, but he was Lutheran, and I'm Catholic. Back then, you know, you married within your own religion. And I figured Harry's parents were directly from Europe, and my parents were from Europe. Harry's family spoke a foreign language at home [Italian], we spoke a foreign language at home [Croatian]. So we just sort of understood one another. A lot of people wouldn't understand that today."

Milly added, "At the time Harry and I started dating, he was also dating a flight attendant from Philadelphia. She wanted Harry to fly to Philadelphia to meet her family. She was serious, he wasn't, and that's when he broke it off with her. He wasn't ready to get married."

Not to the flight attendant, anyway.

New Year's Eve was approaching, and Milly had to choose her date for the big night—Harry or the other fellow she had been casually seeing. "Harry won, and that night, that's when I knew Harry was the one I loved."

Like countless Chicago couples of the era, Harry and Milly felt an instant bond through their shared experience as first-generation Americans. Milly recalled that Harry's reaction to learning of her Croatian background was to name three Croatian officers he worked with—and all three had lived on Milly's block at some point. Whatever the cultural differences there were between Croatians and Italians, Milly and Harry understood one another in hundreds of small ways; their life experiences overlapped. "If Harry came to my house and I was speaking Croatian," Milly explained, "Harry wouldn't mind that, and vice versa. After a while, he learned some Croatian, and I learned some Italian, and that was a good thing."

And they were bonded by worship as well. "Harry and I always went to mass. No one had to tell us to go to church. We went to mass every Sunday. It didn't matter if we were out late the night before. We went to mass. Harry was very devout. He loved saying the Rosary. His parents were very devout, as were my parents. That was our up-bringing. And that meant a lot that we had the same backgrounds. It made for a stable marriage."

All of those factors were enough to form a solid tie between the pretty Croatian girl and the determined Italian boy. But once she took a good, long look, Milly concluded that she was seeing a spe-cial kind of person. For one thing, Harry was highly intuitive when it came to dealing with people. "Harry always knew who was a bull-shitter. He could read people's eyes so fast that it amazed me. And he was usually right about the people."

But even though Harry was smitten, it was Milly who moved things along. After dating for a time, Milly explained, "I had to know where our friendship and courtship was heading. One night we met at Jim & Al's, where we always went for pizza. I told Harry that I was going to apply for a government job as a bi-lingual translator for an overseas office. I told him that I was tired of my job at Motorola, and I needed more excitement." She feigned excitement about work-ing overseas, in Croatia. Harry proposed marriage that night. As Milly sums it up, "We dated about a year and a half before we got married. We dated for six months and then planned the wedding for a year or so, saved our money."

There was fun to be had with the YAH Club before their wedding day arrived. "They always planned outings. We would do candle-light bowling. We'd go to plays and have dinners. It was a fun group of people. Harry's best friends Bob Bernard and Bill Broderick, guys he'd grown up with, both stood up for our wedding, were part of that group."

Milly's reminiscences are rich. "The Halloween parties were always fun. Everyone dressed up. At the very first Halloween party, Harry and I went together; I told him that we were going to dress up as nuns. So I made these nun costumes by sewing them myself. We looked like two legitimate nuns, the two of us, Harry and me. We were driving down North Avenue to the party, and we were both smoking cigarettes, and everyone was looking at us as if we were terrible nuns. When we got to stoplights, we'd just turn and stare at the other people in cars who were all appalled by the sight of two nuns smoking away. When we got to the party, everyone got a look at us and just laughed."

As they shored up their plans for their wedding, they attended pre-Cana consultations in preparation for a Catholic ceremony with the priest at St. Genevieve church. "Harry and I went to pre-Cana, and the priest giving the class asked me, 'What if you're in a boat with your husband and your mother, and the boat capsized? Who would you save?' I said, 'Well, my mother.'" The priest said, "No, you have to save your husband." I said, "Why? I've known her longer than him." The priest burst into raucous laughter.

"Before we got married, my family had a big wedding shower for me," Milly remembered. "Two days before that shower, Harry and his partner went out on a domestic case. His partner didn't back him up that day. And domestic cases can be the worst kind of police call. You never know what you're going to get. Well, the lady at the house they were called to was very angry and threw a huge flowerpot at Harry's head. He was lucky he didn't get killed, but he got a black eye from the incident. So he came to that wedding shower with the black eye, and everyone there was shocked. Harry asked me that day, 'What would you do if something happened to me?' And I said, 'They'd probably put a fund together for me. I'm not going to worry about it.' And you know what? I never did worry about Harry being on the police department. I would always just pray that he came home safely." Then she added a sadly prophetic concern. "But when he went to work at the Dirksen Federal Building downtown, I didn't like that because you never knew what riff-raff went through those doors."

As it is now with police work, the same was true in the early 1960s. Officers had to back each other up, especially in dangerous situations. "After that detective didn't back Harry up on that domestic case where he was struck with the flower pot, Harry never worked with that other detective again," said Milly. "He said the other detective sort of just hung back and allowed Harry to get hurt. Harry didn't talk to that man for a long, long time. I think years later; they began speaking again. But Harry thought it was important for you always to back up your partner."

As rough as Harry's public persona might sometimes appear, he could be a sweet man at his core. "Right before Harry and I got married, maybe a week before, he came to my office [Motorola] and told the office manager, 'I'm taking Milly out to lunch. She's not going to be back the rest of the afternoon.' My boss, a nice little Irishman named Dick Brennan, said, 'You go right ahead.' Harry took me to a restaurant in Barrington. It was a nice Italian place next to a pond. We just had a beautiful lunch together. It lasted a few hours. We were saying things like 'next week we're going to be Mr. and Mrs., you know.' I always thought that was really sweet. It was sort of the calm before the storm because we had a huge wedding. I had relatives coming from all over. Harry would say, in rapid fire, 'Jesus Christ, they're coming by bus, and boats, and ships and planes!' He didn't have that many relatives, and the relatives he did have, he didn't get along with some of them."

Harry and Milly got married on July 7, 1962, at St. Genevieve church in the northwest part of Chicago, in what is known as the Belmont-Cragin neighborhood. It was a big affair, Milly recalls, on "the hottest day of the year. There were 350 people at our wedding and reception. We had the reception at Harmony Hall. Harmony Hall was where my parents had their wedding reception, my older sister Helen had hers there, and my niece had her reception there. I don't think it's there any longer. It was a Polish hall, and it was a fun, fun place." Harry's childhood friend, Bill Broderick, was the best man.

They honeymooned in Canada, where the Cutich family had relatives, spending their time in Montreal and Quebec City. Milly recalled a resort in Quebec where they had made a reservation, that "looked so pretty in the brochures, but when we got there, it was a dump. It was an old ski resort. The room had only two old musty twin beds in it. We only stayed there one night, and then we had to find another place in Quebec. But we wound up having a good time."

And back in Chicago, Milly received uncompromising instruction from her mother. "After we were married, my mom said, 'You have to remember, Milly, your husband comes first before anything, that means before the children or me.' I think a lot of marriages fail because people don't think that way. You have to work at a marriage. It's the hardest job, especially if you're married to a police officer."

As newlyweds Milly and Harry lived in a cute, tiny apartment on north Long Avenue. When Milly's parents moved to northern Wisconsin, Milly and Harry took possession of her parent's home in Chicago. Milly said, "Harry was in uniform from 1957 to 1962. When we met, he was in uniform, and then right before we got married, he became a detective. And that entire time, he was working a side job on a moving truck. I was making more money than him while working at Motorola. I worked at Motorola until 1963 when Karen was born."

It would be wrong to say Harry and Milly were lovers with stars in their eyes—Harry was far too big a wiseass for that, and Milly was too practical at heart—but even their jokes underline just how deeply in love they were. For example, Milly said he often expressed his love in rhyming Italian—"Ti amo, ti adoro, di come di salsa di pomodoro"—and Milly absolutely loved it when he used the expression. But he would never tell her what it meant. "I would always ask Harry what it meant because it sounded so beautiful, but he wouldn't tell me. One day he did. He said, 'It means I love you, I adore you, like tomato sauce.' I thought, oh, you dumb shit. Just hearing him say that phrase in Italian was so beautiful, though."

4

"WE'VE FOUND that people's beliefs about heroes tend to follow a systematic pattern. After polling a number of people, we discovered that heroes are perceived to be highly moral, highly competent, or both. More specifically, heroes are believed to possess eight traits, which we call The Great Eight. These traits are: smart, strong, resilient, selfless, caring, charismatic, reliable, and inspiring. It's unusual for a hero to possess all eight of these characteristics, but most heroes have a majority of them."

—Scott T. Allison and George R. Goethals,
"Our Definition of 'Hero'"

SOME FAMILIES are known for a sense of humor, or great cooking, their business success, or whatnot. Are their shared skills embedded, programmed into their collective familial DNA, or is it a learned behavior? Whatever the source of a shared quality, the Belluomini/ Cutich family is filled with individuals who selflessly serve their communities. Through and through, Harry and Milly, their parents, and their offspring, have lived to serve their fellow humans. Over their years together, Harry and Milly influenced each other in countless positive ways. So to understand how Harry Belluomini operated, we need to examine not only the man himself but also the life of Milly Cutich Belluomini. Without Milly, Harry may have become a different man—and vice versa.

Mildred "Milly" Cutich (cue–tick) was born in Chicago on Friday, June 14, 1940, the youngest of nine children. Unfortunately, two of her older siblings died in childhood from natural causes. Four boys and three girls survived. Milly said, "I was the baby in the house growing up, but I wasn't babied."

Her family lived on the west side of Chicago near Chicago Avenue and Crawford Avenue, and she attended Ryerson Elementary School. The neighborhood was almost a caricature of the Chicago melting pot. "The neighborhood was full of a lot of Croatians, Italians, and then there was a Polish section. On my block, we had a Mexican family, a Black family, Hungarians, Irish, just a lot of nationalities. And everyone got along so well. We all respected one another. And us kids were good. We never really got into trouble. We played a lot of softball in empty lots. I loved going to school. I had a lot of good Irish teachers at Ryerson Elementary that taught us well. When we had the chance, we would go to the show at the Paradise or the Marlboro Theaters on the west side. It was fun growing up."

The Cutich home was near one of Chicago's worst tragedies, the December 1, 1958 fire at Our Lady of the Angels Catholic school in which 92 students and three nuns perished. "I attended Our Lady of the Angels Catholic Church," Milly said. "That's where the fire was in '58. I made my first communion and my confirmation there. There were two children from our old block who were affected. One was David Biscan, who died in the fire. And there was a beautiful little girl named Theresa Whitaker who was badly burned and had to undergo many, many surgeries. It was a very sad time."

Milly's parents both emigrated from Croatia. Her father, George, arrived first. He worked as a miner in Croatia and for a time in America before ultimately changing careers, but Milly said that he worked at various mines in the United States. He then had a brush with fate: He returned to Croatia to visit his family, and he had a ticket on a spectacular new ocean liner named *Titanic*. But his mother begged him to remain in Croatia for just two extra weeks, and he gave in. George sold his *Titanic* ticket to a friend—who went down with the ship. When her father finally returned to America, he went to Hibbing, Minnesota, where his cousins lived. His relatives thought they saw a ghost. "They were all shocked to see him. They thought that he had drowned in the *Titanic* disaster," said Milly.

Milly recalled how her teenaged mother remained in Croatia with her grandparents while her parents—Milly's grandparents—assessed living conditions and job opportunities across the Atlantic Ocean. Milly said her grandparents "moved to Fargo, North Dakota. And then they sent for her. My mom thought she was coming to America to go to school, but her parents had plans for her—they had arranged a marriage for my mom. That happened back then. A lot of my mom's friends had arranged marriages. So my mom got married at 16, which was not unusual back then. My dad was 20 years older than my mom. But they learned to love one another, and they had a big family."

Like so many other recent immigrants to America, Milly's parents searched out familiarity in their new homeland, which meant a particular Chicago area. Milly said, "My parents lived in a neighborhood in Chicago where other Croatians had settled. They were all in the same boat. They all had arranged marriages and big families." There are few opportunities for miners in the Chicago area (read: zero), so Milly's father found work as a coal chute operator at the old Chicago & Northwestern Railroad. But in 1949, he fell into a coal chute and was injured on the job. He spent nine months in a hospital and was never again able to do strenuous work, because, Milly said, "His legs were so badly broken."

Given the age difference between her parents and her placement as the youngest of nine births, Milly had no knowledge of her father as a younger man. "I always knew him as an older man. I really loved him. He would tell me stories about growing up in Europe. He could speak three different languages," she recalled.

Once Milly neared high school age, her family moved to the Kelvyn Park neighborhood of Chicago, and she enrolled at Kelvyn Park High School. "I graduated in June of 1958," she recalled. "I was co-captain of the cheerleaders at Kelvyn Park High School. I got along with everyone. I was voted 'most popular' freshman, sophomore, and senior years. I enjoyed my teen years."

She did not hesitate to forge a way forward for herself in 1950s Chicago. She said, "I went right to work after high school. Two weeks after graduation, I started work at Motorola. It was July 7, 1958. What's funny is that Harry and I got married on July 7, 1962. That's really weird, isn't it? We didn't plan that. It just happened that way."

Motorola became a home away from home for Milly, and the possibilities for her future seemed endless. "I loved working at Motorola," she said. "I worked for six engineers. After that, I was promoted to another office—Military Field Engineering. That was an interesting job. I worked with different engineers who worked at Air Force bases across the United States and Europe. I actually had a government security clearance when I was 19. I think that sometimes my ability to speak fluent Croatian helped me to get my next job at Motorola in the personnel department. That office was located inside the building on Augusta Boulevard, right next to Motorola's international office."

Milly's intellectual prowess, even as a late teen, was impressive. "Sometimes I took their phone calls, and I could understand a bit of Italian, a little bit of German, or Polish. There are a lot of similarities in the Slavic and Germanic languages that you can understand if you're fluent in Croatian. I knew that I couldn't afford to go to college like some of my friends who became teachers or nurses. But working at Motorola was like going to four years of college. I learned so much there. And since I was a 'Sweetheart,' I would have to attend all the important functions at the company."

Milly's cultural horizons were expanding, too. "I had to dress nicely and act nicely. I met so many interesting people at work. I was in the tennis club, the press club. I was in the bowling league. There were a lot of after-work activities. I met people from all walks of life there, important people." Important people, like the president of Motorola, Robert Galvin. "You didn't call him Mr. Galvin. You called him Bob. I remember attending a banquet, and I was at the head table seated next to him and his wife, and we were just making conversation. Bob said, 'Well, we are all waiting.' And I said, 'What are we waiting for, Bob?' He said, 'We're waiting for you to start eating.' I was the 'Sweetheart,' and they all had to wait for me to pick up my fork first. That was all part of the protocol at Motorola."

Being a Motorola Sweetheart was much more than just being a beautiful part of the company's window dressings. "I also attended some very important board meetings, and I met all the executives for the company throughout the year. The first man I worked for was Khaki Bhote, and he was originally from India. What an intelligent man. He said one day, 'Milly, I want you to come into my office so that I can dictate a letter.' I was so nervous that I took down the dictation, and I didn't know what I had written down. I thought, 'Oh, my God. I'm going to get fired.' So I came home, and I made myself so sick trying to decipher that letter. The next day I went to work, and he said, 'Milly, forget about that letter.' Well, that broke the ice with him, and I was never afraid to take dictation again."

Milly's new experiences knew few boundaries. She said, "I loved the Chicago Blackhawks. My brother John took me to my first game. I'll never forget it. It was Thanksgiving Day, 1956. I just fell in love with hockey. After high school, I wound up going to a lot of hockey games. There was a club called the Standby Club where you'd get to meet the players, and we would go on road trips to see the Blackhawks play in Detroit, Toronto, and Montreal. My photo even made the cover of a hockey magazine once. I was photographed with Rudy Pilous, the head coach of the team at that time. I was thrilled. I don't watch too much of it now. I liked when there were the six original teams... But I got to see Gordie Howe, Ted Lindsay, Maurice 'Rocket' Richard, Frank Mahovlich. One time I got to meet Ted Lindsay and Gordie Howe at a little tavern in Chicago called The Cottage. I was so thrilled to talk with them because I have a lot of relatives in Canada. My aunt lived in Canada. I knew all the little towns that they mentioned during our conversation. They were gentlemen and nice to talk with."

There's a caring and nurturing quality that pours forth from Milly Belluomini's every fiber. It's a helping nature that she effortlessly radiates and often puts into practice. It's an innate talent that comes easily to her. That incredible quality was passed down to her from her childhood hero, her mother, Helen. "My mom was a hard worker," she explained. "Everyone just loved her. She was a wonderful woman. She helped so many people. She wound up bringing over two doctors from Ukraine in the 1950s. She signed and vouched for them in the immigration process. One of the doctors became the head of Cook County Hospital. The other became our family physician. During WWII, my mom would send packages to her relatives in Croatia. She helped a lot of people. Whoever came to our house looking for help, she'd find them help. I remember being a little girl, and hobos would stop by our house, and she would feed them. I was four or five years old, but I remember that."

Although looking after her own three young children, Milly also cared for her aging parents. "My mom lost one kidney. She survived that operation, and my parents moved. They bought a farm in Winter, Wisconsin. So that's where my kids and I spent a lot of the summers in the late '60s and '70s. That was my mom's dream, to own a farm. She had some sheep and ducks and chickens and a big, big garden," said Milly. However, her father became quite ill, and they could no longer look after the land in Wisconsin. So Milly's parents had to move back to Chicago. Her father passed away in July of 1969 at the age of 85.

Milly and Helen went back to their family homeland in Croatia to offer a helping hand after a time of political strife in the country, sparked by a decentralization movement away from Yugoslav communist rule. "In 1970 I went with my mom to visit her home village. When we got there, all the villagers would just kiss her and say, 'Here comes America,' because they remembered how much she helped them during those WWII years."

5

FIVE YEARS after joining the CPD, Harry Belluomini was promoted from the uniformed ranks to detective where he worked in Area 5 in the old CPD building at Shakespeare and California Avenues on the northwest side of Chicago. That original building is gone now, replaced with a newer brick structure.

A few of Harry's fellow retired detectives, some now in their 80s, have unapologetically described this era of policing. Political correctness was nowhere on their horizons. There were no female detectives yet, and the men performed their duties in any way possible to keep their community safe from "bad guys." There's a pertinent quote, usually attributed to George Orwell from a 1942 BBC radio broadcast, that some of these same detectives often called to mind. A handful of the detectives even had the selection posted at their desks. *"You sleep safe in your beds because rough men stand ready in the night to visit violence on those who would do you harm."*

The quote was somewhat of a self-directed marching order for the difficult work that lay ahead for the detectives.

The majority of the CPD detectives interviewed were not talkative—made worse, at first, due to their guarded natures. A time-tested tactic for all professional detectives, while on the job, is to keep pertinent information to themselves and only to reveal that information when necessary or when it's required to shake up a suspect and get them talking. Knowing this about detectives, I wanted to add to this volume anything I could get from Harry's friends and fellow detectives, even the less forthcoming types. Still, the few sentences provided by some of the former CPD officers spoke volumes. If they gave me any information about Harry, it was important to them. And if their words had deep meaning for the detective, I needed to add that information here. That much is owed to them and their buddy, Harry.

Retired detective Tom Minasola, a fellow no-nonsense Edison Park-area resident, is the quintessential former police officer, seemingly hardened by the job but with a ready and welcoming smile. He recalled: "Harry was a good policeman. He had my back, and I hope he felt the same way about me, too. He was a gregarious guy. He didn't need a PA system, that's for sure." When fellow officers and Harry would go on fishing trips during their off days, no one wanted to partner with Harry in a small boat. His voice was so booming and commanding, his laugh so loud, that he'd scare the fish away. Minasola added, "It was just his nature and the way he talked. He didn't take any nonsense from nobody." Even the fish, it would seem.

A few weeks before he passed away in the winter of 2019 and in a weakened state, former CPD Commander Ed Wodnicki had this to say about his old friend and neighbor: "Harry was a good friend and one hell of a nice guy. He was a lot of fun to be around."

Frank Radke, a retired Assistant Deputy Chief of the CPD, was also a neighbor of Harry's. When we first spoke by phone, Radke didn't want anything to do with me. He thought I was working for a newspaper. But after I explained, again, that I wasn't working for any publication, Radke began to open up. He said, "I didn't work directly with Harry. I was a homicide detective. But we were friends and neighbors. We lived a block away from one another." Radke is a tall and soft-spoken man with wavy graying hair. The consensus from the other detectives gives an image of Radke as a quite professional and well-liked superior officer.

Radke enjoyed the memories of his old buddy. "If I was in an office on the second floor in the back of the old Area 5 building, you could hear Harry when he came through the front door on the first floor in front. He was so loud. He was loud and boisterous, but he was a good guy. Harry was loud and opinionated. He was not politically correct. He'd say some things that would get you in big trouble nowadays, but he never meant the words in hate. He'd say these things to sort of tear down walls between all of us. He was saying that no one is better than anyone else here." Radke added, "If *Mad Men* were a TV show about cops, the show would star Harry Belluomini."

Radke always marveled at Harry's natural talents. "Harry Belluomini was great at reading people and playing along to get what he wanted from them. He could've been on stage at The Second City. He was that good of an actor. He was rough and brusque and seemed to be in a constant state of readiness to take care of himself and others if things got bad, but Harry was also very empathetic to the public he served."

In the late 1980s, as each man's police career was winding down, Harry and Radke had a heart-to-heart moment in the office one day. "Harry said to me, 'Frank, I'm tired of this city. Maybe it's time for me to retire.' And I replied, 'Well, Harry, maybe the city is tired of you.' That got a good laugh going." He took a few moments to gather his next words, and added, "It didn't surprise me that Harry went after the gunman in the Dirksen Building. That's who Harry was."

Former detective Larry Coffey, a genial and cordial man, was another neighbor in Edison Park, and he also worked alongside Harry. Coffey started his patrol career with the CPD on the North Side near Hayt Elementary School on Granville Avenue, just a block east of Clark Street and not far from Loyola University. I jokingly told Coffey that he might know some of my older brothers. I'm one of the youngest of eight kids, and in the early 1960s our family lived across Granville from Hayt. A couple of my older brothers may or may not have caused minor trouble during their youth. Coffey said, "Wait a minute. Wait one minute. What's your last name?" After giving him my name once more, he asked, "Did your dad go to St. George's High School?" He had, and the ice was broken. My own father remembered Coffey and his sister from their old neighborhood on the North Side.

Coffey is always ready for a spirited conversation about family and friends. He's tall, clear-eyed, and particularly friendly. He now resides on a two-acre horse farm in Woodstock, Illinois, a picturesque town of about 25,000 some 40 miles northwest of Chicago. Nonetheless, he has a family lineage dating back many years with the Chicago Police Department. "I had an amazing career. It was part of my family. My grandfather was a police officer. Two of my grandfather's sisters were married to policemen." His long view of his job and his role in the community gives him a special appreciation for the kind of officer Harry was.

"Harry was a very meticulous fella, a very neat and clean guy. You had to be up to snuff when you were hanging around with Harry. [He] was one hell of a policeman. And he was quite a man. We lived about two blocks away from one another. I moved to the neighborhood first, and Harry came out to visit me and to see my house. He fell in love with the neighborhood, and he ended up buying a house [in Edison Park]. Our kids were fortunate to grow up in that great neighborhood."

Coffey and Harry knew one another nearly from the get-go after they had both become detectives. "I met Harry probably around '62, and he was working in a burglary unit with George Ruckrich." As it turned out, George Ruckrich was Harry's only permanent partner as a detective. Most days, the detectives would partner with whoever was available at that moment. Ruckrich would later enjoy a meteoric rise through the ranks of the Chicago Police Department to become a Deputy Superintendent and the third-in-command of the entire department. Coffey noted that he and Harry "worked cases together, but not on a consistent basis."

Today it can be hard to picture the way the CPD operated in the 1960s. If you were a visitor to the Area 5 offices on the second floor of the old building at Shakespeare and California, or you had run into the detectives of that era on the street, and you happened to overhear them tossing out invectives at one another, nasty little one-liners, you'd think they were all at war. But their ball-busting verbal barrages were only that. There was no authentic malice behind the vocal volleys. The detectives' love for one another manifested in how they looked out for one another. Literally willing to lay down their lives for their fellow officers. Their love ran deep. Their camaraderie was not only the glue that attached them to one another but a form of love that made the men feel safe in a dangerous job.

Coffey said, "We were friends outside of work, too, and whenever he would greet me, whether it was on the phone or in person, he'd say, 'There's that Irish asshole.'" And after Coffey would respond with a counter-zinger, the men would laugh and go about their day.

But they found practical uses for their ethnic differences, Coffey said. "Harry and I were working on some cartage cases where tractor-trailers were stolen and such. We worked on a case where a tractor-trailer was taken, and it was loaded with TVs. We needed extra people working on that case, and Harry was one of them. Most of Harry's cases were for burglaries and stuff like that. One of the suspects was an Italian kid who lived on the West Side. We went over to see if the kid was at home, and his mother answered the door. She's an Italian lady with a thick accent." The woman got one look at Harry, and it seemed as if Coffey no longer existed. "And she said to Harry, 'What you want with my boy? You're Italian. Why do you bother with us Italians?' Harry had her all wound up, [and he] said, 'I don't like thieves, and your son is a thief!' Then Coffey added, "Harry didn't pronounce the word 'thieves' the way I do. Harry would say, 'I don't like teeves, and your son is a teef.'"

Early in their detective days, Coffey and Harry had to partner up on a minor theft case. Coffey said, "Harry and I handled a case where a girl had her purse taken. It was down on the near North Side. A couple of days later, she starts getting phone calls. Harry didn't know if it was the guy who had stolen her purse, but the guy wanted to meet the girl." The young lady was petrified after receiving the phone calls. Belluomini advised the young woman to tell the caller that she would meet him in front of a Walgreens on North Avenue. Coffey continued, "As soon as the guy showed up, Harry grabbed the guy, and they started scuffling. Harry threw that guy right through the plate-glass window of Walgreens. That guy was looking for more than the money he got from the girl's purse. Man, Harry straightened that case out fast. Harry could take care of himself even though he was not that big of a man."

Coffey grew quiet as he considered the memory of his friend. He said, "Any other police officers who came into contact with Harry on the job were affected by him."

Former Chicago Police detective Tedy Nadile, a gracious and warm-spirited man, was one of Belluomini's original detective teammates. Nadile, whose movie-star looks helped him win over crime victims and crooks alike, is a dapper and intelligent man. However, his polished appearance never got past Harry Belluomini's constant, warm-hearted teasing. He remembered his friend quite fondly. "I would say it again, and again—the word 'detective' was invented after Harry Belluomini came on the job. He was the epitome of a big city detective. I could never picture him in uniform. He was cunning. People say he was loud. He wasn't loud, he was in command. He was in command of every scene. And just when the bad guys thought they had him beat, Harry would give it to them. He looked like a detective. He didn't fool any bad guys, but Harry was cunning. He was very smart, very intelligent. He went right to his last breath, being a true policeman. He died too young, but Harry died a hero."

Nadile continued, "I was a vice detective, but if we had something that came outside our scope of work, Harry would help with that investigation. In '62, I was new on the job, and I just went on the vice unit. I remember that I had just finished Thanksgiving dinner, and I got a call from a very reliable informant that some guys had just unloaded a bunch of hot suits from a burglary." Nadile explained that it was the type of case that burglary detectives handled, and he laughingly added the he wanted to unload the case onto them. "Harry showed up and said, "This better be a real job, or you're going to be eating turkey again." But we went over to where the suits were being held, and we wound up making a big, big arrest. But Harry was so mad that we called him on Thanksgiving!"

Nadile became introspective, "Harry was the policeman's policeman. Sometimes he was the hard guy. Sometimes he wasn't. But he was always a cop. Without a doubt, Harry would've been great at improvisation. He didn't need a script, stage, nothing. He was improvising every time he came on a scene." Nadile was always amazed at the fortitude his old friend would exhibit. "He was not afraid, whether it be a boss or not, to tell people what he thought of them. I was very impressed by his police knowledge. Anyone who worked with Harry would've learned how to do the job right. Harry was a good guy. A good guy. They don't make them like Harry anymore."

6

WHEN YOU first enter their tidy home on the far northwest side of Chicago and meet Joe Vuich and his lovely wife Anne Cutich Vuich, you feel like you're visiting your own aunt and uncle's place. They are gentle, gracious people who know how to enjoy themselves and laugh. They miss their brother-in-law Harry very much, but they also love to tell amusing anecdotes about the man. Of course, Harry's job was an essential aspect of his daily life, but his immediate and extended family was his most significant passion project.

Joe is a retired Chicago Fire Department engineer. He and Anne were able to relay some thoughts about Harry and what he meant to them and their family, his wiseass ways, and the warm-hearted companionship they experienced from their brother-in-law on a near-daily basis. Joe and Anne make for an adorable couple themselves, married for decades. They like to finish one another's sentences and talk in rapid succession, all the while offering up delicious homemade cookies, cups of coffee, and sandwiches to their guests.

Joe fondly remembered his brother-in-law and long-time buddy as a fair-minded police officer, one who was there to assist those in need. "There were two men Harry arrested, and for some reason or another, he didn't think about prosecuting the guys. So he wound up helping the men. And he had them up at his house one time for dinner. Anne and I were there. He realized that the men didn't need arresting more than they needed help. Harry was a damned good cop. He was a good cop. He was a good detective. He took his job seriously. Sure, he liked to play jokes and to have fun, but he was good at his job."

Harry Belluomini's mischievous ways were a constant companion at any family function. And Harry's family and friends knew how to "give as good as they got,"' Joe said. "Friends were always playing jokes on Harry, but Harry never got mad. He would say, 'I don't get mad. I get even.' And he did." Joe told a story about a family party in Canada, where a cousin named John hit Harry in the face with a pie. A year later, they were all at another family party, this time where a group from Pittsburgh carried in a big cake. As the party was being set up, John walked by with an armload of pots and pans, Joe recalls, "Harry picked up that big cake and hit John right in the face with it. Harry said to John, 'I told you I'd get even.' The people from Pittsburg got mad because Harry used their cake. They told Harry that it was specially made for their trip to Chicago. Harry said, 'That cake wasn't worth a damn anyhow. You just saved it in the freezer to bring here for your friends in Chicago.'"

Joe mused, "We went to Canada a lot. We had relatives in Hamilton, Ontario. [One time] on the way home, Harry ran out of gas on the bridge from Canada to Detroit. He would not buy extra gas in Canada. He said, 'I'm not spending any more money in Canada.' Milly said, 'Buy the gas, Harry,' but he said, 'No, no, no.' He didn't want to pay for the Canadian gas because it was more expensive. We were in two separate cars, right on top of that bridge coming from Windsor, Ontario, back into Detroit, and he runs out of gas."

Joe and Anne were in the car directly in the back of Harry and Milly, and Joe finally pushed Harry's disabled vehicle across the bridge with his car. Joe continued, "We get to the Detroit side of the bridge, and you have to stop at the customs agent's booth. By this time, Harry was fuming mad. The agent was an African-American lady, and she said, 'Do you have anything to declare?' And Harry said, 'Yes. I'm declaring war.' So I pushed him and the car through customs and when you get off the bridge in Detroit...it wasn't the best of neighborhoods. I pushed him to a gas station where he filled up, and we got going. He just would not get gas in Canada."

Joe giggled as he recalled how Harry dealt with Anne Cutich Vuich. "Harry always played jokes on Anne. My in-laws had a house up in Winter, Wisconsin. Harry knew that Anne was afraid of bugs and other creepy-crawlers. We always stayed on the second floor. Harry took a small rubber ball and stuck some thumbtacks in it. He rolled that down the stairs, and it scared the hell out of Annie. She thought it was some kind of mouse or something."

Anne added, "Up in Wisconsin at my mom's house. Harry told me to go and pick up the mail at the roadside mailbox. So I went to the mailbox, and when I opened it up, a frog jumped out at me. I screamed, and I wet my pants. Everyone else stood at the door to the house laughing like crazy."

She smiled and added, "Harry called my sisters Milly, Helen and I, 'The Bell sisters. Ding, Dong, and Dang.' My husband Joe's nickname, was 'Sogor,'" she added, explaining the pronunciation (sh-wha-gor), "which is Croatian for a brother-in-law." Harry had nicknames for his children, too. His daughter Karen was 'Brat.' His son Mike, 'Bum.' And his daughter Annie was 'Blabber.' Harry also had the endearing habit of calling his loved ones and friends 'dummy.' It was homage to that of the late master comedian Don Rickles.

Joe added, "Harry always had a comeback line. He always had to get that last word in. Our cousin John, in Canada, would make fun of Harry's legs whenever he wore shorts. John would say Harry had chicken legs...John was kind of husky, and Harry said, 'Look at your legs. They're like two tree stumps.' And after that Harry always called John 'Stumps.'"

Joe said that no topic was really out of bounds for a good ribbing. "Harry got to making fun of Milly and Anne's family. He said, 'There's not enough paper to list all the foods Italians came up with. You Croatians can put your food creation on one line: Sauerkraut.'"

The Belluomini/Vuich family duo had extraordinary events that always revolved around good food and company. Joe said, "Harry could cook. Every Christmas Eve, we'd take our kids and go to his house, and on Christmas Day, they would come to our house. That was our tradition. One Christmas Eve, Harry was making polenta. I said, 'Harry, the Croatians like polenta, too.' He said, 'It's an Italian dish.' Harry's polenta dish was constructed in the 'mush' style, completed with grated cheese and sautéed mushrooms on top."

Early in their marital relationships, the Christmas holiday was the most important for the Belluomini/Vuich households. Anne said, "On Christmas Eve, Harry enjoyed making his favorite drink, the White Russian. Milly would have a ham on or roast beef or something. We'd have one drink finished, and Harry would say, 'What the hell, have another drink.' And we would. Well, one of those times, we all got bombed, and we never ate. The food burned." Joe smiled and chimed in, "It was a turkey that burned. We all got stiff before we even ate the turkey. We were just newlyweds back when that happened."

Anne remembered how she and her sister almost got away with a little scam they pulled on Harry and Joe one game night. She said, "We all loved playing poker and Canasta right here in the house. We'd play cards nearly every Saturday or when he was off. Milly and I were partners in Canasta, and we'd blink signs at one another and cheat against Joe and Harry. But Harry figured out what we were doing right away."

Joe recalled an incident Harry had a "near-official" run-in with his son after one misadventure. Joe said, "Annie and I went somewhere, and my son was home alone. My son decided to take my big Chevy station wagon out for a ride. He didn't have a driver's license yet. So my son gets over here by Talcott and Harlem. My son was going one way in the Chevy, and who's going the opposite direction? Harry. They saw one another, and my son, Joe Jr., went right home. Harry came by later and asked my son if he was out with the car. My son said no, and he tried to lie his way out of it. Harry said, 'I just saw you, Joe.' Harry didn't chew my son out or anything. He gave him a nice little talking to."

Harry loved aggravating his sister-in-law, Anne Cutich Vuich. For instance, on snowy days, he'd like to come into her house with his cold hands and put them on her face. Anne said, "He would come to the house here and ring the doorbell over and over. Ding. Ding. Ding. I'd answer the door and say, 'What do you want?!' He'd say, 'I just want a cup of coffee! I'm going to shop at Butera's. I need a fast cup of coffee. Hurry.' He'd drink that coffee real fast and take off. I'd say to Joe, 'My God, he barely drinks his coffee, and then he takes off?'" But within Harry's pestering ways, there was a deep appreciation for his sister-in-law. Anne continued, "Whenever Harry bought something for Milly, he would think of me and buy me the same thing. So when I think of Harry, I think of this." She pointed to a foot-high wood/glass hourglass on a nearby table. "One of those times he got me this. He knew I'd like the hourglass. He'd bring over perfume and lipstick because he worked a side job in security at Carson Pirie Scott & Company, and he'd get an employee discount. He'd be out shopping with Milly, and when they purchased something, Harry would say to Milly, 'I think Anne would like this, too.' It was so nice of him. He was very thoughtful. Very. Harry would take all the kids and go tobogganing at Caldwell Woods. He would tell Milly that he'd get the kids out of our hair for a couple of hours. It was so nice of him to do that for Milly and me."

Frequently, Harry's helpful ways were utilized outside of the department and his home. For example, in the 1960s and 1970s, he was instrumental in helping to set up the Angel Guardian Orphanage fundraising picnic each year. Angel Guardian Orphanage is now Misericordia Heart of Mercy, in the Rogers Park neighborhood on the North Side of Chicago.

Joe became quiet when he continued, "I went to Harry's retirement party. He was never at a loss for words. He was witty. He was a sharp guy. One of the things he mentioned at the retirement party was, 'Now I'm in the K.M.A. club.'"

7

As NOTED earlier, George Ruckrich was Belluomini's only semi-permanent detective partner over Harry's long career. Ruckrich was paradoxically both polite and gruff when we first met at a diner in Norridge. He's a man in his 80s, but he's not a feeble man. He's retired now, but Ruckrich successfully held high commands in one of the largest police departments in one of the most violent cities in the world. His former status as a higher-up is evident in his every movement and stance. It reveals itself even in how he shakes your hand and leads you to the window-facing table at the diner. He's still in command.

As with most of the retired detectives interviewed for this book, Ruckrich wrongfully believed me to be a "newspaper guy," which is a fine occupation—but I am not. I'm a novelist, screenwriter, and storyteller. George Ruckrich fell into the mildly hostile "are you a newspaper guy?" camp at first. There's a reason that CPD detectives tend to dislike "newspaper guys." Most, if not all, detectives feel they have been professedly "burned" by a reporter or three during their careers, and their general reluctance to open up, even about their buddy Harry Belluomini, was fully on display during my initial interviews.

Most of our conversations began on the phone, and almost every one began with suspicion (at best) or outright hostility (at first). The tension didn't begin to break down until I revealed my past working experience as a 9-1-1 Communications Officer. Once that bit of information was on the table—that I had worked for a total of twelve years in "their business"—the retired detectives opened up a tad more. And that hesitant thawing was also the case when I was on the phone with George Ruckrich. But his instincts as a detective led him to trust his quick assessments. He sized me up immediately and concluded I was okay after thirty seconds worth of initial chitchat in the diner. Like Belluomini, Ruckrich carries himself like a former boxer. Only at nearly six feet, Ruckrich is a bit taller. He's confident in his movements, polite but still displaying an authority that he developed while a police officer. His eyes slowly scan as new arrivals step into the diner, probably looking for threats. It's a practice that will never go away for him or any former police officer.

Ruckrich and Belluomini partnered for nearly six years during the 1960s, primarily investigating burglaries and safe heists, working out of the Area 5 Burglary Unit. "We were what the department called the 'safe car,' meaning we went after safe crackers," explained Ruckrich. Unfortunately, in the 1960s era of Chicago crime lore, business was brisk for the detectives. But that was perfectly fine with Ruckrich and Belluomini.

Harry started as a detective a couple of weeks before Ruckrich. As a consequence, whenever they headed out in their department-issued vehicle to perform investigations, Harry would tell Ruckrich, "As the senior officer in this car, I'm calling the shots," Like an "older" twin who happened to leave the birth canal first. The men would get a good laugh out of that running gag.

"Harry was great at writing reports, had a fantastic memory, a photographic memory, but was a shit driver," Ruckrich said. "So I drove all the time. We could be driving down the street at 2 AM, and a car would pass. Harry would see the front plate of the car for a millisecond and say, 'Hey, that's so-and-so. We arrested him a few years back for burglary. Turn around. Let's see what he's up to.' Belluomini's memory was so good that often he'd see a car drive by and instantly recall what crimes the driver had committed in the past, or whether they'd been recently paroled, or even if they were a wanted felon.

Although they weren't even 30 years old when they met, Belluomini and Ruckrich were working at the top of their game, which allowed them a lot of freedom to go about their work in any way they saw fit. "Harry and I were mostly left alone to do our job because we were very good at the job," said Ruckrich. "We were aggressive and made arrests. Harry wouldn't let any little detail go. If he thought a minor detail could lead to a bigger find, he'd chase after it. And I would say, 'Come on, Harry. I want to go home!' But Harry was a bulldog."

According to Ruckrich, Harry was a professional "beefer." "He complained about everything. One time he was talking about quitting the police department and moving to Milwaukee to get a city job there. He loved Wisconsin, so that made sense, but right at the time he was talking about moving, the entire city of Milwaukee went out on strike."

Ruckrich looked out the window and grinned, "I used to call him 'the water buffalo' because he hated the heat. We had no A/C in the police cars back then, and when it got hot in the summertime, Harry would make me drive to this park that had a big fountain in it. Harry would walk over to that fountain and cup water in his hands and splash his face and neck so he could cool off. He was a cold-weather kind of guy. That's why he loved Wisconsin so much."

Driving through Belluomini's old Austin neighborhood on the west side of Chicago was always an interesting trip, Ruckrich said. Harry was something of a local celebrity. "The locals on the street would call out to him—'Harry Bell-Wah-Mini!' His old neighbors loved the guy," said Ruckrich.

But Harry had also grown up around people who wound up on the wrong side of the law. He had a deep disgust for Italian-Americans who had joined Chicago's Outfit. As Harry's friend Bill Broderick said, Harry had hard and fast rules about rights and wrongs. Outfit associates were on the wrong side as far as Harry Belluomini was concerned.

Ruckrich recalled one run-in with an Italian mobster. "We pulled over some Outfit guy. The man was driving a fancy car. When he got out of the car, he was all smiles and wearing an expensive suit. As he put on his fancy hat, he said something like, 'Hey, guys, how ya doing? I'm Joe Bananas.' Or some other stupid nickname. I can't recall the exact name. Harry went right after the guy and said, 'I'm Harry Grapefruit.' The Outfit member never counted on Belluomini being so aggressive and found himself with his face pressed against the hood of his fancy car."

In June 1964, Ruckrich and Belluomini had a deadly run-in with an ex-con with an extensive burglary arrest record. According to a June 17, 1964, *Chicago Tribune* article titled "Stolen Auto Suspect Shot During Chase," a 25-year-old man named James Caparusso was shot and killed by Ruckrich after he and Belluomini stopped the suspect in a stolen car and a foot pursuit ensued. The suspect was initially pulled over in a vehicle on Grand Avenue, but once stopped, he fled on foot and was pursued by the two detectives to a trucking terminal lot on north Union, about two blocks away. There the suspect lunged at Ruckrich from a hiding spot behind a parked trailer. Caparusso then attempted to grab detective Ruckrich's gun, but Ruckrich managed to get a shot off, striking the convicted felon in the head. After the shooting, a loaded revolver was discovered near the parked trailer where the suspect had been hiding, and another loaded gun was located in the stolen car left on Grand.

Milly Belluomini had this to say about the Caparusso shooting, "Harry would never talk to me about that incident. I didn't even know about that until later." She explained, "Harry never told me what was going on, where other detectives would tell their wives, you know, the cases they were working on. Harry would say, 'That's not for you to know, Milly. That's my job.' When Harry walked out of that police station every day, he left that behind, and he came home to his family." During our time together in the Norridge diner, Ruckrich never spoke of the Caparusso shooting, either.

That wasn't their only moment of shared risk. On September 25,

1964, the Almira Savings and Loan Association at 3434 W. North Avenue was robbed. A responding CPD detective witnessed as the four robbery suspects left the bank building on foot, and he directed, via his car radio, the route of travel two of those suspects were taking. Harry Belluomini and George Ruckrich had been in the area on another matter but responded when they heard the radio call.

It was a dangerous situation, where one of the bank employees had been pistol-whipped. Nevertheless, Belluomini and Ruckrich quickly apprehended two of the suspects as they hid under a porch of a home a block from the bank. The performance of Belluomini, Ruckrich, and the other CPD detectives drew a commendation from the FBI. Special Agent in Charge M.W. Johnson wrote on October 6, 1964: *The teamwork, aggressiveness, and initiative in answering an alarm immediately, although these officers were engaged in other investigative matters, resulted in a successful early solution to this armed robbery. These four vicious robbers had pistol-whipped one of the employees and had locked all the employees in the vault before leaving the association. It is indeed a pleasure to commend these officers for their performance and actions in this matter.*

The Belluomini/Ruckrich partnership and aggressive tactics would churn up other dangerous, life-and-death incidents, Ruckrich recalled. "One very snowy night, we were tailing a man and woman who were notorious pharmacy-safe crackers. They'd break into a pharmacy safe and take all the narcotics so they could use some and sell the rest." It was common knowledge to officers at the time that the couple traveled with their small baby in the car with them. "We learned later that they had gotten away with a few burglaries even after the police had pulled them over by hiding the drugs in their baby's diaper. No police officer is going to check a baby's diaper," said Ruckrich.

Belluomini and Ruckrich followed this couple through the snow to a motel on Harlem Avenue on the city's northwest side. Ruckrich said, "It was one of those no-tell motels. It's still there. The motel was across the street from a big pharmacy. This happened in about

1966. The couple and their baby checked into the motel, and we figured that they were going to get a room, break into the pharmacy,
go back to the room, get some sleep and leave the next morning. We
didn't have a radio in the detective car that night, so we found a pay-
phone and called our supervisor and asked if we could get a room at
the same hotel so we could set up surveillance on the couple."

After Belluomini and Ruckrich got the go-ahead from their boss,
"Our supervisor sent over two other detectives to help out," said
Ruckrich. "We'd take turns watching the pharmacy burglar's motel
room door. While one of us kept an eye on the burglar's room door,
the others would play cards or take a nap."

Directly next to the motel was a large cafeteria called the Holloway House. The well-liked cafeteria was closed for the night. "It's
not there anymore," said Ruckrich. "But when it was open, it was a
very popular spot to eat. Back then no one used credit cards when
they went out to eat. It was all cash. It was a cash-rich business, and
I remember this happening around the holidays, so there was probably a lot of money in the safe there. It was about 2 AM, and I was on
watch. I kept my eyes on the burglar's motel room door and window,
but all was dark and quiet. The burglars were probably sleeping."

Movement on the edge of the darkened Holloway House's building, though, caught Ruckrich's attention. He said, "I saw a man
dressed all in dark clothing in the gangway on the side of the cafeteria, peeking around the corner. The guy backed up and then the same
man and another man, also dressed in dark clothing, walked out
into view. Each was carrying what looked like a heavy canvas bag
of tools. The first man angled towards the front door of Holloway
House. The other guy went around to the back and out of my view."

Ruckrich alerted the other detectives and directed Harry and one
of the other detectives to go around to the back of the Holloway
House cafeteria. Then, Ruckrich and the other detective would take
the front door. Ruckrich grinned as he recalled the scene, "I quietly
stepped through that deep fresh snow and up to the suspect who
was working away at the front. He was trying to pry the front door

open. I stuck the barrel of my .38 revolver in his ear and said, 'Don't move, motherfucker'—and that guy gave it all up. He immediately told me his name, the name of his partner out back, and where their car was parked. All of it."

Ruckrich cuffed the burglar, and as he, the suspect, and the other detective made their way to the back of the building through the deep snow, he said, "We heard a muffled gunshot." When Ruckrich got to the back door of the cafeteria, he discovered that Harry had shot the other suspect in the abdomen after the man pulled a gun on him. "It was a serious wound, but the guy survived," said Ruckrich.

That's when all of the detectives at the Holloway House heard police sirens angling their way in the darkness of that snowy night —a lot of sirens. "We all sort of relaxed a little. More help was on its way from the Chicago PD," recalled Ruckrich. But as the several police cars started pulling up to the Holloway House cafeteria building, the detectives began to notice that the cars arriving were distinctly Norridge Police cars and not CPD cars. "We were in the suburb of Norridge and not within the city limits of Chicago...and we were now in big trouble," said Ruckrich.

Chicago is a crowded metro area. The transition from the city's streetscapes into the first ring of its suburbs is almost invisible. The only difference when you cross the boundary, generally speaking, is a change in the streetlights and the street signs. And that isn't true in every case.

Ruckrich shook his head, "We were so hot on the safe-cracking couple that we hadn't noticed we were out of our own jurisdiction. By a block. And Harry had shot a guy." To the responding Norridge Police officers, Belluomini, Ruckrich, and the other two CPD detectives were heroes for stopping a burglary in progress. However. "When we got into our own office the next morning, we were in big, big trouble. We were maybe looking at being fired," said Ruckrich. A few hours after repeatedly getting chewed out by their bosses, though, the Norridge Police Chief hand-delivered a complimentary letter to those same bosses telling them how appreciative the city of Norridge was for their detectives' efforts. Ruckrich smiled, "That letter saved our ass. The guy Harry shot was a real professional burglar, too. We heard afterward that he would have a bunch of combination locks affixed to his bed's headboard at his apartment. He'd lay in bed and practice opening those locks by working over his head and backward and never looking directly at the locks. He'd work by feel and open those locks over and over again. These were the type of people we were up against."

As we spoke, Ruckrich recalled one episode after another from the late 1960s. "We were following a brother and sister robbery team from Tennessee. They were known to be violent and heavily armed, and they were staying at a third-floor apartment at the corner of Belmont and Kimball on the northwest side. There was an old Italian immigrant who was the building manager, and we set it up with him to clear the building so that we could arrest the brother and sister in a peaceful manner. We told the building manager that everything would be okay and no one would get hurt. We had a team put together to surround the offenders and to take them down."

The violent brother and sister robbery team had other ideas, Ruckrich said. "On the day we hit the apartment, the brother and sister opened fire on us, and we had a long shootout. No one got hurt, and the suspects finally surrendered. The building manager was in his own apartment when the shit hit the fan, and a round went through his wall and into the pantry he happened to be standing in. The bullet caught a can of peas on his pantry shelf, and the building manager said the water leaking from the can ran down the back of his neck as he cowered in the pantry. He thought he'd been shot, and the can juice was blood. He was fine, but when he came out to talk with us, he said in his broken English, 'You said everything be okay.' He pointed to his wet neck and continued, 'This is okay?!'"

The detective partners had some fun on the job, too. "A year or two after we made detective, the department had a memo come from on high about having all officers pick up trash from the streets when they were out on patrol. We thought, what kind of bullshit is this? We're putting bad guys away, and we don't have time for this shit. A couple of days after the memo came out, Harry and I braced some Streets & Sanitation guys and borrowed a couple of their uniforms," said Ruckrich. Complete with long wooden sticks with nails in the end for picking up paper and oversized, shoulder-slung canvas garbage bags. "Harry and I wore those garbage-man uniforms to roll-call the next day. When our sergeant saw us, he said, 'What the fuck are you guys doing?' Everyone laughed. We didn't get in trouble because we were good at what we did every day. No one really wanted to discipline us."

Belluomini and Ruckrich had a creative approach that they'd use when trying to get sneaky suspects' attention. Ruckrich continued, "We were trying to get this high-end burglar in for questioning on a string of crimes we'd been investigating. The guy lived in a fancy Skokie neighborhood, and he was never home. We got sick of his family covering for him and saying he wasn't home when we knew he was, but we didn't have a warrant to get the guy because we needed more information before we could arrest him." That was the night they crafted a simple, effective plan. "Harry and I got an idea on how we could get the guy to come and talk with us," Ruckrich said. "We found some old cardboard and rigged a big sign together using the cardboard and a magic marker. We planted the sign in the guy's yard just before the sun came up. It read, 'Call me. Harry Belluomini, CPD [and his desk phone number].' That guy didn't call—he came into our office an hour later. So that worked out."

Belluomini and Ruckrich succeeded in part because they were always able to roll with whatever particular situation they had been handed. Ruckrich said, "One time, we were given information about a guy selling a lot of drugs from the second-floor apartment of a building directly across from a Chicago firehouse. The fire department allowed Harry and me to set up our surveillance from the second floor of the firehouse." As they watched the suspected drug house, they noticed many people going up to the building and entering another apartment on the second floor—across the hall from where the drugs were dealt. "Every time the other apartment door opened, we could see racks of suits. Literally. Like racking from a retail store. The place was filled with new suits. We called around and discovered that an entire semi-trailer load of suits had been stolen a day or so before. We got a warrant and took the place down. That was the second time Harry and I discovered a separate crime while investigating another one," beamed Ruckrich.

As we wound up our conversation, Ruckrich became reflective. He said, "After those nearly six years of working with Harry, I put in for the sergeant's exam. I needed the extra money, is all. Some people thought I was ambitious, but it was always about making more money for my family. Harry never wanted to take the tests for advancement. He just wanted to keep his head down, do his job, and go home to his family. He loved his family very much. When I got my promotion, I took over a tactical arrest team, and we'd go after some real bad guys. Harry sort of worked as our go-to detective for getting warrants and doing research, things like that. He was kind of our 'on call' detective. Harry separated the job from his family and his family from the job. And even at the many police parties we went to, Harry would never talk about the job. His family came first."

8

BOTH MILLY and Harry grew up on Chicago's West Side, which has historically had a reputation as a breeding ground for undesirable types. They lived near the neighborhood that nurtured members of Chicago's Outfit, and for ordinary, working-class Chicagoans in the area, the criminal organization often intruded on their daily lives.

"When we were first married," Milly recalled, "I worked a part-time job at a dry cleaner on Chicago Avenue. I worked there two or three days a week, from about nine until noon." At first, Milly never seemed to have any issues working in the dry-cleaning business and felt it was a great place to earn some cash to supplement their household income. She said the owner "was very, very nice, but that was where the Mafia brought their cleaning in. One day, [the owner], in his thick Italian accent, said to me, 'You. You go upstairs.' I asked why, but he never answered and told me to go. That was when some of those Mafia guys came in."

But interaction with Outfit members turned out to be impossible to avoid. Milly continued, "One day, two Mafia guys came in when I was at the counter. One of them said, 'Oh, we hear that your husband is a detective.' And I told them yes, he was. He next asked, 'Is your husband's name Harry Belluomini and his partner is George Ruckrich?' And I said it was. They just nodded and never said anything else. At the time, I thought that was really funny. I didn't tell

Harry right away, but I did tell George a couple of days later. I called him because it started to bother me, and Ruckrich said, 'Milly, don't work there anymore. Harry and I arrested those guys. And you never know. To retaliate against us, they could put a bomb in your car.' So I never did go back to the cleaners after that. I didn't tell Harry until quite a long time after that happened. I really liked [the owner] and his wife, but I didn't want to put my life in jeopardy working there."

Just the same, the experience fascinated her. "They had a truck driver who would bring in the clothes from River Forest, where a lot of the Mafia guys lived. I had to go through those clothes making sure nothing was left in the pockets, but those clothes were absolutely beautiful. When the clothes were cleaned, I had to hang them perfectly so that the sleeves hung a certain way. We cleaned both the men and women's clothing, and wow, they were beautiful. Working there was an experience." She added, "I never found anything in the clothing except soiled hankies. I worked there for two months, and that was it."

Her negative memories revolve more around corruption within the CPD than with organized crime, she recalled. "In the late '60s, I received a phone call at home. A man said something like, 'If you come up with...five thousand dollars, Harry could become sergeant.' And I said, 'Listen, if I had that kind of money, we'd put a down payment on a house. And there's no way that my husband would do what you're asking.' That voice was so familiar. It was a man, but I couldn't place a face to the voice. Until this day, I still think about that call." Once Milly shut the man down, there were no further mysterious calls. Milly knew that Harry wasn't one to delve into things that didn't directly concern him. That type of corruption-busting was the bailiwick of the officers in Internal Affairs. Harry kept his head down and did his job, went home, and cared for his family. Milly said, "I don't think that Harry knew exactly that there were officers doing illegal things. Maybe he thought they could be doing things. I think that Harry didn't want to cause excitement over things he wasn't sure about. But when I think back to that time now, there were certain guys he'd stay away from. [But] Harry tried to remain friendly and respectful with everyone in the long run."

Milly, however, had additional worries of her own and voiced them to Harry. She said, "I would ask about things that bothered me, and Harry would tell me not to worry about it, 'Let's just worry about ourselves,' he'd say. I think he knew that some things were [criminal], but he'd never [go into detail]. I know that [other officers] would meet at Joe the Tailors, and I don't know if they were good guys, bad guys, I really don't know. But Harry knew things were going on there, and that's where those guys would meet."

In October 2000, the *Chicago Tribune* published an exposé about CPD corruption. The article was titled "Sordid Ties Tarnish City Police." The story revolved around a crowded little tailor shop located at 5257 N. Central Avenue. According to the article, that shop, owned by Joseph Rozenberg, a man who had escaped a Nazi labor camp in France and found his way to America, was the alleged meeting place between Outfit members and CPD top brass. The *Tribune's* information was obtained from a joint FBI/CPD Internal Affairs investigation of Outfit members meeting in the tailor shop with a few of CPD's top cops, particularly Superintendent Matt Rodriguez.

George Ruckrich was retired when the article was released, but he was also mentioned as visiting the tailor shop. Ruckrich's own home was less than a mile away. One could contend that Ruckrich may have simply been dropping off his clothes for cleaning or repair. No further law enforcement action came as a result of the exposé. Superintendent Rodriguez had resigned three years before the report was published. That resignation came after it was learned that one of his close personal friends was an Outfit associate.

There was a strange ethical gray area, it seems, within the department, where officers had to wrestle with the collision between their trust and respect for fellow officers and the fact that some of those officers ended up accused of criminality. Milly added, "A man who was one of Harry's pallbearers, he had a beautiful home. We'd go there for Christmas parties, and I thought, 'My God, how do they afford such a beautiful home.' And Harry would say, 'Don't worry about it.' It turned out that that other officer went to prison later."

George Ruckrich, in a bit of unprovoked conversation at the Norridge diner, tossed out a couple of comments at the end of our discussion about the detective Milly mentioned, former CPD Chief of Detectives William Hanhardt. Ruckrich seemed genuinely hurt by what had transpired for his former boss and coworker. Ruckrich said, "He was a good man and a great cop." Ruckrich explained that apparently, Hanhardt may have been in gambling debt, and he possibly started committing crimes himself to pay off those debts. Hanhardt wound up serving a lengthy prison sentence after being convicted of running a theft ring that targeted several traveling jewelry salespeople. Hanhardt passed away in December of 2016. Ruckrich concluded, "I was heartsick by what became of Hanhardt."

9

HARRY BELLUOMINI was a professional investigator to his core. And he appreciated it when he and his fellow detectives completed their work at the highest levels of competence. There would be no small detail ignored when performing their job. Belluomini would make sure that new detectives got 'on-boarded' and up to speed on proper tactics as quickly as possible, so that meant he would make sure he showed newly promoted detectives the professional ropes himself when he could. It would be a task that he'd accomplish many times over during the second half of his CPD career.

Jack Lorre, now retired, was one such officer. Lorre, who started with the CPD more than a decade after Harry Belluomini, said, "I came on in 1970 and retired in 1997. Harry was just so well-liked. I was partnered with him one day, and he said, 'Come on, kid, we're leaving.' So we get out to the unmarked car, and Harry tosses me the keys and says, 'Here, kid, you drive.' So I start the engine, and Harry says, 'Look at this thumb.' And he shows me his left thumb. 'When this thumb moves to the left, you turn left. When it moves to the right, you turn right. You got that, kid?' That's how he introduced himself to me. He was just kidding, of course. We laughed, and I never took offense to what he did."

Lorre continued, "So we were driving later in that day, and we stopped back at the district building to see if anyone needed anything." It was the time well before cell phones. Lorre said, "When you walked into a district building with Harry Bell," using Belluo-mini's commonly used nickname among his fellow officers, "it was like you were walking in with a movie star. He knew everyone, and everyone knew him. Commanders, captains, everyone."

Lorre laughed as he recalled another moment he had with Harry. "We were working a case, and I had the file in front of me. I was going to call the victim to get more information. So I'm talking to the victim, and Harry grabs the case file from my desk, sees the victim's name, and he takes the phone right out of my hand. He says into the phone, 'This is Harry Bell. Don't you ever call the police again, or I'm going to come out and arrest you.' Harry hung up, and I said, 'Harry, what are you doing?' Harry said, 'He's a burglar. I've arrested him five times. He's just making this story up.' But here's the thing, Harry never treated anyone like that unless it was called for. He was an experienced burglary detective. That guy never called back or complained. Harry was right."

It's a well-known fact that police officers of all stripes tend to socialize with their ilk. Not one hundred percent of the time, of course, but often enough. There's a comfortable shorthand that officers enjoy when they gather outside the department. They don't have to explain anything to anyone about what they do, especially with non-officers, and that sits well with most police officers, especially when they're trying to unwind and get away from the "office." Lorre said, "Harry always organized baseball games, where everyone would go to the park after work and play some ball. Everyone would bring their family. Harry would bring his children. He organized picnics with the unit, so we'd go there with our children and our wives."

Evident to Harry's fellow officers, when they were working side-by-side with him, was one simple universal truth. "Harry adored his family. He was one of those guys who wouldn't go out for a beer every day after work. He wouldn't do that. There was a bar right next door to where we worked. Harry always just wanted to be home with his family. It's a shame that he wasn't able to spend these past years with Milly...because they were a great couple," said Lorre.

Lorre continued, "One day at the station, Harry's sister called and told him that her son needed to see an eye doctor, a specialist. All I could hear was Harry's side of the conversation. Apparently, it was a complicated situation, so Harry said he'd call the doctor for his sister. Again, I'm only hearing Harry's side of this conversation when he calls this eye doctor. All of a sudden, Harry's on the phone, and he says, 'Two months? The kid will need a white cane and a cup! My nephew needs to see someone sooner than that.' He would say blunt things all the time, but he was right."

Lorre recalled in particular how Harry's experience deflated a fantasy "big case" the young detective worked. "We had a kidnapping that we had to investigate. You have to understand. I'm a 26-year-old kid. I had hardly been out on the street at all. This was exciting! A kidnapping! That's a big thing. So Harry and I go to see the victim, who said that she was kidnapped and kept hostage before being released. So we're talking to her, and Harry was very good with people, especially victims of crime. All of a sudden, Harry says, 'You weren't kidnapped, were you? You were with your boyfriend, weren't you?' And she said, 'Yeah, you're right, I was.' She just didn't want her parents to know that she had spent the night with her boyfriend. But I was thinking, 'Boy, you just blew my kidnapping case, Harry!' I thought I was going to have a big caper, you know? Harry just knew. He was a great detective. You could tell who the good detectives were, and you picked up stuff from them. Harry was one of those detectives. When I look back, I always think of the detectives I've learned from, and Harry was one of those great detectives for sure." Lorre and his co-workers would go on to help show newer detectives the ropes, so Harry's ways live on even to this day among the CPD ranks.

Retired CPD detective Stan Golucki, like Jack Lorre, met Harry years after Belluomini joined the police force. Golucki was one of the new detectives that Harry had a large part in coaching over the years. By the time Harry met Golucki, Harry had been appointed to be a General Assignments detective—meaning, he would investigate pretty much any crime in his geographical area except for homicide. Golucki communicates from the heart. He is an extremely personable and friendly man willing to speak freely about Belluomini. Another officer who lived in Edison Park, Golucki was called "Hutch" among the officers' kids in the neighborhood because he resembled the actor David Soul, who played the Hutch character in the TV cop show *Starsky and Hutch*.

"I first met Harry in the early 1970s when I first made detective," Golucki recalled. "We were assigned to Area 6 at Damen and Grace. I worked as a sworn officer for 33 years, and then I retired but was hired back as a civilian investigator in the personnel division. In the 51 years I worked for the CPD, I had never met any other officer as professional as Harry Belluomini. He was the best detective I ever met."

Golucki particularly enjoyed Harry's wit with other officers. "Harry was a funny guy. He'd like to aggravate his co-workers sometimes. I'd get to work, and he'd talk out of the side of his mouth with this even gruffer voice and say, 'Hey, Polack, how you doing?' And I would laugh and say, 'Leave me alone today, Harry.' And he would reply, 'Come on. Let's go for a cup of coffee.' I loved that guy."

Ribbing within the group of CPD detectives was an ongoing proposition. Golucki said, "The only thing Harry would really get pissed-off about was when I'd tease him about the color of his hair. He had jet-black hair. And a full head of hair. I kept busting his balls, asking, 'What kind of shoe polish do you use to keep your hair looking like that?' I had never seen a hair out of place, and I had never seen a gray hair. How was that even possible? He'd reply to my teasing by saying, 'Hey, fuck you, Polack!' All kidding aside, I had nothing but respect for that man." Golucki even asked me, in all seriousness, to tell him about anyone who worked with Belluomini who had anything bad to say about the man.

Golucki paused briefly, gathering his thoughts before he continued to discuss his old friend, "Harry was a little rough around the edges, but deep down, he had a heart of gold. He was kind of an organizer for our unit. He kept everyone together." Golucki continued, "We had wives and kids, and we didn't always socialize together, but

Harry would make sure we did things together. He used to organize a picnic every year at Griswold Lake," a local resort lake in McHenry County far to the northwest of Chicago. "We'd all go. We'd get the kids, the wives, and we'd barbeque and have a good time. He also liked to get us all together at a little pizza place, and they had a juke-box with the Jim Croce song 'Bad, Bad Leroy Brown.' Harry loved that song. I can see him with a slice of pizza and a beer in his hands and singing along to the song."

Attempting to lord over a group of independent-minded detectives is a delicate balance for any commanding officer to pull off. According to Golucki, most of the other detectives in their group would follow Harry's lead over their official supervisor. He said, "We were in General Assignments. We handled a little of everything. Harry was not a brown-nose. He didn't kiss any boss' ass. He was independent. He was kind of a bulldog sometimes. He didn't give a damn about some of the bosses. We had a new lieutenant in General Assignments that came from Homicide. He had us fill out these forms with a lot of unnecessary detail as if we were investigating a homicide when we were actually investigating a property crime. You know, things like what were the lighting conditions at the crime scene? What were the weather conditions? Now, if somebody pulls away from a gas station without paying, what difference does it make, the lighting and weather conditions? Did you get a license plate number? That was all we needed. But this new boss wanted us to go into detail for a lot of things that were unnecessary." He shook his head. "I called a lady up because she was an armed robbery victim, and I asked her if she was married. It's a question on the new form we were required to use. She got upset and asked, 'What does that have to do with anything?' And I tell our new boss that the lady got angry, why are we asking these types of questions? She thinks I'm hitting on her, and I'm just trying to do my job. Now here's how Harry would handle that type of situation. A lot of the work was done on the telephone. Harry had a case and had to call this one man up who was part of the case. Using the new boss's form, Harry asked the guy what his birthdate was, and the man on the other end got angry and asked why Harry needed his DOB. Harry replied, 'Because I want to send you a fucking birthday card. What do you think? It's for my report.' The boss was sitting right there, and he said, 'Harry, you can't talk that way to people.' Harry replied, 'I wouldn't be asking these stupid questions if it wasn't for you asking us to ask these stupid questions.' Harry wound up moving areas not long after that."

Stan Golucki and Harry got into their share of dangerous duty as well. One example came in the 1970s when they investigated extortion. It was a case where Harry and Golucki volunteered to place themselves squarely into the middle of a risky situation. Golucki said, "There's a place called The House of Glunz on Wells off of Division. I believe it's the oldest wine or liquor store in the state of Illinois. Mr. Glunz got a phone call from an unknown person stating that they were going to burn his building down if he didn't come up with $50,000. Mr. Glunz was an older man who emigrated from Europe. He said to the caller, 'What do you want, a check or cash?' And then he hung up on the caller." But the calls kept coming "Glunz finally called the police," Golucki went on, "and we were assigned the case. It was difficult, at that time, to put a tap on the phone because we never knew when the people would call again, and they wouldn't stay on the phone long enough [to successfully track them]. Harry and I decided that we would stand-in for Mr. Glunz's sons, and we would be the ones to drop the money for these extortionists. Harry wanted to be the person who met these people in the parking lot where the drop was to take place. So here came the car, and the bad guys smelled a rat. I was in an observation vehicle, but the bad guys had changed the location for the drop at the last moment, and we weren't in a good position. The cameras we had set up weren't in the right position due to the drop location change. I heard gunfire, and we later discovered that the bad guys tried to run Harry over. Harry had emptied his gun into the vehicle, which we found abandoned a couple of blocks away. There was no blood in the vehicle, so Harry probably didn't hit anyone, and we never figured out who the people were. They never called Mr. Glunz again. But it was scary for the Glunz family."

Golucki grew quiet once again as he remembered his old friend. "Harry had balls. He didn't take shit, and he was loyal. He was a stand-up guy." Then he told a story about a side job he took early in his career to help make ends meet. "One of the other officers was running security for a motorcycle show at the old Chicago Amphitheater down on Halstead Street. They hired us to do security because a lot of the people coming to the motorcycle show were...Hell's Angels and the like. Our job was to make sure they didn't cause any problems, to search them, and to make sure they didn't have any weapons on them."

Harry was not associated with this part-time arrangement. Still, he would be deeply involved a few weeks later after a confrontation erupted between the off-duty officers and the wealthy man running the motorcycle show. Golucki said, "It was just me and a couple other coppers working there. And at the end of the week, we were supposed to get paid. But one of these other coppers got drunk that night, and the wealthy man running the show refused to pay him. Now they were in a side room, and I was out in the general area, but I heard their argument. There were threats being made, and then I heard a tussle, and that was it. The drunk copper walks out and leaves, I go into the office to get paid, and the copper running the show has this big mouse on his eye. So I can only assume that the drunk copper punched the copper running the security detail. The drunk copper also threatened the millionaire who was running the whole motorcycle show. So I got my money, and I left."

Unfortunately, only days later, a criminal complaint about the incident was filed with Internal Affairs by the wealthy man running the motorcycle show. It turned into a larger investigation, and Golucki ended up in front of a grand jury. He soon found that his job, perhaps even his freedom, could be at risk. The wealthy promoter of the motorcycle show testified that Golucki was in the room when the altercation took place. The grand jury returned an indictment of all of the off-duty officers who were involved.

A couple of weeks after the fiasco at the motorcycle show and after the grand jury had done their work to jam up Golucki and the others, Harry was assigned a rather large felony theft case. Golucki said, "The millionaire running that motorcycle show made a police report that his wife lost about $50,000 worth of jewelry. Harry was in charge of the investigation. So I told Harry, 'That's interesting. That's the jerkoff who's trying to put me under the eight-ball by saying I was in that room, and I wasn't.' Harry said, 'Come on with me, we're going to conduct an interview.' So we go to this millionaire's office, and he looks at me and says, 'What the hell are you doing here?,' Harry said, 'That's my partner.' The millionaire said, 'I don't want him here.' And Harry said, 'If you don't want him here, you don't want me here. That's my partner. I'm conducting a criminal investigation, and you are an alleged victim, and you're telling me he can't be here?' Well, anyhow, this millionaire had some clout. He made a phone call, and the chief of the Dicks called Harry and took him off the case. But that's the kind of stand-up guy Harry was." Golucki's voice broke when he added, "Harry put himself on the line just to help me."

Golucki's fondness for Harry Belluomini is palpable when discussing his old friend and workmate and the lengths he would go to look out for his fellow detectives. "Years ago, my wife and I had two phone numbers coming into the house. There was a little switch on the phone to change from one number to the other. My sons were quite young at the time, not even teenagers. They kept getting calls at our home where a male caller would ask them if they've ever seen their mother's bare breast or if they've ever seen her naked." Golucki immediately turned to Harry for help. He said, "I called Harry, and I said, 'Listen, I need a favor. My wife and kids have been getting phone calls at the house from some moron. The calls have sexual content.' Harry talked out of the side of his mouth sometimes, and I could tell he was doing just that when he said, 'I'll look into that for ya.'"

Harry had a call-tracing 'trap' placed on the Golucki's home telephone number. "So the guy calls, and my wife told him to hold on, and she switched over to the other line. She called Harry and told him to start the trap. So my wife kept the individual on the phone for a while." Harry was listening in now with the help of the phone trap. Once he got the location of the phone the individual was calling from, he escalated the investigation. Golucki said, "The calls were coming from the main U.S. post office building. The big one that straddled Congress Boulevard. Harry went over there and found that the phone was in an office that several people had access to. Harry looked at the times of the calls and the dates of the calls. Harry found out that they had regular service calls for their vending machines, and one particular man would come out to the facility to do those calls. Harry asked my wife if she'd recognize the guy's voice if she heard it again, and she said that she thought so. So Harry told my wife to call the number from the trace and tell the guy who answers that she's an accountant and that she needed information about 'this or that,' or some bullshit. So my wife called this individual and had a conversation with the male who answered the phone. She then called Harry and said that was the same voice. So Harry couldn't exactly prove that that was the guy making the phone calls. But if I remember correctly, Harry told the individual, 'I'll break your fucking fingers if you ever dial that phone again.' We never got another phone call. That was Harry."

As Jack Lorre had observed, Harry was famous in the department. But Belluomini was well-known among the criminal operators working in the Chicago area, too. Golucki said, "Harry was a character. Most burglars, the street guys, knew Harry by name. They called him Harry Bell, or Harry Bells. I heard about this incident in Evanston. Evanston PD had shot a burglar, and Harry went to the scene to check it out. It was right on the Evanston and Chicago shared border. The bad guy got shot in the ass by one of the Evanston police officers." Harry had heard about the incident on the police radio and quickly drove to the scene to see if he could offer the Evanston Police a hand. The guy was lying on his face, handcuffed, and he wouldn't turn over so Harry could see who he was. Golucki continued,

"So Harry sort of used his foot to persuade the guy to roll over. So the bad guy flipped over real fast, saw Harry, and said, 'Bells, what the fuck are you doing here? I'm in Evanston. You're not supposed to be in Evanston.'"

Retired CPD detective Luis Alviso not only worked with Harry, but he was another Edison Park neighbor of the Belluomini family. He's is a tall man with a full head of white hair and an even golfer's tan, but he still sports the bushy mustache he's had since working as a detective. Alviso said, "Harry was a happy-go-lucky person. He was always singing. But he was one hell of a ballbuster. I first met him when we were both working in Area 6. He was in General Assignments, and I was in the Youth Division. His office was right across from mine. Any juveniles he came in contact with, he'd have to bring them over to us. That's how I met Harry. We used to call him 'Harry Bell' or 'Harry Ding-Dong.' What? You think we're going to say 'Belluomini' every time we interacted with him? Once you met Harry, you'd never forget him. I don't think you'll find a person who'd say a bad thing about Harry. And his kids are the same. Good people."

Retired CPD detective Brian DuFour fondly recalled working with Harry and socializing with him and his wife, Milly. DuFour is one of the few former detectives who was immediately forthcoming with information about Harry. He's a friendly man, with a shock of white hair. He wears designer glasses, and he conducts himself with a professional demeanor. DuFour said, "I worked with Harry in the old Area 5 General Assignments detectives division, which was on California Avenue. I knew Harry for a number of years, and to use a quote, he was a 'character.' He had a certain persona about him. He had an ability to stick with something and bulldog it to the end. If he wasn't happy with something, he'd let you know. He'd read you the riot act."

DuFour recalled how Belluomini handled formidable suspects, "I would get a kick out of the way he handled prisoners. He would just kind of intimidate them by roaring at them sometimes. He was a real bull. Harry was a smoker, and he'd have a cigarette dangling from his mouth, and he'd be kind of growling at people." DuFour remembered him jumping up on one of the tables while he interrogated a suspect. "He got so frustrated with a guy he just jumped up on the table and growled at him like he was an animal. It was unbelievable. It looked like he was sort of losing it, but he wasn't. He was just attempting to intimidate a suspect."

Like other officers, DuFour said that Harry sometimes seemed a bit rough around the edges, but he was a professional to the core, doing what was necessary to solve cases and set victims' minds at ease. "He went out and did his job. He took things seriously. When he went out to get a perpetrator...he'd bring them in and handle them very professionally. But you know he didn't take any BS from anybody... He was very street-wise and conscious about what it was like to get people off the streets that were doing wrong to people. You know— get the bad guys. He was very conscientious when dealing with victims of crime. He had a heart. If something was wrong, I mean, he reached out to the people to try to help them. He handled people appropriately. He handled them appropriately as a victim, and he handled them appropriately as the criminal. But I really enjoyed just watching him at work because he was so entertaining."

DuFour continued, "We socialized on a number of occasions, and we used to have watch parties and get-togethers... One of the places we used to go was The Cardinal Club over on Addison and Laramie. I remember Harry's wife, Milly. She was a very lovely lady. They really seemed to love each other."

Ed Pyrcioch, another retired CPD detective, didn't work with Harry daily, but he was pretty familiar. Pyrcioch said, "I worked on a tactical team run by a sergeant named George Ruckrich. Ruckrich was Harry's old partner. We worked in the 20th District, and Harry was assigned to Area 6 General Assignments. He was a detective that covered that area. He would come into our office periodically if he needed information or to give us information. Or if he was looking for any particular bad guys...we would give him a hand in finding them. That was in a period of, say, 1968, '69, and '70. Back then, we used to have what they called crime cars, and then they switched [the terminology] to tactical units. We worked in plain clothes in unmarked cars. Our basic job was to go out and make street stops and catch bad guys. That was the job. Harry investigated cases, and we assisted him. He'd come into our office several times a week because he worked with Ruckrich, and he would say, 'Listen, guys, I'm looking for this particular guy. If you find him, grab him, and call me.'"

Pyrcioch has fond memories of Harry from their time together. He said, "Harry was a very upbeat person. He had a very unique sense of humor. He was an interesting guy. He was a very good police officer. He was a very good detective. He was tenacious. Harry would be one of the last guys—if you were a bad guy—you'd want looking for you because he just didn't give up. He was a tough guy. And he had this sarcastic sense of humor, and he would throw out these lines, and he was quick-witted. He was an interesting individual."

Pyrcioch continued, "When I think of Harry being unique, he came into the office one day, and he looks at my partner and me, and he says, 'Hey, do me a favor. Take a ride with me. I want to grab this guy who lives over by Wilson and Racine. He's supposed to be a bad guy.' So we go over there, and the guy lives on the 4500 block of Clifton. We go there and get into the old marble-lined vestibule of the building with the mailboxes and the doorbells. And the guy's name is on the mailbox. I'm with Harry, and my partner goes around the back of the building in case the guy comes out that way. The guy lived on the second floor. Harry rings the guy's bell, and he said, 'Well, we'll see what happens. Either he's going to come out here, or out back, or we won't get any response.' So we hear a door open beyond the security door, and a muffled voice call out, 'Who's there?' All of a sudden, Harry yells out in a sing-song voice, 'It's Bell-Waaaaah-Mini!' Harry's voice was echoing off those marble walls. And the guy yells out from the second floor, 'Who the fuck are you?' And Harry called back, 'I'm your worst nightmare, asshole. I'm the police. Get down here.' And the guy actually came down! Basically, without incident, we took him into custody. I will never forget that. Harry was a character."

Pyrcioch, along with George Ruckrich and a few other detectives on a tactical team, helped Belluomini handle yet another precarious case. Pyrcioch said, "Harry had some information about two guys coming up from the South who were going to rob a couple of banks. These guys were supposed to be hanging out at a couple of taverns up north in the 5800 or 5900 block of Broadway. As fate would have it, my partner and me spot these guys in one of those bars. These guys are supposed to be heavily armed, and we were told to use caution. We were all in plain clothes, and we would go into the bars separately."

On his solo reconnaissance tour of the bar, Pyrcioch said, "I walked in, and I saw the two guys. I recognized them from the description, and Harry also had an old photo of one of the men. In those days, our radios were in our cars. We didn't have portable radios. I had to walk a block back to the car, call for backup, and also keep an eye on the tavern door to make sure the two suspects didn't come out. I fired up the car, and of course, it took like 30 seconds for the radio to warm up. Luckily someone else was listening to the damned thing. So the troops came, including Harry, and we took the suspects into custody. We find their car, and they have several guns and maps of two particular banks in the district where we worked."

The suspects were more professional than most criminals and seemed well prepared for the robberies they were about to pull off. Pyrcioch said, "They had the guard schedules, the hours of operation [of the banks]. So Harry brings them into the office. They were Southern guys, two hillbillies. Kind of tough guys. Bad guys. They both had rap sheets and had both done time in prison for armed robberies and things like that. These two suspects had also shot a police officer down South several years before. As Harry was handcuffing one of the suspects to a ring in a table, he tried to take a swing at Harry. Harry clocked the guy. The other suspect looks over and says, 'So now it starts, huh? You're going to beat confessions out of us.' Harry said, 'I don't have to beat it out of you.' Harry showed both suspects all the bank robbery plans that we got from their car. The suspect said, 'Those aren't plans to rob a bank.' And Harry replied, 'Well, what are they then, plans to build a playschool?' It turns out the suspects were also wanted in another state."

Retired detective Ken Berris came on to the CPD in 1969. He retired after working a total of 38 years with the department. He said, "I was a detective for 29 years. I got promoted to detective in August of 1977. I was assigned to the Area 5 Homicide, Sex Crime, and Aggravated Assault unit. Area 5 was on the northwest side of the city of Chicago. We had six detective areas that were divided up over the entire area of Chicago. I got to know Harry Belluomini. He was in Burglary or General Assignments." Berris is an exceptionally professional individual. He describes himself as an average Joe—an average Joe with blonde hair, blue eyes, and glasses. Interestingly, Berris relished taking on the more minor cases in the office, which weren't significant crimes. These were the types of petty crimes against people who couldn't fight back.

Belluomini made quite an impression on the young Berris. He said, "Harry stood out. He was a very professional, well-spoken, serious, but not an overbearing man. He was old-fashioned in the sense that he could relate very, very well to people. A lot of times, people think that old-time detectives are from a 1940s movie where they get a guy in a dark room, and they're pushing him around. They're mean to him and physically abusive. But that was not the way the old-timers worked. I never even saw anything like that. They were brought up during some tough times, and they were instilled with middle-class values. Right is right, wrong is wrong, and you treat people decently. Things like that. And that's the kind of guy Harry Belluomini was. He knew what he was doing, and he stood out from other guys. If you had a case where one of your relatives was a victim, you'd want Harry or the guys like Harry to work on it. Other detectives would *try* to do a good job. Harry would just *do* a good job. Whether it was a suspect, a witness, or a victim, he could relate well to anyone. Harry was able to sell himself to people. That was all by his personality. People had confidence in Harry that everything would be done the best as he could, and that included white people, black people, Hispanic people. In those days, with guys like Harry working, the public rarely ever complained about them because they knew he was doing the best he could."

Ken Berris and Harry worked on an actual kidnapping in the 1970s. Berris said, "There was an Italian girl who was abducted... Somehow the girl's father was asked to meet with the bad guys. Well, we're sure not going to send the father and put him in jeopardy now. So we had to get someone who appeared to be Italian, and Harry fit the part. But it was more than just Harry being of Italian descent. There were other guys who could do the job. Harry could carry it off. He would do the job the best it could be done. After Harry posed as the girl's father, everything turned out okay. The bad guys were apprehended, the girl was returned safely. Everything worked out as smooth as silk. Harry was the officer on the line in that situation. Things could've gone bad for him. I mean he could've got shot if things went sideways. The girl could've been placed in worse jeopardy."

Berris understood how vital Harry's family was to him, more important than his job. He said, "Harry wasn't going to go around after work and tell his family about what he was doing. This was all in a day's work. This is what he had to do today, and tomorrow is tomorrow. He wasn't going to sit around and talk about things like the Italian girl being abducted. He did his job. He did it right. And tomorrow, he's going to go out and do it again. Harry was a real family man. After work, he wanted to go and be with his family. Harry was a wonderful father."

Curt Blanc, a retired Homicide Sergeant with the CPD's Detective Division, was another young detective who worked alongside Harry Belluomini in the 1970s. Blanc is a large and imposing man, with a size and carriage that suggests he was once a middle linebacker. However, he is gracious and patient with his time, making sure that what he has to say about Harry is truly heard. He seems to be in charge of any room without being overbearing. Blanc said, "The old Shakespeare station wasn't that big. You couldn't hide in there very well. The morale there was great, which contributed to a lot of interaction between the different units. There was no infighting between those units, like between General Assignments and Homicide, or Burglary and the Homicide people. Even though we'd tease everybody and say that we did all the important police work."

When it came to Harry in particular, Blanc said, "If you didn't know Harry, he'd walk into a room, and you'd think you were looking at a little bulldog. Your first impression would be, 'you know, I don't really know if I want to talk to this guy or not.' But your first impression would be entirely wrong. He was very gregarious. Harry didn't hold back on any topic, and he had an opinion about everything. But if you didn't know him, and he had to approach you to discuss something, your whole first impression of him would turn 180 degrees. You'd think to yourself, 'boy, did I make a mistake misjudging this guy.' Harry was personable. Respectful."

Blanc continued, "Whether it was a raffle, or a fundraising dinner, or the guys gathering at the Buck-Eighty," referring to a tavern next to the district building, for example, to raise money for an officer in need, "Harry was always there. Any fundraiser. And he was always the lead man. You could tell he was sincere. He enjoyed doing these events, and he wanted to do it to help the individual who happened to need help."

George Ruckrich mentioned that even after Harry was retired, he would call his busy CPD headquarters office to make sure he would purchase a ticket for an event or show up at a scheduled fundraiser. "He'd bug the shit out of me, but I'd buy the ticket or show up at the fundraiser. Harry was always a bulldog," said Ruckrich.

Harry Belluomini's passion was evident in both the ways he celebrated his life and his job and in the manner in which he disagreed with you. Blanc said, "Harry was very compassionate. And that always came out in your conversations with him. It was his manner. He would listen first and then respond. But boy, if he didn't agree with you, you'd hear his opposing opinion, too. He never held anything back. You always knew where he stood."

10

THE BELLUOMINI family began to grow about a year after Harry and Milly got married in July of 1962. Each had wanted children in their marriage, and they wasted little time achieving this particular life goal. Milly rattled off a list: "Karen came along in May of 1963, Mike in May, 1965, and Annie in November, 1967."

As Karen's birth approached in 1963, Harry was on a temporary furlough from the CPD, but he worked his side job on the big day. Of course, if he had known that that specific day was The Big Day, he wouldn't have left Milly's side. Milly said, "It was the day of the Kentucky Derby, and Harry did go out to work on the furniture moving truck. I couldn't get a hold of him, and no one knew where he was. My mom and dad were away that day, and my sister lived way out in Wheeling. So I had to call the police station and ask Harry's buddies if they could find him."

Harry worked with CPD detectives, so they had an excellent chance of locating him. Milly continued, "Somehow they found him, and Harry came home to take me to Garfield Park Hospital. Those two detective buddies came along to the hospital, and when the nurse came out and asked who the father was, they all three stood up and said, 'We are.'"

Milly recalled how lucky and appreciative she and Harry were to have an extremely diligent doctor working with them when Karen was born. "The doctor we had was supposed to go to his daughter's graduation from the University of Illinois that day, but he stayed with me because he knew Karen was a breach. I didn't know that. That doctor stayed with me all day and missed his daughter's college graduation. That was amazing. I don't know how many doctors would do that. And then when I had Michael, Michael was one of the last babies that same doctor delivered before he retired. He was so excited that we had a son. The next day that doctor got me roses and snuck up a steak, lobster, and champagne dinner—at the hospital. How many doctors would do that? He retired to Tucson, and he and his wife just loved Harry and I. We kept in touch with him until he and his wife passed away. His name was Dr. Sidney Wise."

Two years later, son Michael was born, and Annie completed the family in 1967. All three children were born at Garfield Park Hospital. Milly laughed, "When Annie was born in November of 1967, we had had that big snowstorm in late January of that year, so there were a lot of babies born nine months later." Just the same, Harry still went to work during Chicago's "mini-baby-boom" 1967 blizzard. "Harry actually walked most of the way to work in that big 1967 snowstorm, and then he got a ride, part way, on a Wonder Bread truck. He was determined to get into the station."

Harry was keenly aware that Milly had a demanding job dealing with their household. Milly recalled, "I was a stay-at-home mother, which I loved. We always had family dinners together every night. On his days off, Harry would take the kids down to the lakefront to fly a kite or something similar. He'd say, 'You take it easy, Milly, and relax. I'll take the kids for the day.' He'd take them to the zoo, and for walks. He was really wonderful to me. He respected me, even though I didn't have a job outside the home."

The summer of 1969 was a busy one for Harry and his work with the CPD, so Milly and Harry decided that she and the kids, would go ahead and spend the bulk of the summer with her parents in Winter, Wisconsin. But Milly had an independent streak that would sometimes reveal itself and cause minor rifts in the Belluomini household. One such occurrence happened during that busy summer. While she and the kids were in northern Wisconsin, a small nearby cabin was for sale. It was a simple structure, built in the '20s or '30s as a hunter's camp, located in Loretta, Wisconsin. It really wasn't much more than a roof with four walls, a window or two, and a doorway. The interior walls were adorned with yellowed and tattered, 1940s-era pinup posters. A wood-burning stove and large bunk beds completed the sparse interior design. The cabin was located a few miles down a dirt road from the main highway. The only marking pointing visitors toward the place was a hand-painted yellow and black sign attached to a tree with the word "Hideout" and a small arrow directing visitors to the tiny structure. Once you traveled down the dirt track for several hundred feet, another posted sign, this one aqua-blue colored and hand-painted as well, read: "This is it!"

Milly made an executive decision. "I bought the cabin without telling Harry about it. It was in the woods about three blocks from the Chippewa River. So Harry called one day and asked how things were going and if we were having a good time at my mom and dad's farm. I said we were and that I had purchased a little cabin. He said, 'You what? Wait a minute. Start all over again.'"

So she did.

"I told him that we bought a cabin, and he said, 'Are you crazy?' We had a little money saved at that point, and instead of putting it into the stock market, I thought this might be a good use for our savings."

There was a method to Milly's apparent madness. She said, "A few years earlier, one of Harry's workmates had talked him into buying stocks, and I was angry over that. I thought, you know what, land is always a good investment." When Harry finally came up to see "the cute little cabin" that Milly had purchased without his input, he told his wife, "Put a match to it and burn the damned place down." Milly laughed as she continued, "My brothers and I fixed that cabin up to look so cute. It didn't have indoor plumbing. There was a two-seater outhouse. And there was a well with a water pump outside.

We had the best summers up there. No TV, no radio, no telephone. We just loved it."

A few years later, when they decided they needed a bigger vacation space, Milly said, "The property had tripled in value. That's how we were able to buy a nicer cabin in Mercer, Wisconsin. So my buying that cabin worked out okay. But when I first bought it, Harry had a shit fit. At the time, he said, 'I can't believe you did that without telling me.' Well, I did it, Harry. He wound up really liking that little cabin. The kids were happy, and Harry liked that. Having that cabin was what made Harry want to move north after he retired. There was all the fishing and all the walking through the woods. It was a simple, simple life. There were no Disneyland vacations for us, and my kids, to this day, still talk about how much they loved those summers at the cabin."

The family purchased a second property in 1986. This time together, to Harry's delight. It was located on the Turtle Flambeau Flowage. The cabin had initially been a part of the Sleepy Lagoon Resort. The Belluominis bought after the resort was sold, and the lots were portioned off to individual buyers. The second cabin was originally built as a seasonal summer structure, but it was winterized for year-round use. The setting was beautiful. The family had nearly 200 feet of waterfront property, and their cabin was complete with a small dock to park their pontoon boat. Across the flowage from the place were many acres of wooded land owned by a Wisconsin utility company. The land across the way was a natural buffer that would never see commercial development. A friend in the area made the Belluomini's a wooden sign for their new home away from home: *Harry & Milly's Summer Place. Established 1986.*

In the years to come, the same plot of land would eventually be used to build a larger, more permanent home for Milly.

11

KAREN BELLUOMINI, Harry and Milly's oldest child, is a charming person, going out of her way to make others feel welcome when first meeting her, but she's also not one to be verbally tested. It's not that she's imposing physically, but you get the sense that she has no problem letting you know how she feels—about any topic. Like her father before her, Karen has an air of command. It's a trait that would suit her well once she was solidly placed into her chosen profession in her late 20s. Karen said, "I thank God every day for my parents. We were so lucky to have parents like them. They were fun, but they were strict when they had to be. They were strict, and I was kind of stubborn. They instilled in us what we are today."

For the first few years of Karen's life, the Belluomini family lived with Milly's parents in their house on Deming Place in Chicago. Karen continued, "I had a great childhood. I wouldn't trade it for anything in the world. I was the first grandchild, so of course, I was spoiled. My parents loved going away for the weekend, so I would sometimes spend the weekend with my dad's parents. I loved my grandma and grandpa, and I also loved my mom's parents, who we called Baba and DeDe. When I spent time with my dad's parents, they showed me how to make ravioli, taught me how to play the piano, and doted on me."

Karen and her siblings all have a sense of having been cheated out of experiencing their father's individuality and parental advice as they matured, and they miss that presence in their lives. Karen said, "I always thought of my dad as being strong and very dedicated and loyal to his family. He loved us and put us before anything else. We weren't rich, but he always made sure to try and do the best he could by taking side jobs. And even though we didn't get to go to a lot of vacation places when we were little, he'd make sure to take us down by the lake. We'd go to the beach where we'd fly kites and things like that. He liked to take us to Lincoln Park Zoo. He'd try to spend a lot of time with us because, you know, he was working all these different shifts as a detective. My father was always a hero to us. We all looked up to him because he was the smartest man I ever knew. He was also hilarious."

As for growing together with her siblings, Michael and Annie, Karen said, "We all got along as kids. I loved my brother and sister, but as we got a little older, we started fighting. That happens."

Karen, the elder sibling, held sway over her younger brother Michael and coerced him into performing stunts that were ill-advised at best. "I'd talk him into climbing out of his crib and, bonk, he'd fall right on the floor. That's the kind of kid I was," she said with a giggle.

As with most families with three or more kids in the house, the Belluomini offspring formed temporary alliances, as the coalitions seemed to fit. Karen said, "The kid fights would always turn into a two on one. And when we were little, they called me the 'ring leader.' It would be me and Michael against Annie—or Annie and me against Michael. But those two never ganged up on me. If me and my brother and sister were fighting, as kids do, we'd have to sit at a table and write out 100 times 'I will not fight with my brother and sister.' Or 'I will not talk back to my Father.' Stuff like that. It didn't really work, of course. My dad was very strict, and because I was the oldest, I was kind of rebellious. We had the same kind of personalities. He was stubborn. I was stubborn. I was always questioning, which he hated. If I smarted off to my dad, I either had a bar of soap shoved in my mouth, or I was grounded. I was very mouthy."

Karen is also realistic about it, "I deserved what I got. I admit I deserved it," she said.

One tumultuous event occurred during her childhood that Karen still recalls rather vividly. "My mom went and adopted a dog when we were little kids and living on Deming. At first, my dad didn't think we needed a dog, but he grew to love her. One day, the dog went after our mom when she went to spank one of us. My mom brought the dog back to the pound that day, and when my dad got home from work, he was very upset that she was gone."

Harry was miserable knowing that Milly had returned the pet. "My dad went back to get her," Karen continued, "but she was already gone. We were heartbroken. We loved that dog. She was a mutt. Her name was Tootsie. She was a little German shepherd mix. Whenever we had liver and onions for dinner, we'd feed her under the table."

Harry Belluomini was leery of trying another dog adoption. "My dad didn't want any more pets in the house for a while after that. He took that whole situation badly. And then my mom came home with another dog, and my dad was upset about it at first. But, man, that dog became his. One of the ladies at my mom's work had a dog that had puppies, and she took one of them. Her name was Buttons, and she was so cute. My dad would call her Buttoni. She was a little poodle. It was hilarious watching my badass dad whistling and walking a little poodle down the block every day. He loved that dog. They had her until she was really old. She slept on their bedroom floor every night. They took that dog everywhere they went, to Wisconsin, everywhere. The dog was my dad's world. She was 14 when she died. I never saw my dad cry, except for when his mom and my mom's mothers died. He cried when Buttons died. That was the last dog my dad had."

Everyone pulled their own weight around the Belluomini household. Karen added, "We had a schedule for doing chores around the house. Oh, if you didn't do your chores, you'd be in trouble. You'd get grounded. There was no chart for scheduling chores. If my dad told you once to do it, that was it."

Being the eldest child had benefits but also a downside, Karen said. "If my parents went out and then came home to find a window broken, or whatever, I was blamed whether I caused the damage or not because I was the oldest. I should've known better or stopped it from happening."

Harry Belluomini worked many different shifts as a detective, as is the norm for police officers. However, there were some perks for the Belluomini kids when their father worked cases on the north-west side. Karen said, "He usually worked afternoons or midnights. I remember my mom telling us, when we were little kids, to be quiet because my dad was sleeping. But when he worked afternoons, the big treat for us was when my dad would call the house and ask my mom if we were still awake because he was coming home early with Jimmy's Red Hots. Jimmy's was on Grand and Pulaski. We used to love those hot dogs."

In the early 1970s, the Belluominis left their home on Deming Place and purchased a brick home on Pratt Avenue just off of Harlem Avenue. When not in Wisconsin at their cabin, the family's summers were full of warm days exploring the beautiful, neat, greenery-enveloped, tree-lined streets of the Edison Park neighborhood. "In Edison Park, there were a lot of neighborhood kids," Karen recalled. "There had to be fifteen kids on our block. And then, on Farwell Avenue, there was also a bunch of kids. We called them the 'Fartwell' kids. We played in the street all the time. You'd go home for dinner and then go right back out and play. We'd play softball, kickball, hide-n-seek, and things like that at the elementary school down the block." But not all of their kid games were as innocent as pickup softball games in the schoolyard. "We'd take large rubber bands and stretch them across the street and tie them down, so when a car drove past, it would snap the rubber band. There was a crab-apple tree down the block, and we'd take those and throw them at the buses going up and down Harlem Avenue. We'd do stupid stuff like that. The neighbors would yell at us and say we were going to break a window, which we did when playing baseball in the front yard." In short, they enjoyed an idyllic childhood in the neighborhood.

At times, Harry and Milly were part of the game playing at the house, too. Karen continued, "My dad started playing tag with us around the house when we were kids. You know, the last one tagged was 'it.' Can you imagine your mom and dad racing around the house before going to work, or wherever, playing tag? That's what we did. We called it 'last tag.' That game lasted for a long time, and we got maybe too big to be playing. But it was fun. We always had a Ping-Pong table in the basement, and we'd have tournaments. My parents used to ice up the back yard and make a little skating rink back there."

As Karen grew a bit older, entering her teen years, some of the games she was part of were a bit more mature, and they had consequences. At 14 years of age, she entered Taft High School on the northwest side. Karen said, "I never did drugs or anything, but a lot of my friends drank. And that's what I did. I had such a good party at my house one time, and my mom and dad never knew."

Or so Karen thought.

She continued, "My mom bumped into one of my friend's mothers at the Happy Foods grocery. The lady said, 'Oh, my son had such a great time at your daughter's party.' My mom was like, 'What?' That's how I got caught. I had made my brother and sister take all the empty beer cans and dump them in someone else's garbage cans. At the time, I thought my brother and sister had ratted me out, and I still think that maybe my sister did, that my mom wouldn't give her up and said she bumped into someone at Happy Foods. That was when I was about 17 years old."

Karen's wayward path narrowed and lengthened all at once. She said, "I barely graduated high school because I was always out with friends drinking and stuff like that. I actually had a job too. I'd rather have just gone to work than to school. My grades were okay, but when I graduated and got a set of luggage as my graduation gift, I saw the writing on the wall. My dad wasn't happy with me at that time. My parents had wanted me to go to Good Counsel High School, and I told them, 'Sure, send me there. I'll get thrown out, and you'll waste your money.' I hated school. There was an economics class at Taft, and as part of the class, they helped you find a job in the neighborhood. But my dad actually got me a job at Fannie May Candy on Northwest Highway in Edison Park. He came home and said I should go over and apply at the candy store.... So I went to fill out an application and to get interviewed, but I wrote down the wrong phone number on the application. No one would ever call. My dad probably got wise to what I was doing, and one day he came home from work and said, 'You got a job. You start Friday at Fannie May.'" Karen worked at Fannie May Candy for a time, sometimes having difficulty dealing with a few more-entitled female customers from nearby suburban Park Ridge. Karen knew them by sight after a time working there. It wouldn't be the first time the Belluomini kids had love/hate experiences with some folks from the upscale suburb that bordered their Edison Park neighborhood to the west.

After graduating from Taft High School, Karen found solid employment on her own, though. She said, "My first real job was at an office on Northwest Highway in Park Ridge. They taught me how to take care of accounts, and phone manners, and things like that. It was a billing center for doctors. So I took care of the billing accounts for about fifteen doctors."

Nowadays, when thinking back about her dad at home when she was a kid, Karen recalled, "He loved watching golf on TV. He'd lie on the couch and fall asleep to it. We'd sneak into the room and try to change the channel, and he'd wake up and tell us to change it back. As we got older, we'd laugh and say that the reason he had kids was to change the channel on the TV when he wanted to watch something else. We could be outside, and he'd call for us to come in and change the channel for him. If my dad didn't have a cigarette in his mouth, or he wasn't doing something around the house, he'd be laying on the couch watching a golf tournament on TV. He'd be wearing a pair of jeans and a t-shirt. He had this jacket he wore when he went to walk the dog, and I still have it, and I still wear it. It's like a quilted windbreaker with pockets. It zips up the front. It's just beat to hell. I wear it...when I'm working around the barn. I wear that jacket every single day, except for in the summer. He wore that jacket when he was whistling down the block and walking our dog. Now I wash it separately, so I don't ruin it. I love it, and it's my favorite."

12

THROUGHOUT THIS book, there have been, and will continue to be, concerted efforts to allow Harry Belluomini's family and friends to directly convey the bulk of information about the man. That approach continues with Harry's son, Michael. Harry and Milly's middle child is a highly personable man, pleasant, and a remarkable conversationalist. And like all of the Belluominis, he is not afraid to speak his mind. It's true of everyone, Milly and the three children alike. They are not rude in their approach, just forthright and honest in their assessments.

Michael was named after his mother's brother, Michael Cutich. When we first met face-to-face, he graciously handed over a stack of photos and important papers relating to his father's life, trusting me to take control of and safeguard the priceless cache. He said, "You appreciate these old memories now. It was tragic what happened to my dad. He was way too young to die. He never got to really enjoy his retirement."

Milly, Karen, and Anne have also provided pertinent documentation and photos for this book.

"My dad had, obviously, a different childhood than I had," Michael said. "When I was growing up, we had little league and did different fun things. He grew up with immigrant parents. He was in the first generation here. So he had probably more of a traditional upbringing. Probably a harder upbringing when he was a kid because his parents spoke mostly Italian. His father worked at The Italian Village restaurant as a waiter, but before that, he and my grandmother had a tavern on Madison Street. My grandmother was a great cook. She made the best chicken tortellini soup I've ever had. I wish I had those recipes."

Michael continued, "I remember growing up at 4451 W. Deming Place in Chicago. It was right by Kelvyn Park High School. We lived there until I was five years old. My mom's parents lived upstairs from us. My grandfather passed away when I was four. Both of my grandfathers died around that same time. We always had a lot of love in the family because the grandparents were upstairs, and we always had parties in the house. I remember big get-togethers around the holidays with all my aunts and uncles and cousins coming over. We always had a house-full."

Michael's memories are mostly warm, and he has no trouble recalling the best parts of growing up. He said, "It was a happy time.... Things were simple. I remember that my dad worked a lot. He didn't really talk about his job at home. When we saw him, we had a great time. We weren't too far from the lakefront, and I remember he'd take us down to the lake when we were little." Harry would always have a jazz music station on the car radio as they traveled from one point to the next. According to Michael, the Miles Davis Quintet song "Airegin" and its driving drum and bass lines evoke memories of his dad's sometimes frenetic pace as he went about his day, either tending to his children or chasing down bad guys.

Michael echoed Karen when he said, "We used to go to the Lincoln Park Zoo. And afterward, a lot of the times, he'd take us to Jack-in-the-Box. Jack-in-the-Box was the first fast-food restaurant that I remember. We liked the clown and the onion rings, and the burgers. He used to take us to the lakefront at North Avenue and fly kites."

Michael also recalled his father's love for model trains. "He had old Lionel and American Flyer train sets. He must've gotten them when he was a kid because one is a pre-WWII model. The other was produced just after the war. I still have the train sets. I always wanted to set them up for my son, but I never had my basement set up the way it needs to be. But in that old house, my dad had that Lionel train on a 15-foot-long by 8-foot-wide rectangular platform. There was a 4-inch-tall glass wall all around the edge of the platform so that the train wouldn't fall off. When I was a kid, my eyes would light up when I saw that train set. He had a rotating beacon on the backside and two trains going at once. It had switches with red and green lights that activated when you switched tracks. My dad set that train up at our house in Edison Park on an L-shaped platform. I wanted to buy this one engine when I had a paper route, so I saved up my money to get it. He took me to the hobby shop, and he said, 'Get this one instead.'" Michael laughed as he continued, "Looking back, I think he wanted me to buy the one he picked out because he liked it more than the one I chose."

"I liked Matchbox cars when I was little, and my dad wound up making this little town that he painted on top of a piece of plywood. He then placed a Matchbox firehouse and a gas station on top. Those two items would be worth some money nowadays. He painted roads on the plywood and hand-built a church and a little bridge. He painted a river and a little lake. There were stop signs and stoplights. It was really cool, and it kept me entertained for hours." Michael passed down his love for Matchbox cars, "I did the same sort of thing for my son when he was little."

Things weren't always train sets and Matchbox cars, though. Michael experienced some instant justice from his father when he was in elementary school. He also learned a life lesson after uncharacteristically leaning to the wrong side of a precarious childhood situation. Michael said, "I was in the third grade at Ebinger Elementary School, and there was this one girl there named Karen. She lived in the 6700 block of Oconto. Karen and I had the same birthday. She was going around school that day saying, 'Mike's my boyfriend because we have the same birthday.' I didn't like hearing that, because I liked another girl. After school, I followed her down the street to where our houses were. When she crossed Pratt Avenue to go to her house on Oconto, I crossed the street right behind her. I wound up getting mad at her, and I pushed her down onto a driveway of what would become the house I live in right now." The tumble ripped a hole in the little girl's pants. Michael added, "She ran home crying, and I felt bad. I knew I was going to get into trouble when my dad got home. Sure enough, her mom called my mom—and then my dad got home. He started screaming at me and then dragged me down the block. He rang the family's doorbell, the mom answers, and the girl's still crying, which made me laugh. And I still hadn't apologized. My dad slapped me in the face right in front of her. My dad gave the mom the money for the pants, apologized, and dragged me back home. It was after that that I pretty much became a gentleman. My dad's favorite quote while we were growing up was, 'I'll give you so many rights, you'll be begging for a left.' I remember my sister Karen sitting at the dining room table crying when my dad was teaching her fractions. He saw me and said, 'You just wait, dummy. You'll be crying too when I teach you.' And sure enough, when I learned fractions, I was in the same seat, crying."

Harry Belluomini's own humorous and wiseass ways were often experienced at home, too. Michael said, "At my eighth-grade graduation party, I started opening presents. One wrapped package was a four-pack of toilet paper. One was a roll of paper towels, and one was a box of cereal. I was sort of scratching my head. My mom's laughing, and my dad's laughing, and he says, 'Okay, put that stuff back in the pantry on the back porch.' Of course, there was a brand-new Schwinn Traveler III 10-speed back there."

Milly Belluomini encapsulated her son Michael's persona as she recalled one of his earlier birthday celebrations. She said, "At Mike's seventh birthday, I asked if he wanted a party. He said no, he wanted to take a train ride. We held hands as we walked to the Edison Park train station, and we went all the way out to Crystal Lake, where we stopped and had ice cream. But I remember him asking me that day, 'Mom, when I was born, did I hurt you?' And I told him, 'Oh, no, Michael, you never hurt me.' But that's just how thoughtful that kid was. To this day, he's still like that." She hesitated and then continued, "Yesterday, I got a photo in the mail of Michael's son, who is also named Michael." Milly's grandson is a graduate of Notre Dame High School in Niles, Illinois. "When I looked at that picture, I cried... and then I laughed. He looks almost identical to Harry. It's unbelievable. I just kept staring at that photo." After Michael heard his mother's recollection of his seventh birthday, he added, "My mom is a hero to me."

Michael's tenth birthday was a special occasion, as well. Michael said, "My dad was a big Bears and White Sox fan. He never took me to a Cubs game or a Bears game, but I remember he took me to White Sox games. One time it was a fireworks night for my tenth birthday. My sister Annie was there, too. My dad said, 'Keep watching that scoreboard.' So at one point, Annie had to go to the bathroom, so my dad takes her, and I was sitting there looking around. On the scoreboard, it says 'Happy Birthday to Mike Belluomini.' My heart was pounding, and I was thinking, 'oh, my God,' but no one else was there to see it. When they got back, I told my dad that my name was on the scoreboard. It was so nice that he did that for me. That was crazy. It was the little things, you know."

Just like his parents, Michael was quite enterprising, even as a kid. Michael said, "I was in the fifth grade and walking home from Ebinger School after playing baseball with my friends, and a guy in a big four-door Olds pulls up and says, 'Hey, kid. Want a job?' I should've went running and screaming, but I said, 'Doing what?' He said he had a paper route for me. I told him I had to check with my mom. So he followed me down the street and was waiting in front of our house until my mom came out. He said he worked for Edison News Agency and that one of his paperboys quit. The guy said it was a morning route, and he asked my mom if that was okay, and she said yes. He said that he would pick me up at 5:30 the following morning. So the guy picked me up and drove me around the route. I had a three- or four-block area around my house—sixty-five customers. I rode with that guy for three days while he showed me the ropes, and then on my fourth day, I was soloing. At first, I was walking with a wagon full of papers. From the wagon, I went to a bike with the newspaper bag hanging off the handlebars, but on Sundays, the papers were so heavy you couldn't use the bike or the wagon. I would be struggling. One day, my dad told me that he'd gotten me a baby buggy. I told him, 'I'm not pushing that buggy.' What kid wants to push a girly-looking buggy? My dad said, 'Use the buggy, dummy.' So I ignored him, and I used the wagon. One Sunday, I was hauling that wagon around a corner, and it tipped over, and all the papers went flying. So I went on to use the buggy, and it was the best thing I ever did. The buggy was great. I had that paper route from fifth to eighth grade. Every year at Christmas time, the news agency would give you these little Christmas cards to put inside your papers to get tips from your customers. My dad went to work and put together a better-looking version of a card with a personal message on it. I didn't want to put those in my paper inserts because I felt embarrassed. My dad said, 'Put them in there, dummy, I'm telling you.' I put them in my inserts, and I got good tips. It worked. I remember that sometimes when the weather was really bad, my mom or dad would drive me on the route. It was my first real job."

Like his sisters, Michael recalled that Harry Belluomini existed on his CPD salary, but with a mortgage and three growing children to take care of, the police department paycheck wasn't enough sometimes. Michael continued, "My dad worked a lot of side jobs over the years. When I was a little kid, one job was working security at Carson Pirie Scott's department store on State Street downtown. He'd catch a lot of shoplifters and investigate employees who were stealing merchandise. He'd take me down there when he had to pick up his paycheck. I loved going downtown with him because we'd go on the L-train. He always would try to get us into the front car, so I could get that one side seat next to the conductor and look out the front window. It was a big thrill. One time when we were getting off downtown, and this was when they had the older cars, my dad started walking off the train, and I was right behind him. But the conductor closed the doors on purpose, leaving my dad on the platform and me stuck in the door. My dad turns around and sees me stuck. The conductor was sticking his head out the window laughing. My dad grabbed that conductor and pulled him halfway out the window, and said, 'Open that damned door!' That conductor knew immediately that he messed up. He wasn't trying to hurt me. He was doing it as a joke. I mean you do that to some kid whose dad happens to be a cop? Watch out."

All of the pretty ladies at Carson Pirie Scott's made it all the better for Michael, though. He said, "When we went to Carson's, the first stop was always at the cosmetics counter where my dad knew all the women. He'd always pick something up for my mom there. And every time we went there, all those women would come up and start kissing and hugging me. I was in my glory."

One of Harry's side gigs led to a series of quick weekend getaways for the family and later full-blown driving vacations. Michael said, "One of my dad's side jobs was working at a Holiday Inn in the security department. He did that for a while. So whenever one of those new Holidomes opened up, my folks would take us for a weekend getaway every once in a while. Just to get out of the city. It was kind of nice." The entire Holiday Day Inn Holidome idea was ahead of its time in the 1970s. The Holidome buildings had a hotel, but under an attached large glass dome were other amenities, like an indoor pool, restaurants, arcades, and sometimes, kitschy Tiki bars.

Michael said, "Growing up, the kids I know, their parents would take them to places like Disney World. My parents never took us to Disney World. I remember them taking us to historical places. In 1977 we went to Lookout Mountain, Tennessee, and the Civil War battle site of Chickamauga. As a kid, you may not always appreciate a trip like that, but we saw where some history occurred. We went to Ruby Falls, Lookout Mountain, and places like that. The other kids in the neighborhood would say, 'We went to Disney World. Where'd you go on vacation?' Ah, we went to Tennessee. But I learned to appreciate where my parents took us. I went on a motorcycle trip a few years ago with a buddy to Chickamauga. They put up a museum there now. It's beautiful. Here's the funny part of this. I've never been to Disney World, and I took my kids a few years ago when they were younger. And I felt like the biggest sucker there. It was just a big marketing campaign. I mean, Mickey Mouse was there and all that. My kids didn't know who Mickey Mouse was. They grew up with Sponge Bob Square Pants and different cartoon characters. I felt like such a chump walking around Disney World because it was so expensive. I really didn't miss anything, and I felt like a dummy for being there. I took my kids on a better vacation. We went out to Glacier National Park on the train. I just never liked the big Disney thing and their marketing. Now I know why my dad took us on similar vacations. In a sense, I find that I'm turning into my dad, in the things I do and say."

One of those extended Belluomini family driving vacations happened in the summer of 1979. Michael continued, "We went to Lake Placid, New York, the year before the Olympics. While we were there, we went to Fort Ticonderoga on Lake Champlain. And I remember seeing the construction crews building the Olympic Village for the games. That was also the summer that Ernie Banks was inducted into the Baseball Hall of Fame. My dad took us to Cooperstown. So we're driving down the road, and we're passing a golf course in our two-door Plymouth Fury. It was a big boat of a car, Mom and Dad in front, and the three of us in back. So we see a putting green, and my mom says, "Oh, my gosh. That's Ernie Banks!" My dad stops the car, and we all look. Ernie Banks was on the putting green. My mom got her camera out and took a photo or two. So fast-forward, and I'm a sophomore in high school working as a stock boy at the Osco Drug Store at Milwaukee and Oakton in Niles. They had a grand reopening of the store, and who was the special guest? Ernie Banks. He was going to do an autograph signing as part of the event. So I bring this Cooperstown baseball book I got while we were there on vacation and one of the photos that my mom took of Ernie Banks on the golf course. He signed the book, and he signed the photo, and he said, 'Where was this?' I said, 'It was in Cooperstown the weekend you were inducted into the Hall. We had driven past the golf course and saw you on the putting green.' He said, 'Yeah, I remember that. I made that putt.' And I said, 'No, you didn't. We were all watching you.'"

After returning from that upstate New York trip, the Belluominis' other family car was struck by a hit-and-run driver overnight while it was parked on their side street. Harry was a detective to his core and would wind up working the case to its satisfying conclusion. Michael said, "Pratt Avenue goes through Edison Park from Harlem to Northwest Highway. People use it like a thru street. We had a 1979 Dodge Monaco, sort of like the Blues Mobile, but nicer. It was parked on the street in front of our house. My dad woke up, and someone had sideswiped the car in the night. There was debris lying all over. My dad caught the guy within a day. I asked him how in the hell he figured that out. He said he heard the dog barking at three in the morning, and he figured it had to be someone from the neighborhood. He drove up and down each street in the area and the alleys, and he found the car four blocks away on Olympia. It was the street where one of my best friends lived. My dad said the paint from our car was all over the side of that car. He took a sample of paint off the car, and I guess he knew someone at the crime lab. It came back as a positive match. Our car's paint was on the other car. So my dad went to the guy and told him, 'You hit my car the other night.' The guy tried to deny it, but my dad said he had proof. I told my friend that his neighbor hit our car, and my buddy said, 'That guy's the local drunk. He's always hitting cars.'" Michael constantly marveled at his dad's bulldog ways—especially when someone, even himself, was wronged. He said, "You or me, we would've just filed the claim with our insurance company, but my dad? He caught the guy. That was the detective in him. He would always tell me, 'Someone's always watching. Someone always knows something about what happened.'"

Harry was a veteran detective with the CPD, but he was also an average 1970s dad in many ways. Michael continued, "My dad loved the old *Looney Tunes* cartoons. Bugs Bunny, Tweety Bird, all of those. He loved *The Honeymooners.* And he loved *Barney Miller.* He said that that was the most realistic cop show on TV. He liked *Get Smart.* It's funny, the things I remember now about him."

Michael also noted that the "real" Harry's fashion sense reared its head when he was comfortably inside his own home. "When he was around the house, he looked like a bum. He wore a white t-shirt like Ed Norton all the time, and he wore the worst blue jeans that he got from Goldblatt's or somewhere. They were the shittiest-looking jeans you'd ever see. And as we all get older, we lose our ass and gain a potbelly. So my dad had this little potbelly and no ass. He'd walk around in his boxer shorts in the morning, and you'd see his bony legs. It was so comical, you know, but I know I'll end up like my dad someday. I just wish I had his hair. He had a full head of jet-black hair. People would ball-bust him and say he used Vitalis or something in his hair, but he didn't. He just had great hair."

The public-facing Harry Belluomini was, of course, a slightly different animal. Like Harry's CPD detective teammates, Michael remembers his dad making an effort to look good, especially at work or special events. Michael said, "My dad was kind of like a more-dapper version of Columbo. He'd drive you nuts until he got what he wanted from you. He was relentless. That's how he was on the police department. When my dad was on the job as a detective, he had to wear sport coats, button-up shirts, and ties."

Michael continued, "When I graduated the eighth grade, he took me shopping and picked a nice suit out for me. He'd pick up clothes and say, 'This'll look good on you.' He was a great dresser. He'd dress up for parties and all that. He always looked nice in those situations. But when he went golfing, most of the guys he went with would wear their nice golfing attire, their golf hats, and polo shirts. My dad would wear those shitty jeans and a sweatshirt."

Harry's cooking chops came to light, especially after Milly returned to work in the late 1970s. Harry picked up his culinary skills at his own mother's hip, of course. He employed a variety of cooking styles, top-flight Italian fare among them. Michael said, "When my mom started working more, my dad was the cook. He was a great cook. They were both good cooks. You couldn't go wrong with either of them making you a meal. My dad was good at the BBQ." But according to Michael, Harry excelled when it came time to prepare pasta dishes. He said, "One of my favorite things he made was his Fettuccini Alfredo. I love pasta. He'd always make a pound of pasta. He'd always say, 'You don't want to go out to an Italian restaurant and pay what they charge. You can go to the supermarket and get a box of pasta for fifty cents.' You get Alfredo sauce in a restaurant, and it's really heavy. My dad's sauce was so light. It was fantastic. That's a recipe I wish I had. I could eat like a horse when I was younger. I'd finish and ask why there wasn't any left. He said, 'Jeez, you ate two plates.' So he started making more, a pound and a half of pasta. I'd ask him to make two pounds, so I'd have enough to eat the leftovers the next day. When I was in the Cub Scouts, we'd have a spaghetti dinner every year to raise money. I had all these tickets to the dinner I had to sell, so my dad would sell all of the tickets to the people he worked with. One year he volunteered to make garlic bread for the event. The people running the event said that they didn't need garlic bread, but sure as shit, he made great garlic bread. He made so much garlic bread in a church kitchen where the event was taking place. People loved it. It was a big hit. I loved when my dad cooked. He made great stuff. My dad would go to one grocery store for meat and another for this and that. He had all these little stops he'd make. I find myself doing the same thing. My wife will go to one store and get everything. I go to the butcher for chicken and steaks. I buy certain things at certain places."

When Michael was 14 years old, he had to make a significant change in his daily routine, one his parents thought would be best for him. Michael said, "I went to Weber High School. It was by Area 5 where my dad worked as a detective. The kid of a friend of my dad's went to Weber, and I think that's why there was a push for me to go

to there. All my friends went to Taft High School in our neighborhood. My sister, Karen, was doing a work program through Taft
High School where every few days, she'd leave school early to work at
the Fannie May Candy Store on Northwest Highway in Edison Park.
Well, she was cutting class a lot and wasn't going to graduate. My
dad had a work-related problem with one of the kids at Taft about
a property crime. So my dad had to go to Taft and talk with the prin-
cipal. My dad said something like, 'Listen, I'm going to take care
of this kid for you. You make sure my daughter gets her diploma.'
So after that, my dad told me, 'You're going to Weber.' I was like,
'Where the hell is Weber?'"

Weber Catholic High School, which has since ceased operations
(the building has now become Northwest Middle School), was located on the northwest side, some eight miles south of the Belluomini
home. It's the alma mater of Mike Krzyzewski, the famous former
Duke University head basketball coach. Michael Belluomini continued, "I really didn't know anyone there. I didn't like high school because I didn't have a bond with anybody. I couldn't wait to get out.
I mean, I thought high school would be like the show *Happy Days.* I
mean, it's co-ed, you're going to dances, and you're meeting people.
It's high school. All you're thinking about is girls and hanging out
with your friends. Here I was taking a one-hour bus ride each way
to school. I understood what my parents were doing. They wanted
me to have a better opportunity. They didn't want me getting into
trouble, hanging out with the burnouts at Taft. Of course, there are
burnouts everywhere, wherever you go to high school. At Weber,
there were drugs and gangs. I had to try and hang out with kids I
had a common interest with." One of those fellow students was actor
Dennis Farina's son, Dennis Jr. The actor Farina Sr. started his professional life as a Chicago Police officer before turning to the enter-
tainment world.

Once Michael Belluomini graduated from Weber High School,
he sought work in the marine and boating world. As it turned out,
this would eventually become a main environmental component of

his future chosen profession. He said, "I really didn't know what I wanted to do. I hated school, so I didn't want to go to college. My dad had a friend named Terry Lamb, who had a boat shop in Wilmette, Wilmette Boat Works. He built and repaired boats, did a lot of woodworking, and he was an engine mechanic. He came up with his own design and built his own type of sailboat—it was called a Wilmette Five Meter. It was a 17-foot sailboat. I started working with him right out of high school. I learned a lot.... My dad was hoping that I would eventually go to this mechanics school called the Outboard Marine Corporation. It was located in Racine, Wisconsin, and they taught you how to work on outboard boat motors. I didn't, but I learned a lot in Wilmette. Lamb eventually moved his shop to Glenview because he got a contract to build a big 24-foot sailboat that was designed by a guy out in Washington State. So Lamb won the contract to build the boats, but he only had me and two other guys working for him. He wound up going bankrupt because he had to order so much inventory to keep up with the contract. He was probably better off just staying down by Wilmette Harbor doing repair work."

The Belluomini men prized their playing card and boards games, and competition could become fierce sometimes. Michael said, "My dad and I liked to play games of Cribbage. The weekend before he died, I wound up playing a couple of nights in a row with him. I think I beat him one of those nights. I never beat my dad at that game. That was kind of weird. It was the Saturday before he died. And he didn't let me win. He'd never let you win. You didn't want to play Monopoly with him. He had no mercy. He'd always have to be the car. He'd win that game so fast, and if you owed him rent, he'd take that money, like, right now."

Michael's memories of his father are fond. He said, "My dad was laughing and ball-busting all the time. And today, my kids say that I'm fun. I try to be the same way my dad was with us. I try not to be serious with everything. I try to have fun. My wife thinks that I'm still as funny today as the day we met."

Michael always appreciated the effort his dad put into maintaining relationships with retired workmates and old friends. He said, "My dad kept in touch with all the old-time officers. He would do anything for those guys. He'd throw the retirement parties for people or put benefits together for people who would need help because they were sick or a family member was sick. My dad respected the common man. He wasn't impressed with athletes and people like that. It's funny that I find now that I have some of the same similarities as my dad. He always liked going out for Chinese food and eating chow mein and egg foo young. Today I find myself always getting the same foods he always got." But Harry wasn't above playing a food-related practical joke on his kid. "Oh, I remember he gave me hot mustard once when I was real small. Oh, man." But Michael takes heart in how his father would verbally spar, playfully, with anyone willing to test him. "My dad was so quick-witted. My wife always wonders where I come up with snappy one-liners. That's from my dad and his quick-wit. He would always say, 'Don't try to match wits with me. You're only half armed.'"

Michael became quiet and reflective as he recalled his upbringing. He said, "The love my parents showed for us kids by doing the simple things was important. They wanted what was best for us, to grow up and do things the right way. I tell my kids the same sort of things. Treat people the way you want to be treated, don't rip people off, don't be a thief. Everything my dad did was right. He had the right frame of mind for the things he did and the way he treated people. He was just an honest person. He would never screw anybody over. The most important thing to know about my dad is that he was a simple man, a common man, and religious. He wasn't a hero for what he did that day in the Federal Building. He was a hero for what he did every day. He was a great son to his parents and my mom's parents. He was a great husband and father. He was a great friend. He would do anything for you. He would sort of bitch about things he was asked to do, probably because you would seldom see him relax, but he'd do whatever you needed done. I think this is true with a lot of men. I do this same thing every time my wife asks me to hang a picture on the wall, but I do it."

For the family, Harry would do anything, especially his aging mother. Michael said, "He took his mom to Mass every week, and he'd say, 'I have to take Mom to confession. I don't know what in the hell she's got to confess, but I'll take her.' His mom had this little apartment near Western and Irving Park Road. We'd go there every other Sunday for dinner. Later on, he had to move her to a nursing home in Niles, where he'd visit her all the time. She had dementia. She didn't remember anyone, and she only spoke Italian. So my dad would go over and speak Italian with her. She died there in Niles. It was difficult for my dad when his mom passed away. He was crushed."

Michael continued, "My dad and I would ball-bust each other a lot, but we got along overall. I respected him. I was afraid of him. He kept me in line. I never got arrested. I never hurt anyone. He was so street smart, especially when he was reading people. But he was always a gentleman. He was polite and held doors for women and older people. So that's what I did. My son is doing the same thing."

As Harry began to age, Michael tried to keep an eye on his father's health. He said, "My dad would walk all the time. He'd walk and then smoke. I'd get on him all the time for smoking because it defeated the purpose of the walking. As he retired and got older, I worried about his health. I wanted him to have a long, healthy life. And that was the saddest thing. He finally quit smoking, and then he got killed at the Federal Building. I felt so bad for getting on his ass for the smoking."

13

ANNE BELLUOMINI, Harry and Milly's youngest child, may be diminutive in stature, but she's big on earned confidence and in command of herself and seemingly any situation she encounters. She achieves this dynamic combination of personality traits while also exhibiting a very fair-minded and pleasant disposition. She's upfront, honest and humble in her appraisals of herself and her family. She was named after Milly's sister, Anne Cutich Vuich. Anne echoes her siblings in her first description of their father: "My dad was funny. Usually, he was jovial. He was always joking."

One year, when his kids were young, Harry had a Halloween gag in mind for them. Anne continued, "He told us he was going to tell us a ghost story. We all went into the basement, and it was dark, and he proceeded to tell us a story about a ghost sitting in a rocking chair. There was a rocking chair set up in the basement. After the scary story, the rocking chair started rocking back and forth. I started screaming and ran across the basement and up the stairs." Harry had, of course, tied a fishing line to the rocking chair and was pulling it so the chair would rock. "As funny as he was, he was very clever," Anne added.

When Anne recalled her father hanging around the house back when she was a kid, she said, "He was always dressed in a white t-shirt and jeans, or he was always wearing these pajama shorts. And he loved to whistle. He was always whistling. To this day, Michael and I are always whistling, too. All of our old neighbors could hear my dad in the yard whistling while he worked in his garden."

Anne added, "My dad loved nature and animals. He was not and never would have been a hunter. I'm not saying that hunting is wrong, but for a detective who most likely saw everything, he loved animals and would never harm one."

And Anne also echoes Michael's observation that Harry was not only an excellent detective, he was utterly proficient in the kitchen. "He made a great frittata. He made great salads. I don't know what it was about his salads, but they would taste so good. He used just vinegar and oil, but it was always perfect. He washed the lettuce in the morning, and it would sit in the fridge all day. It was just so crispy. Family nights were for pizzas. He'd put the whole thing together from scratch. On Holidays we'd have BBQs for friends and family." The entire Belluomini family would get involved when the holidays came around. Anne said, "My mom would prepare for days. She'd make potato salad and macaroni salad. My dad made great garlic bread. We were always taught, and to this day, I'm like this, if you're going to have people over, then do it 100%. So if you're having 20 people over, have enough food for 50. And make sure you supply your guests with everything or don't do it at all."

Anne's earliest memories are joyous ones, beginning when her family lived on Deming Place. She said, "It was fun living at the old house because I was very close to my grandmother, my mom's mom. I was really close to her, and I liked to visit her. So even after we moved, I'd go back to the old house and visit and spend the night or even a few days there. My grandmother's and my birthday were two days apart, so we always celebrated our birthdays together. I don't think that the other cousins realized that I was the favorite, but I was," she laughed. "We used to ride the bus to go to the grocery store. She would let me get my favorite cereal. I'd always get the cereal with the marshmallows in it, like Count Chocula or Lucky Charms. And then, I would pour all the cereal into a big bowl and pick out all the marshmallows and eat them. My grandmother would get mad at me, but I told her that that was a normal thing to do. I'd put the cereal back in the box, and when my brother and sister would come over to visit, they'd get mad because all the marshmallows were gone."

When things got out of hand in the Belluomini household, justice came quickly and swiftly. Anne said, "My dad was very strict. We got spanked, which to me is not abuse. I think you deserve what you got. He was very loving and kind, but he didn't tolerate nonsense from us. He called home a lot to check in because he worked so many different shifts. So if he learned that we had gotten in trouble, he'd say, 'When I get home, that's it.' And we'd be like, 'Oh, Jesus.' I can remember times when one of us would be fighting like kids do. We'd get in trouble from my mom, but we'd get another round when he got home. So if Michael and I were fighting, or if Karen and I were fighting, he'd say, 'Okay, you're going to write one hundred times, "I will not fight with my brother or sister."' And if that wasn't done by the time he got home, it would be doubled. We'd get soap in the mouth if we were mouthy. We'd get grounded if we weren't behaving."

And everyone in their home pulled their weight, no matter their age. Anne said, "We all had chores we had to do and responsibilities. In our family, there was no waking up in the morning and just hanging out all day. Before you went out, you had to do chores. We all took turns doing dishes, pulling weeds or sweeping, taking the garbage out, making our beds, vacuuming. That had to be done before we could have fun for the day."

Anne continued, "My parents used to joke around all the time, too. They used to play jokes on us. I remember one time when we all came home from school, and they left us a note saying they left us. My sister and brother, Karen and Michael, were laughing. I was crying. My parents were hiding in the closet. It wasn't mean. I was just kind of a baby."

Harry and Milly would nurture their relationship and work toward extending that adoration to their children. Anne said, "My parents would go on date nights without us. They'd get us a babysitter. But then we'd do things as a family together. They'd take us places, or we had game nights. Rather than sit in front of a TV all day on a Sunday or at night, we would play games." The Belluomini family would play all manner of games—card games, Aggravation, Sorry, Boggle, and Yahtzee, Anne said. "It was so much fun and really brought us together as a family. I don't think a lot of families do that anymore, but I remember it as being so important. Sundays were always 'big dinner' days for us when my mom would cook. So a couple of times a month, on a Friday or Saturday night, my parents would have date night. The other weekends we'd all be at home and make homemade pizzas. On Valentine's Day, we'd wake up and find flowers for my mom and Fannie May candy for us kids, and cards with notes saying 'we love you.' My parents always wrote notes on the napkins in our school lunches."

Again echoing Michael, Anne said driving vacations were the only way to go for the Belluomini family of the 1970s. "We used to go on vacations, but we never went to Disney World like most kids. We usually drove to the East Coast and the historic places. Places like Fort Ticonderoga, Stone Mountain, Cooperstown, and Lake Placid. We'd pack salami sandwiches with mustard and eat them the whole way. We also went to Wisconsin in the summers. We had a small cabin, and my aunt and uncle had a place around the bend, and my mom's mom had a small farm up there. We'd spend, like, a month in Wisconsin, and my dad would drive back and forth to see us. Our cousins would be up there. We'd go out and pick berries so that my mom and her sisters could make jams and jellies."

Harry Belluomini kept things interesting for the kids with little competitions here and there. Anne said, "My dad liked to fish, so to make it fun for us kids, he came up with little contests, just so that we'd want to go, too. Like whoever caught the first fish would get a dollar, whoever could keep the quietest would get a dollar, whoever caught the most fish would get a dollar. So that was a way to make it fun for us. But one of us would always drop someone's sunglasses in the lake or something."

Anne recollected the time she overindulged while on vacation to the North Woods with her parents. She said, "When I was in the seventh grade, my parents took me with them on vacation in Minnesota. I met some other kids there. I remember running to the lodge to get ice cream, and I didn't have any money. The people working there said that I could just charge it to my cabin. So once I found out that I could charge it all to my cabin, I began to treat all the kids at the pool. I would eat like four ice cream sandwiches in a row. When we checked out of the resort, the people at the desk said that we had a tab. My parents were, like, 'A tab?' This was in the early 1980s, and the tab was $50 or $70. It was a lot of money. My dad asked what the tab was for, and the people said that I had been charging for ice cream and candy. So my parents weren't really happy with me. I really liked sweets, and when I found out that I could charge it all to my cabin, it was like a smorgasbord for me. I don't remember having to pay it back because I was little, but I probably got my ass kicked."

Anne continued, "Growing up, we hung out mostly with the kids on the block. We'd play tag and hide-n-seek. I don't know if a lot of people did this, but if we wanted to play with another kid, we'd go to the back door of their house and yell, 'Call for Anna,' or whoever. Instead of ringing the bell, 'Call for Jimmy. Call for Billy.' We'd just keep yelling until someone answered. We did stupid stuff as kids. I'd follow my brother, and we'd throw snowballs at cars, and people would chase us. We'd play jokes on cars driving down the street. One time I remember my brother walked out into the middle of the street pretending he was blind and almost got hit by a car. We just did the stupid stuff that kids do. We'd laugh, but we didn't realize how serious the stuff was. If our parents knew we were doing that stuff, they'd probably kick our ass."

Like her sister Karen, Anne mentioned that Harry would often call home to see if his kids were awake so that he could bring them a treat while on his way home. Anne said, "He would call from work and tell us to stay awake as he was going to stop by Superdawg and bring something home for us." As everyone on Chicago's northwest side can tell you, Superdawg is a Chicago-style-hot dog paradise. It has been in business since 1948 at Devon and Milwaukee Avenues —and still going strong. On its roof are statues of male and female hotdogs. The male is in a Fred Flintstone type of jerkin. It's a local landmark. Anne continued, "The hotdogs come in a box, along with French fries packed on the bottom. We were always excited when he would bring those home for us. It was a huge treat."

When it came time to enroll in school, Anne and her siblings simply walked a block from their home to the neighborhood elementary school. The school's placement was a significant factor in Harry and Milly choosing their home in Edison Park. But Anne initially felt the same way about school as her siblings. "I went to Ebinger Elementary School, and I hated it. I hated school. I didn't want to leave home. And then my kindergarten teacher made fun of the way I drew. I'm not a good artist. I can't draw to this day. My dad and I had that in common. Neither one could draw. My brother, sister, and Mother are all very artistic, and my dad and I were not. I remember that I had to draw a tree, and the teacher held it up for all to see and said, 'You call that a tree?' So that experience set the tone for school for me. I was also one of the youngest in my class, so I think I remember my mom and dad talking about holding me back because of my age. I also had a hard time sitting still. And I liked to socialize at school. But the way schools were laid out just wasn't conducive to how I learned—just sitting for 45 minutes. I'm more of a get up and move-around type person. But later on, when I decided to go to junior college, I did very well in school."

Instead of going to the public middle school in their area, Anne enrolled at a Catholic school in a nearby suburb. Anne said, "I went to middle school at St. Paul of the Cross in Park Ridge. I generally had a hard time at school. I'd say that most of my school life was difficult. I was horrible at math, and we had a math teacher who would make fun of you if you didn't understand. But I think that's how teachers were back then."

She continued, "My dad was very smart. He was very good at

math, which I am not. Yesterday I went to the phone store, and the guy there said, 'You can get a new phone for a dollar a month for 30 months.' And I said, "So, it's $300?" He said, 'No, it's $30.' Damn it, I knew it was $30, but I just wasn't thinking. My dad used to tutor us in fractions and adding, subtracting, and dividing. He could figure out math problems in his head so quickly. I would get anxiety before going to class. I was also probably very rambunctious. I talked a lot. I had notes sent home saying that I talked too much in class. And the principal at St. Paul would always say that the Chicago kids were the bad kids and the Park Ridge kids weren't. We Chicago kids would get blamed a lot for some of the stuff we didn't do. But I was rambunctious. If I look back, I think I was a different kind of learner, and I just don't think schools were set up for that. Even to this day, if I have to sit through an hour-long training class, my mind wanders, and I lose focus."

Anne was also quite enterprising, even at 13 years of age. She said, "When I was in eighth grade, I knew someone who worked at the local grocery store. The store's still there, but it's under new management. They had me working in a backroom, clipping coupons from newspapers for $2 for a few hours a day. I thought, 'Man, I could make $6 if I did this three days a week.' It was probably illegal what they were doing. It was horrible. You'd sit in this upstairs stinking room with stacks of newspapers. All you did was cut the coupons out. The store was probably sending the coupons back to the manufacturers for rebates. It probably wasn't legal. I hated it, and I quit, and my dad told me that I wasn't going to quit and that when you sign up to do something, you do it. I went back, but I didn't last long there."

After her days at St. Paul of the Cross Anne moved on to her next educational adventure. Anne said, "I went to high school at Good Counsel in Chicago. My experiences there were pretty much like my other schools. I did make a lot of good friends there. I still stay in touch with them, and we go out together sometimes. Maybe not as much as we'd like because we're all busy with work and them with work and families. I had a couple of different groups of friends in high school. I had changed friends over the course of high school. When I first got there, I didn't know anybody, and I kind of gravitated toward the first person I met. And then, as I got to know other people, I just sort of clicked with them. I had a best friend, and then we met another good friend, and then we'd all just branch out. One of my good friends started hanging out with the stuck-up girls who I didn't like. I started hanging out with one of the girls in homeroom, and she and some others from high school I still hang out with now. There were two girls I hung out with in sophomore and junior year, but I realized that they were not really nice people. There were a couple of times when we'd go out and do stuff, but then they'd leave me at the bus stop. They weren't a good influence. I stopped talking to one of those girls in particular. I gravitated towards the girls that I still keep in contact with today."

Anne's first official jobs were not instant successful matches. She said, "We all had to get jobs when we turned 16. I had a job at a fast-food place that I didn't like in the Harlem/Irving Plaza. I didn't last long there. I hated it. The first few working years of my life, I had this 'quit job thing.'" Anne may have quit one job but would almost immediately have another lined up. "I went to work at another restaurant in Jefferson Park. It was where my high school friend's boyfriend worked. It was called Uncle Charlie's. I worked there for a few years. I worked the cash register, and I had to mop the floors and scrub the toilets," she said.

When Anne considers her teen years, she recalls Harry's intolerance for people attempting to bullshit him. This intolerance would extend to others outside the house, as well. Namely, neighbor kids. Anne said, "At times, there would be parties thrown on the block by neighboring teenagers whose parents were out of town, or just out. If the parties go out of hand, he would go out there and break it up. I think one time, a few teenagers were mouthing off to him, and one said, 'My dad is so-and-so.' Trust me, my dad did not give a shit who that kid's dad was. My dad wasn't tolerating the nonsense and handled the situation."

Anne added, "My dad never brought his work home. He never had an ego about doing what he did and being in law enforcement. He did his best to leave that at work and never talked about it. Once in a while, he would ask us if we knew some kids in the neighborhood. He would do that if he was working on some case, I'd imagine."

Finally, Anne completed high school. At first, it seemed like a relief, but things were just beginning to get more challenging for her. Anne said, "After high school, I went right to work. My dad said, 'I wasted my tuition money on you because you didn't apply yourself, so if you're going to live at home, there's no free ride. You're either going to go to school full-time, or get a full-time job, or a part-time combination of the two. You're going to pay rent. I'd help you, but you wasted my money while you were in high school.' Which was fair. I went to work at a small brokerage firm downtown, and worked there from May through the fall, and quit. I hated it. I was making $10,000 a year, and I thought I was rich. I was acting like a baby. I felt like it was so far from home, I had to travel downtown. I missed being around my home. I wanted to be closer to home. So I quit without telling my parents. When my dad found out, he was pissed." Her father began to keep track of Anne's rent payments on a bulletin board—the board had one column for "back rent" owed and one for "current rent" due. Anne said, "He told me that he was still going to charge me back rent." So Anne had to get to work to make up the back and current rent payments. "And I did it. It took me a while. I babysat for some of the people I used to play racquetball with. And then a man at the racquetball club owned a small business and heard that I needed a job, and he hired me as a secretary/receptionist."

Anne's fortunes seemed to be changing for the better. "It was a family-owned land-surveying company. It was a great place to work. The man and his wife ran the company with their two sons. They ran it like an old-school business. At Christmas time they paid us two weeks' salary as a bonus, and they bought us nice gifts. It was on Elston Avenue, just north of Montrose. It's still in business these days. The man passed away, but I think the sons still own it. I worked there for three or four years."

However, Anne began pining for better opportunities. She said, "I was getting bored. I thought, 'Is this what I want for the rest of my life?' I felt like there had to be more out in the world. I wanted to go to college, and I signed up at Wright College, and I got a job at Jim Beam Brands in Deerfield. I worked there for one day. Oh, God, I hate change. I was a little immature. I walked out after my first day, and I never went back. So I quit, and my dad got pissed again. I remember he was talking to my mom, and he said about me, 'What in the hell's wrong with her?' My mom said, 'But she didn't like it.' He said, 'Well, that's too God-damned bad. She's got to get her ass out there and get to work. What's wrong with this girl?'"

Anne, tail tucked firmly between her legs, went begging at her old job. She said, "I went to get my old job back at the surveying company, but they had already hired a new person. My dad was so furious with me. I told him Deerfield was too far away. And now that I say this, it sounds so stupid because I went to Deerfield all the time." And once more, Harry had his "back rent" and "current rent" bulletin board out again. Anne continued, "I don't remember how long I was out of work, but I was getting used to it. Maybe I was a millennial before my time." The passing years and gaining more maturity can change a person. She added, "Now, I like working, which is unbelievable. I think my dad would be surprised that I like working so much."

Anne's professional pursuits were finally progressing down a solid career path, and her strong work habits were firmly in place. She said, "There was a job opening at a company called Duo-Fast in Franklin Park. It was a manufacturer of staples, nails, and tools. I thrived there. I started as a receptionist for all the salespeople, and then the two vice-presidents recognized that I could get the work done with a quick turnaround. I'm kind of a type-A. Then the VPs were like, 'Hey, if you're not busy could you do this for us?' They would be happy because I'd get the letter typed or whatever right away. They'd say that they had to wait for the next day to get the work done from the others in the office. They sort of bypassed the other receptionist/secretaries because I had a quick turnaround. And I didn't make mistakes. So I started doing their secretary's work, and then she left, and I took her spot."

Anne's determinative ways suited her operational style—especially when working with sales-minded individuals. She said, "I was still going to classes at Wright College, and I asked the bosses for a raise, but they didn't want to give me one. I found out that they gave four other guys at the company $10,000 raises. I didn't bitch about it. Instead, I came up with a plan. I wanted to transfer from Wright College to DePaul because they had an adult program, but it was too expensive for me. So I asked one of my bosses for a meeting. I had a whole presentation. I said that they didn't give me a raise, but there's a program at DePaul that I wanted to attend. But I can't afford the program because you didn't give me a raise. However, if I go to DePaul and take the classes, it would help the company. I asked that the company pay my tuition. They'd get a tax write-off. I could still go to school and still work at the company. And so they agreed. I said I'd take on more responsibilities, and I'd be taking classes that could help the company in the future."

Anne's professional fortitude and interpersonal talents would help launch her into a new civic-minded opportunity a few years down the road. But first, she had more maturing on her horizon and challenges to overcome.

14

AFTER LEAVING the boat repair job in Wilmette, Michael Belluomini started working with the natural gas utility company that services the Chicago suburbs. There was better pay to be had and benefits. The job could mean some security for the young man. What he'd discover was that his most valuable benefit was living right under the same roof, in the form of a seasoned CPD detective.

Michael said, "I ended up getting on with the gas company in their Glenview facility. They hire you as either a meter reader, where most people start, or, if you were like me and you had a mechanical background, they'd put you in the garage doing vehicle maintenance. I worked the 3-to-11 shift in the Glenview garage. My job title was Mechanic's Helper. I would alternate jobs doing oil and grease changes on fleet vehicles. Then the following month, I would deliver company mail to various gas company locations around the Chicago area. The following month I'd be making sure the fleet vehicles were filled with fuel every day. I was there for four months, and I had just gotten into the union."

That's when his perceived security suddenly evaporated. "One day, the bosses came into the place and called a meeting in this one room. Myself and eight others were waiting our turns to be called into the room. Three people had gone in so far, but no one was coming out. Finally, they called me into the room, and the person in charge, the vice president of our division, said, 'Michael Belluomini, have a seat.' So I'm sitting there, and he starts reading off a paper in his hand. He said, 'Michael Belluomini, we are terminating you for the following reasons.' I was in shock. Terminating! I was a 19-year-old kid. I'd never been fired from a job. I've always held down a job up to that point."

As Michael's shock and pain just started to settle in, an extra jolt of agony was right around the corner. He said, "So he read off charges like stealing company property, being signed in when I wasn't there, using marijuana, drinking on the job. The list went on and on, and I was thinking, 'What the hell is going on?' So they then escort me out to my locker, and there are two Glenview Police Officers going through my stuff in the locker. I was thinking, 'Why are they going through my locker? Did they plant something in my locker, like marijuana, too?'"

The search would come up empty, of course. "They didn't find anything. So they put my stuff into a box, and they escort me out to the parking lot, and I'm on my way. I get home, and I'm crying. My dad saw me, and I told him what happened. He said, 'Did you do these things?' And he's screaming. I told him I didn't do any of the things I was accused of. I've never tried drugs my whole life, I never smoked weed, none of that kind of stuff. I knew my dad would kill me if I had. It was a good thing I got into the union because I now had their protection." He also had his father in his corner.

Harry Belluomini's detective instincts kicked in right away. Michael said, "So my dad goes over to the gas company's Glenview facility, and he sees my foreman sitting under a tree. He had just gotten fired, too. He was a nice guy. The foreman told my dad that I was a good kid and that I had kept my nose clean, and that I had gotten railroaded. So it turns out that some of those fired were doing stuff, and it all started before I got hired. Four of those fired were mechanics, and they were working on their friend's cars in the company garage during hours. Some of them were drinking, and I had seen a couple of them smoking weed. What started this whole episode was that an arc welder mounted on a truck had been stolen from the facility. The truck was recovered, but the arc welder was missing from it. So the gas company had hired this older guy to work in the garage after the equipment was stolen. I remember training this guy on how to do a couple of the duties at the place, like how to drive the tanker truck to fuel up the fleet vehicles. This new employee asked me what was in all the trucks we were working on, and I told him that I didn't know. My job was to fuel up trucks and to do oil and grease changes. I knew something was up with this guy. I didn't know it at the time, but he was a mole for an investigation company that the gas company had hired."

Some of Harry's investigative instincts had rubbed off on young Michael, but he hadn't put things together before it was too late. Michael said, "I knew something was up, and I was a 19-year-old, and these other employees at the facility are hanging out with him, going on their breaks with him, drinking with him. I had seen what was going on, but I didn't say anything. I was just minding my own business. All nine of us filed an official grievance, and right after that, my dad had us all meet at one of the guy's places in Evanston. He was one of the mechanics. A nice guy, too. My dad got us there and said, 'Listen, somebody here may be a mole. So don't say anything about any of this stuff to anyone unless you have your union rep or a union lawyer with you.'" Well, that new hire, who was...'fired' with the rest of us, started getting angry. My dad said, 'What did I just say? Keep your mouth shut.' So my dad knew then that something was up, and sure enough, after my dad did a background check on this guy, he had an unlawful use of a weapon charge against him. The new guy had been arrested. All kinds of stuff was dug up on this guy."

Among fellow employees of the gas company at that time, Michael and the others who were fired would be known as "The Glenview Nine." Unfortunately, Michael's nightmare would last a while. He said, "We went to the arbitration hearings, and this went on for three years. During that time, I wound up going to Wright College and working a part-time job because I knew I'd be getting my gas company job back. I got my associate's degree at Wright College. So all the arbitration hearings finally came down to the company admitting that they were wrong. Three of us got reinstated with full back pay. Some of the others were reinstated with no back pay because they had actually violated some of the rules they were accused of breaking. So I got three years of back pay and my seniority. I was promoted when I started back to work. Those others fired that day told me that if it weren't for my dad, they wouldn't have their jobs back. The union lawyer, who was from St. Louis, even admired my dad for being smart about things. One of the union guys thought we won the case because of the lawyer, and the lawyer and others were saying that it was my dad who won the case for us."

Michael's secure job was back once again. "When I went back to the gas company, I worked on a street crew and worked on the gas mains. I helped to install new service lines to new residences. And I worked on gas leaks, digging up the ground, and stuff like that. It was ball-busting, but it was a good job."

15

AFTER 31 years with the Chicago Police Department, working primarily as a detective, Harry Belluomini retired. The date was August 2, 1988. He had amassed many commendations, honorable mentions, and complimentary letters for his work throughout his career. Harry displayed his keen sense of what's right and wrong time and time again over his entire career. And regarding Belluomini's many commendations, Milly said, "Harry never really told me when he got written commendations. He usually tossed them out. One time he said, 'I'm just doing my job. What do I need this piece of paper for?'" Having clerks search the CPD archives gained very little information about Harry's "official" career record, other than a one-sheet abstract listing the number of his commendations, honorable mentions, and complimentary letters he received, not the specific details of each entry.

When I asked George Ruckrich about the lean file left behind after Harry's career had ended, he said, "I was the third in command of the entire department for a time, and there's not much information for me, either. That was all before they had computers to store the stuff. It's all gone." However, at our meeting Ruckrich did hand me the actual commendation letter that he and Harry had received from the FBI for handling the robbery at the Almira Savings and Loan Association in 1964. He said, "Please give this to Milly."

Life was, happily, going to change for the Chicago natives, Harry and Milly Belluomini. Now came the time for the construction of a new ranch-style, waterfront home in the north woods and a permanent move to Wisconsin. Frank Radtke said, "Harry wanted to build a house in Wisconsin at a place he called the Loon capital of the world. I said, 'That sounds perfect for you.' Harry laughed. We were always joking around like that."

Harry's childhood buddy Bill Broderick said, "Harry looked forward to moving to Wisconsin after retiring. He talked about that a lot."

Milly was ready to move north, too. Except for her sister Anne, her entire family already lived in the same area where they would build their new home. "Harry loved northern Wisconsin," Milly explained. "He didn't want to move to Florida. He didn't want to go out West. He loved to fish and to go for long walks. He just loved it there. There were the Friday night fish fries with friends. It was just a relaxed way of life, and you didn't have to constantly look over your shoulder all the time. You could leave the keys in your car and your front door unlocked all the time."

First, there was a formal retirement party to attend. The gathering, organized by Harry's many friends on the department, kicked off on Friday night, September 9, 1988, at the Venice Banquet Hall on Fullerton Avenue. A few hundred of Harry's closest friends and fellow police officers assembled to send him off in a Rat Pack-like old-school roast. Harry's son Michael said, "When you have that many people show up to ball-bust, most of who were bosses, you know you were well thought of and respected."

Specifically for the event, one of the CPD's sketch artists did a rendering of the "suspect" Harry Belluomini. Copies of the drawing were distributed to those attending the party. In the image, by expert sketch artist Leo Feltman, Harry exhibits a clear-eyed expression, with just the hint of a farewell smirk on his lips. That same sketch adorns the cover of this book.

CPD Sergeant Joe Greco was one of the roasters. His chop-busting bit revolved around the hypothesis: Is Harry Belluomini an alien?

Greco's premise contained seven items listing clues as to whether Harry was, indeed, from another planet or not. Greco said, "Number one. Wearing odd or mismatched clothes. Some aliens do not fully understand styles. They wear combinations that are bizarre or in bad taste. Two; does the subject display a bizarre sense of humor. Misunderstanding earthly humor, they may laugh at or tell jokes that make no sense. Three, Harry was always very protective of his papers. Aliens are always gathering information. Number four: They constantly question their coworkers and their customs. Aliens may ask questions that seem stupid. Five, they are secretive about their personal lifestyle and home life. An alien won't discuss domestic details or talk about what it does at night or on weekends. Number six, Aliens frequently talk to themselves. An alien may be practicing our language. And number seven; does the subject display a change of mood or a physical reaction when near a golf course or Wisconsin."

One of the gifts that Harry received that night was a check from his coworkers, who had all pitched in for their buddy's joyful send-off. The note attached to the check read: "Harry, your friends, and others who have attended this affair to make sure you leave, wish to extend to you the best of times. This check is to be used specifically for one of two purposes—The Irish Relief Fund or a trip to Las Vegas (Milly deserves it!!!). Good traveling, (signed) your friends."

After the retirement party was over, and once Harry and Milly had arrived back at their Edison Park residence, and taken off their formal clothing, and settled in for the night, Harry wept. A new chapter in life was about to begin for the former detective. He was both melancholy and excited for what his future would hold.

In November of 1988, Harry Belluomini applied for a Court Security Officer's position with General Security Services Corporation (GSSC) of Minneapolis, Minnesota. The Federal Government had recently privatized some of its security services in facilities all across the nation. GSSC had the security contract for the Dirksen Federal Building in Chicago. But Harry still needed to be trained by the U.S. Marshals Service in security techniques. He completed that course work locally, in Chicago, shortly after applying for the position with GSSC. And then he began his part-time Court Security Officer job in the Dirksen Federal Building in downtown Chicago. Harry intended to keep his part-time job until he and Milly could firm up their plans to build a home in Wisconsin and sell their Edison Park home.

On the job with GSSC, Harry was a front-row witness to the goings-on at the Dirksen Federal Building. When not working in the secured garage beneath the building's 30 stories, he checked visitors through the metal detectors in the lobby. Milly said, "The famous Chicago news anchor, Walter Jacobson, came to the Federal Building once, and Harry made him show his ID and empty his briefcase. Harry said Jacobson said, 'Don't you know who I am? I'm the WBBM news anchor,' and Harry said, 'I don't watch the news. I watch cartoons.' He pissed off Walter Jacobson, but Harry said, 'That's too bad. He's just like everyone else going into that building as far as I'm concerned.'"

Harry liked to pull reporters' chains whenever he could. Milly added, "Whenever newspaper reporters would try to interview Harry for something, he'd tell them that his name was Harry LaPorte. That was the name he used. He never wanted his real name in the paper. He said he didn't want any criminals to know what he was doing."

Harry Belluomini and his mother Ruth in the 1930s.

Baby Harry and his mother Ruth.

Two-year-old Harry.

Harry Belluomini's CPD academy photo.

Harry and Milly dressed as nuns for a Halloween party.

An injured Harry and Milly at their wedding shower.

Milly and Harry's wedding day.

Retired CPD detective Tom Minasola.

The Belluomini family's first cabin near Winter, Wisconsin.

Retired CPD detective Tedy Nadile.   Retired CPD detective Louis Alviso.

Retired CPD detective Brian
DuFour.

Retired CPD detective Stan Golucki
and his wife, Carol.

Retired CPD detective Curt Blanc.

Milly's sister Anne and her husband
Joe Vuich.

Milly and Harry enjoying their pontoon boat in Wisconsin.

The toy car town Harry built for his son Michael when he was a young boy.

Anne, Harry, Karen, Michael, and Milly Belluomini celebrate Christmas in the 1980s.

Harry enjoying one of his social gatherings.

Milly and Harry at their Wisconsin cabin in 1990.

Milly and Harry celebrate New Years in the late '80s.

Milly and Harry playing bags at their Wisconsin cabin.

Karen and Harry at Karen's CPD academy graduation ceremony.

Former CPD partners Tammie Pena Arroyo and Karen Belluomini.

CPD sketch artist Leo Feltman prepared this rendering for Harry's retirement party.

Former Palatine Police Officer Kevin Maher. Maher was injured in a shooting by the Bearded Bandit.

Retired Park Ridge Police Officer Dick Paul.

Retired CPD commander Tom Argenbright was one of the first detectives on scene at the Dirksen Building.

Harry's grave at St. Adalbert Catholic Cemetery, Niles, Illinois.

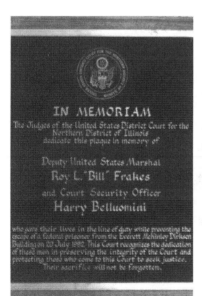

The Dirksen Federal Building plaque dedicated to Belluomini and Frakes.

Michael, Anne, and Karen at the plaque dedication ceremony for their father.

The Wisconsin home Milly had built after Harry's death.

Milly's Wisconsin home in the aftermath of the fire.

Milly, Karen, Michael, and Anne at Michael's CPD academy graduation ceremony.

Michael Belluomini under the street sign bearing his father's name at the Dirksen Federal Building.

CPD officer and Anne's academy instructor, Michael Simi.

Karen, Milly, Anne, and Michael at Anne's CPD academy graduation
ceremony.

Anne, Michael, family friend actor Dennis Farina, and Karen at the CPD's
Gold Star memorial wall.

Maureen Kowalski, Milly Belluomini, and Kathy Paddock at a Wisconsin
get-together.

16

Not long after he retired, Harry was once again called upon to apply his commanding ways on behalf of his son Michael in what could've become a significant purchase fiasco. Michael said, "I bought my first new vehicle, which was a brand new 1989 Ford Bronco XLT. I had to order it."

The total price of the truck came out to $16,999, and Michael gave the dealership a down payment of $2,000, leaving the balance at $14,999. When the car arrived at the dealership, they called Michael to provide him with the good news. Michael was excited, and it was on a Friday night, so he was looking forward to driving his new Bronco around all weekend. When Michael got off the phone with the dealership, Harry asked, "Do you want to go and get the truck?" Michael knew that his father had a retirement party to attend at the Snuggery Pub in Edison Park, so he told Harry that he'd have a friend drop him at the dealership instead.

"So I go into the dealership and find my salesman," Michael continued. "I hand him the check for $14,999, and he says, 'No, the balance is $16,999.' I was like, 'Wait a minute. The original price was $16,999. I gave you a $2,000 down payment, and the balance is $14,999.' The salesman then told me that they couldn't sell me the truck at that price. I showed him the original, agreed-upon paperwork, but he still said no, that I couldn't get the truck at the original price." Michael was, of course, angered. "So I asked to get my $2,000 back. The salesman said he couldn't do that because the business office was closed. I told him that I'm either getting the truck or my money back. He said that I'd have to come back Monday morning when the business offices were open again. I felt like a sucker. And it was my first experience buying a new vehicle."

The incensed Michael stormed out of the dealership and went home to stew. But that didn't last long. Michael said, "I wind up going over to the pub where my dad is, and I hated to bother him. He had a couple of beers in him, and he was asking, 'Hey, did you get your truck?' I told him the whole story, and he and I got into his car and drove to the dealership. He's pissed. He's steaming after I told him what happened. So we both walk into this dealership on a Friday night, like a bar scene from an old Western, and my dad calls out in the loudest voice, 'Where's Joe [the salesman]?'" And everyone in that place just stops and looks at my dad. Some guy came over and asked what he could do for us, and my dad said he wanted to see the manager. The guy said the manager wasn't there, so my dad asked to see Joe, the salesman. My dad laid into the guy and told him that I either get the truck or I get a check. The guy said if my dad didn't calm down, he was going to call the Niles Police. My dad said, 'I don't give a shit who you call.'"

Within minutes, the Niles Police arrived at the dealership to find an irritated Harry Belluomini, pacing back and forth on the sales floor among the shiny new cars. Michael said, "We showed the police my contract and the dealership's contract, and you could tell that the dealership changed the number on their copy of the contract. The Niles policeman said that he could definitely tell that the dealership fudged the number on their copy. Even after the Niles officer showed the salesman the differences, he still said he couldn't sell me the truck at that price. So my dad, again, said, 'Give my son the truck or his down payment money back.'"

The dealership miraculously found an employee in the building who could cut the refund check for Michael Belluomini.

Michael giggled and added, "As we're walking out, we stepped past a room where a couple was sitting with another salesman looking as if they were about to purchase a car. My dad stopped, stuck his head into the room, and said, 'You gotta be fucking nuts to buy a car from this place.' It was the funniest thing. Even the Niles coppers were laughing. Hey, my dad was sticking up for his kid. I ended up buying my truck from a dealership in Wisconsin. That dealership in Niles is no longer there." Mamma bears are a force to be reckoned with, but don't mess with an Italian-American Papa bear, especially one who's a time-tested CPD detective.

17

MOST PEOPLE experience growing pains while navigating their 20s. There's attending college (or not), finishing college (or not), finding jobs, possible marriages, etc. Karen Belluomini had a rough go of it finding her place in the world during her 20s. But she was tenacious, intelligent and kept trying to better her standing in life. She also had excellent tour guides to life in the form of Milly and Harry Belluomini.

Karen worked as a bookkeeper for Consolidated Stamp Company in Harwood Heights, not far from her parent's home. She said, "I was married at 21. It was sad moving out of the house. And then the marriage didn't work out. I was only married for a few months. My ex-husband hated my family. It was bad. He was controlling and abusive. I was close with my family, and my ex would take the cord off the phone and hide it so I couldn't call them. I didn't want to tell my dad what was going on because my dad would've killed him. Annie, my sister, knew what was going on."

Once the marriage was over, Karen moved back to her parent's home. She said, "It was kind of uncomfortable and kind of embarrassing for me because I was divorced. I was one of the only ones in my family to get one. I finally got back on my feet and got myself an apartment of my own. I decided that I had to get my life in order after the divorce. My ex left me with a lot of bills that I had to pay." Karen experienced a life jolt again when she was fired from Consolidated Stamp after discrepancies arose with employee time cards and her accounting skills were questioned. Her firing led to a better-fitted administrative job at Comdisco in Rosemont. Comdisco operated on a Business-to-Business model, and their forte was computer product leasing and asset management. Karen said, "That was a great job. They treated employees well, but when they started to get larger and larger, I saw the writing on the wall for me and my position." The company seemed to be growing so rapidly that it couldn't keep up with its expansion. Customer care fell by the wayside, and that's a recipe for disaster in the corporate world. She was at Comdisco from the ages of 21 to 25. That's when another significant life change appeared on her near horizon. It was an advantageous move for the young woman because Comdisco would eventually file for bankruptcy.

She considered joining the family business, specifically the Chicago Police Department. "I thought about taking the police department test. A friend of mine had talked me into it. He was a guy who I had gone to grammar and high school with. His dad knew and worked with our dad. His name was Lenny Muscolino. I was hesitant, but Lenny said that I could do it and pass the test. I took the test, and my dad was pissed. He was not happy. And the more he got pissed off, the more I wanted to do it. If he doesn't think I can do this, I'm going to do it."

Karen's sometimes obstinate personality traits were set in stone when she was a toddler, but now her pushback had some serious upside and a dangerous downside. She said, "I've always been pretty rebellious, you know. The more I thought about being a Chicago Police officer, the more I liked the idea. You get a pension, and you get health care. I was 25 years old when I got on the job. All that stuff I went through before joining the police department, like dealing with those other jobs and my ex-husband, it made me stronger. I mean, with each job I had before, I bettered myself. I think that's what you're supposed to do. And I did it."

Karen did it, all right, but the journey to a badge and a blue uniform was not an easy one. Karen continued, "I got to the police academy, which I hated. Oh my God, I couldn't stand it there." She said she was like the Goldie Hawn character in the movie *Private Benjamin*. "I had the nail polish on and the long hair. All of that had to go. For me, I hated being told what to do. I'm sure I wasn't the only person like that there. I'd tell my parents that I was going to quit, and my dad said, 'You're not quitting.'" In Harry's mind, if Karen was going to go through the trouble of applying to be on the CPD, and she was fortunate enough to be invited to the police academy, she'd see her next professional move through to fruition. There was no backing out now. Karen said, "I used to go to my aunt and uncle's house and cry at their kitchen table, saying, 'I don't think I can do this anymore.' It was brutal. So I told my dad at that time, 'Well, I made it to the academy. I did it. Now I can quit.' And he said, 'You're not quitting now.' I finished, thanks to my aunt and uncle and some friends, who all helped me get through the academy."

One academy test had to be accomplished before Karen and her classmates could graduate and be awarded their stars. And it was a difficult one. It was what the police academy called the "red man" test. First, one of the instructors would dress in a red-colored padded suit to avoid injuries. Then, the students would be required to work in pairs to take the "red man" offender to the ground and place him into custody utilizing proper techniques. Karen Belluomini and her fellow academy student, Dale Willingham, were only a few of the students to achieve their goal of placing the "red man" into custody. And because Belluomini and Willingham had been successful, they were awarded their stars early.

Karen was thankful to have made it through the demanding mental and physical coursework, and she was also honored with a surprise from her formerly disapproving father. After taking the "red man" test, she was handed a manila envelope in her police academy classroom. "When I opened the envelope with my star inside, it was my dad's old star. I started crying. I didn't know, but my dad had gone to the guy who had gotten his old star and asked if he could switch with the star I was supposed to receive. The other officer was nice enough to do that for us. That really surprised me. Then I knew that my dad was proud of me." As a result, Karen and Dale Willingham were able to wear their stars on their uniforms at the academy before the official graduation ceremony. In contrast, some of the others in their class had to retake the "red man" test. Once they had passed their final test—the rest of the students were awarded their stars at the graduation ceremony.

The first area of operation Karen Belluomini was assigned to was the 13th District, also known as the Wood District. It was the same one Harry Belluomini was assigned to when he graduated from the academy in 1957. Karen said, "When I was first on the job, I was supposed to go to the 16th District, which is the Edison Park area, which is not a training district. My dad found that out and did not want that for me. He said, 'I don't want you sitting behind a desk and becoming a do-nothing fat ass.'"

Harry called in a favor with the brass and had some strings pulled for his daughter, but not in the sense that his offspring would be working in a less dodgy area. Karen continued, "He had me transferred to the 13th District. And I thought, 'Holy crap, the 13th District. He really hates me.' The 13th District is at Wood and Augusta on the west side of Chicago, near the old Chicago Stadium and the Henry Horner projects." The 13th District, historically, has covered one of the most dangerous parts of the city of Chicago.

Karen said, "It was the best thing that my dad ever did for me. I worked in that district for nearly ten years. I learned everything I ever needed to know working in that district and with a bunch of great guys. That was the same district my dad started in when he came on the job, too. It was like the whole world gathered in that district. You had the projects. You had Ukrainian Village. We were near Humboldt Park, so you had the Puerto Rican neighborhood. You had the Italian neighborhood over near Grand Avenue. You had some hillbillies, and then the Yuppies started moving in on the east part of the district. You had all sorts of people there. You had everything there, and it was a nice little district."

One of Karen's former patrol partners, Tammie Pena Arroyo, said,

"Karen is very funny and very sarcastic. She's also a very consistent person. She was a sort of a voice for the underdog, like the homeless and the stray animals or the police officer that other officers made fun of. Any time she saw an underdog, she came to the rescue. She was always empathetic to the underdogs. She was consistent—consistent in that way. She was a protector."

When she met Harry Belluomini, Arroyo immediately saw that Karen and her father were very much alike. She said, "Karen's just like her father in many ways. She was a great partner, and she had the biggest heart. Especially for the homeless and stray animals, stray dogs particularly. If she saw homeless people, she would stop and give them a couple of bucks, or if she had food, she'd give it to them. If she saw a stray dog, she'd stop and try to get the dog to come to her. She had some type of dog food with her all the time in the trunk. She'd always have dog food or treats. She was always trying to coerce stray dogs to come to her, which drove me nuts at the time because I was not a dog person. I'd say, 'Karen, what are you doing?'"

Drawing further comparisons to her father, and as much as Karen loved taking care of wayward animals in her district of operation, she had one sole purpose in life. Arroyo continued, "Her number one priority was always her family. On Sundays, they would get together and eat, play games, and watch football games. She was such a sports fanatic. I always thought it was a cool thing, and a bit unusual, for anyone I knew to say that they had any consistent family time once a week."

Arroyo recalled their time together in a patrol car. She said, "We both liked working on midnight shift. She worked side jobs, and I worked a combination of side jobs, and I went to school, too. We knew each other's routine, and we understood when one of us was tired and needed to have a quieter night." And when their meal break times came, the partners were always on the hunt for unique places to find good food. "We both loved to eat. We'd get comments from the other officers saying that they'd never seen anyone eat as much as we did. On midnights we'd sneak over from the 13th District to the 14th District and get Father and Son pizza. We'd eat burritos at a Mexican place on Chicago Avenue. We'd do burgers at a place I don't think is there anymore, on Milwaukee Avenue. There was a bar that had great bar food and pasta. It was an actual bar with music and people drinking. We didn't care. We'd go in wearing our uniforms and order because the food was great. I'm telling you, nothing got in the way of our food."

Arroyo said that one of their calls she remembered fondly seemed as if it came straight from an episode of the TV police comedy *Brooklyn Nine-Nine.* Arroyo continued, "We responded to a domestic situation one time where the homeowners must have just laid those square vinyl tiles on the floor. I remember walking into that place, and there were a few other officers there, as well as the family's dog, a little Chihuahua. We were all walking around with square vinyl tiles stuck to our feet, including that dog."

Karen was on the solid path to a long career with the CPD. However, after getting her fill of the action in the 13th District, it was time for a change. Karen said, "After nearly ten years of working in the 13th, I started seeing the same crap over and over again, and I was just sort of sick of it. The final straw for me was dealing with a dog that was hit in the head with a machete. It just kind of broke me. I needed a change, and I needed to get the hell out of there. A friend of mine, who has since passed away, a man named Miles Myers, suggested I transfer to O'Hare Airport. He had done it a few years earlier." However, Karen hesitated and never made the call to try to start the transfer process. So her friend Miles did the next best thing. "Miles threatened to make the phone call for me if I didn't do it myself. So I called my dad's friend Frank Radke, who was the boss at O'Hare, and put in for the transfer. It was the best thing I ever did. I dealt with goofy tourists and stuff, but nothing real ugly. You're away from the gangs and other ugly parts of the world."

18

THROUGHOUT 1990 and heading into 1991, police in the Chicago area, and the FBI, began noticing a pattern from one of several bank robbery suspects plying their dangerous trade at the time. Unfortunately, business was booming for bank robbers, and more than a few were crisscrossing the area. It was a record-breaking bank robbery moment in time for the Chicago area. The unique robber in question, though, was operating in an exceptionally professional yet terrifying way. He was always described as a tall, Caucasian man— a menacing man who operated with extreme precision. The physical descriptions of this man would change slightly, sometimes dramatically, from robbery to robbery. Occasionally, the bank robber was described as being svelte, other times as being rather heavy-set. The police would later determine this was due to the suspect frequently using padding under his shirts, coveralls, and jackets. One similarity in all the robberies was that the male offender always wore a fake beard, sunglasses, and gloves. In his non-gun hand, he held a portable police scanner, which he listened to intently.

This same robber had an identical modus operandi nearly every time he'd take down a bank. He would approach a teller, make his intentions known, and order that teller or another teller standing nearby to open the bank's vault—all the while pointing a large caliber pistol at their heads. The robber had a verbal countdown to hurry the tellers along and make them bend to his will, starting at

30 and working back to zero. If the bank employees didn't have the vault opened and the money, sans a dye pack, in the robber's duffel bag by the time he reached zero, he would threaten to kill the tellers. The robber would listen to the police scanner in his hand, and if he heard a bank robbery call dispatched out to patrol officers in the area, he'd know that a silent alarm had been tripped and that he had mere seconds to get the money and make his escape. The pattern that emerged from the spate of crimes also revealed that most of the bank jobs pulled off by this Bearded Bandit usually took place on a Monday and that a stolen Japanese- or Korean-made vehicle was used in each of the robberies. The stolen cars would later be found within a block or two of the initial robbery scene. The authorities assumed that the actual getaway car would be staged at that secondary location.

The authorities also noticed something more troubling in the images captured by bank surveillance cameras during the robberies. The evidence seen in the photos could make their job a lot more complicated and deadly if they ever had to confront the Bearded Bandit. The unsettling development was only evident when the bank robber momentarily placed his police scanner on the bank teller's countertops. It was the way the offender held his pistol when aiming at bank employees. The robber utilized a two-handed "Weaver Stance." The Weaver Stance requires that the shooter hold the trigger controlling hand straight, forward, aimed at their target. The non-controlling hand is wrapped under the shooting hand, and the non-shooting arm is bent forward at a nearly 45-degree angle for support and to create a more stable platform. The foot opposite the shooting hand is placed ahead like a right-handed football quarterback when he plants his left foot before launching a pass. The overall stance adds stability to the shooting platform, not allowing the shooting hand to hang in the air and be thrown off by recoil when firing the weapon. In the early 1990s the Weaver Stance was a type of shooting stance taught only to those in the military and police departments. If the offender was military or police trained and had an accurate shot, the authorities might be facing a deadly situation for themselves or any passersby if a shootout took place.

While this book focuses on Harry Belluomini and his family, some information about the Bearded Bandit is required for context. Who was Jeffrey Erickson? What was Harry Belluomini up against on that day in July of 1992? Finding people to speak with about the suburban cop turned alleged bank robber, proved a near-impossible task. One former neighbor from Morton Grove didn't even know the Bearded Bandit was his neighbor, and they were the very same age, and they'd grown up close to one another. Another individual was pictured standing next to the Bearded Bandit in a high school yearbook photo, and yet, this person claimed they had never heard of the bank robbery suspect.

After more than a year of trying and subsequently contacting more than a dozen people from his past, almost no one associated with the Bearded Bandit wanted to talk about the man. And those who spoke did so with apprehension.

Betsy Weiss-VanDie, a former classmate of the Bearded Bandit's at Niles West High School in Skokie, Illinois, said, "He graduated in 1977, and I graduated in 1976. He was just such a quiet kid. You never would, not in a million years, guess that he would have a life of crime. He was on the swim team, and he just blended in. He wasn't popular. He seemed like a loner and stayed to himself. But he seemed normal, you know?"

In 1990 Weiss-VanDie had several antique and vintage books she was looking to sell. By happenstance, she saw an ad in the newspaper touting a new bookstore in Roselle, a northwestern suburb of Chicago. Best Used Books on Irving Park Road was looking to buy old books. The store would possibly purchase what you were selling if the transaction didn't occur on a Monday. The store seemed always to be closed on Mondays.

Weiss-VanDie had no idea that when she spoke with the man at Best Used Books, she talked with her former high school classmate, even after he identified himself. It had been years since she had heard his name, so she hadn't recognized the connection. Weiss-VanDie said, "I saw an ad that they were looking to buy books, and I had a number of antique and vintage books that I wanted to sell. I called, and he picked up the phone, and he actually even said his name. I said I have these books that I would like to sell and how will this work. Do I have to make an appointment to come in, and where are you located, etc."

The Bearded Bandit asked Weiss-VanDie which volumes she had in her possession, and they discussed the books and how the purchasing process could work. Weiss-VanDie said, "He was very soft-spoken. He sounded very intelligent. He was very straightforward on the phone. Very professional." But when Weiss-VanDie attempted to lighten their conversation, she said, "He didn't have a sense of humor. He said he had to go and to call him back to make an appointment to show him my books, but I never did. I mean, not in a million years would you think that his bookstore was a front for a criminal. Of course, the following year, I heard the news about him being arrested, and I thought, 'oh, my God.' And when it was published that he went to Niles West, I was again thinking, 'oh, my God.' It was unbelievable." It was only at that time that Weiss-VanDie had finally figured out that she knew the Bearded Bandit.

Dick Paul, a retired Park Ridge Police officer and a police and fire communications equipment specialist, had quite a different experience with the man who would allegedly become the Bearded Bandit. Paul said, "He worked at the 7-Eleven on Oakton Street in Niles." The 7-Eleven in question, where the Bearded Bandit worked at the counter in the late-1980s, was located directly across Oakton Street from the Park Ridge municipal border. Thus, it was a convenient location for patrolling Park Ridge officers to get their coffee fix for their shift. "Some of the other guys and I used to go out there and hang out with him, and he seemed to us to be a nice guy. He worked the afternoons and evenings." Dick Paul and his fellow Park Ridge officers knew that the man who would allegedly become the Bearded Bandit was in the process of trying to get onto the Hoffman Estates

Police Department. Paul said, "I know he mentioned Hoffman Estates, and he was very proud about joining the department out there. He even brought part of his uniform into the store."

Paul continued, "He was very nice. Cordial. That was the thing, he sort of interacted with us, and we all talked. We used to go there and get our coffee and talk with him, and he would say, 'Hey, look at this,' and he'd show us part of his uniform. He was very proud of it."

The massive Chicago metropolitan area has a population of nearly 10 million residents and covers more than 10,000 square miles. Yet, Harry Belluomini and the Bearded Bandit had lived only three miles from one another when the alleged robber was living at home with his parents in Morton Grove. The 7-Eleven where the Bearded Bandit worked before becoming a police officer in the suburbs was even nearer, just two miles from the Belluomini family home in Edison Park. Harry and the Bearded Bandit may have crossed paths during their day. They could've met one another at the 7-Eleven when Harry was picking up a pack of cigarettes while on the way to a round of golf with his police buddies. Is it possible that the Bearded Bandit knew Harry to be a police officer and had talked with him about his upcoming job as a cop in the suburbs while working at the 7-Eleven? Or had the Bearded Bandit ever proudly displayed his police uniform to Harry, as he did for the Park Ridge officers? Come July of 1992; there was one hard fact—the viciousness wrought in the basement of the Dirksen Federal Building that warm evening was basically, and quite unfortunately, neighbor-on-neighbor violence.

19

THE BEARDED Bandit's first alleged bank robbery occurred on January 9, 1990, in Wilmette, Illinois. It may have been the start of a crime spree, but the beginning of the Bearded Bandit's end got underway on the morning of November 4, 1991, in the northwest suburb of Palatine, Illinois. It would become an event that would be the catalyst in launching a much larger effort to capture the dangerous criminal.

Former Palatine Police officer Kevin Maher is a highly cordial and professional man. When we met at a Barrington diner, he was quick with a smile and a pleasant joking manner. Maher's the youngest of five from an Irish-Catholic family. He grew up in nearby Mount Prospect, and attended St. Viator High School in neighboring Arlington Heights. He graduated from Northern Illinois University in 1990, and four months later, at 24 years of age, he was hired by the Palatine Police Department.

Of November 4, 1991, Maher said, "We got into roll call that day, and they told me I'd have a rider with me. My beat was the southwest section of Palatine. The ride-a-long's name was Jim Dunning. I told him that if I saw any type of violation, I'd make a traffic stop. It was about 11 AM, and it was sunny. It was a typical November day."

Jim Dunning, now the IT Coordinator for the Vernon Hills Police Department, and I spoke by phone the day after Maher and I met in the Barrington diner. Dunning was brand-new to the police- and fire-dispatching world in 1991. He was excited about the prospect of working alongside officer Maher that sunny November day. He said, "When I worked at Northwest Central Dispatch (NCD), they encouraged us to go out and ride along with officers in the various towns that we dispatched for. We were to pick up geography, special notes about the particular villages. At that time, we were dispatching for eight or nine police and fire communities."

Maher continued, "I was driving south on Quentin Road, south of Euclid Avenue. I was in the left-hand lane when I saw a car pass me. I thought it had an expired registration, so I turned around. The suspect car turned right on Euclid Avenue, so I turned right on Euclid. We were going eastbound on Euclid Avenue, and I was punching in the license plate information on my car's computer so that I could get a return from the state if the plate was expired or whatever. While I waited for the computer information, the suspect car took a very calm right-hand turn onto Smith Street."

Smith Street has a slight incline and decline as you travel south from Euclid Avenue. Dunning said, "The street went down into a little dip, so we came upon it, and before anyone was able to do anything, Kevin hadn't even stopped the car yet."

Maher continued, "I saw him jam on his brakes and reach for something that was on the right front seat. I saw him produce a rifle. I had a rear-side view of the weapon. Up until that point, it was all very nondescript. He was driving normally. I assumed that he just lived on Smith Street and he was going home. Nothing had tipped me off that he was [the Bearded Bandit]. When I jammed on my brakes, I had put my car into park so I could get out. But once I saw him reach for the rifle, I grabbed Jim Dunning's head and stuck it down in between his legs. By the time I had done that and looked back toward the suspect's car, [The Bearded Bandit] was standing alongside the car with the rifle at his shoulder. He was already firing on me. It happened so fast."

Jim Dunning said, "[The Bearded Bandit] got out of his car and started walking back towards us. He started shooting at the driver's side. As soon as the shooting started, Kevin threw the car into reverse and lit up the tires, and all I saw was the smoke from the tires as we were backing up. [The Bearded Bandit] got off a few shots, but as we backed off, he stopped shooting, got into his car, and took off."

Maher said, "I put my car into reverse and sped backwards. I had my head down, and all I could see was the white smoke that my spinning rear tires was producing. I didn't really hear the gunshots. It may be part of audio exclusion, something your body does when it goes into a fight or flight situation. I never heard the gunshots. I reversed back over the top of the hill all the way back to Euclid Avenue. To this day, I don't know how I did this because I never saw where I was going when I reversed at high speed, but I stopped just short of entering a busy Euclid Avenue."

The distance from the shooting location to the point where Maher stopped his reversing patrol car is approximately 500 feet. He was able to keep his car moving, in reverse, at a high rate of speed, practically straight backward for nearly the distance of two football fields. Maher added, "I don't know how I stopped where I did. I just did. For years after those events, there were still deep tire burn marks ingrained in the street leading from where the shooting occurred all the way to Euclid Avenue. While reversing, I never saw that I was approaching Euclid Avenue. I can't say that I planned it. I can't say anything about that. For lack of a better term, it was God's will that I stopped the car where I did. If I had backed out onto Euclid Avenue, we may have been hit by cross traffic." The speed limit on busy Euclid Avenue in that area of Palatine is 45 MPH.

Dunning added, "Kevin immediately got on his radio. And I don't know how to describe this, but Kevin that day was slouching to his right side as he drove. Sort of leaning over towards the center of the car." Once Maher had stopped the patrol car, they noticed that the windshield had damage. Dunning said, "He wasn't leaning real bad, but later when we saw where the shots went, neither one of us would be here today, especially if he'd been sitting up straight."

"There was a large red 'emergency' button on the mobile computer keyboard in my car. I hit that button," Maher recalled. Dunning also hit the red button. "I hit the button and drew my Glock pistol, and I called on the Palatine radio band for help. We also had a central communications center that would dispatch for several suburban departments. It's called the Northwest Central Dispatch System. The downside of having the central dispatch center is that the organization rotates dispatchers, and it's possible that the person dispatching may not know the details of the geography of your town."

Moments before the shooting started, fellow Palatine officer Larry Canada came upon a disabled car in another part of town. Maher said, "So as I was about to call in for help, Larry was calling in information about his disabled car. Larry Canada was about two miles away, and he got to me in, like, 30 seconds, it seemed. Kirkpatrick [another Palatine officer] was up in the northwest section of the city. But Palatine guys knew where I was. There was no delay from the other Palatine officers. But in the radio transmission, when NCD is keying up, you can hear the other dispatchers in the background telling all the other departments what's going on. So that's why those departments started to arrive, obviously."

Maher kept his calm the best he could and switched radio frequencies. He said, "I then went onto the Illinois State Police Emergency Radio Network (ISPERN) and called in [the shooter's description]. That's when Cook County Sheriff's Police and Illinois State Troopers and everyone else started rolling in my direction."

Thirty years after the events, Maher can remember the scene as it all played out, recalling it step by step. "I thought that maybe he was going to be coming back over the hill back after me. So I sat there facing forward with my pistol resting on the steering wheel. I was using the car for cover, and as I was talking on the radio, that's when the blood from my ear hit the microphone on my shoulder-mounted radio. I thought at that time that I got hit in the head, so I looked into the rearview mirror, and the side of my face was red. Every time I tilted my head to see the wound, the blood would trickle toward my cheek and chin. It probably looked worse than it was. But with my adrenaline pumping, it was helping with the blood flow."

Maher would realize a bit later that the blood flowing on the left side of his face was from where his left earlobe had been struck by bullet fragments or flying glass. He hadn't felt any pain up until that point, either. Maher continued, "I saw that my shirt was ripped. I knew that he fired multiple shots, but I didn't see any blood on my shoulder where my shirt was ripped. Quite honestly, I was focused on my face. I didn't know if he had hit an artery in my neck. I didn't know. I did know that he had fired through the windshield. I could see that. I could hear all of the sirens, so I knew help was coming. So as I'm waiting, I started giving out a description of the offender on the radio."

The following is from the transcript of the actual police radio traffic on November 4, 1991. Maher's call sign is 8140. Officer Canada's sign is 8154:

Northwest Central Dispatch (NCD): Go ahead 8154.

Officer Maher: Shots fired. Shots Fired. Officer down! Smith and Euclid. Officer down. Shots fired. I've been hit. I need an ambulance at Smith and Euclid.

NCD: 10-4

Officer Maher: Central, 8140.

NCD: 8140.

Officer Maher: Suspect's got an Uzi. Last seen... Hold on.

Officer Canada: 8154 en route.

Officer Maher: Hold on.

Officer Kilpatrick: 8144 is en route to that location, central.

NCD: 10-4. 44 we got Euclid and Rand. What's the cross-street there, Rand, and what else?

Officer Maher: No, Central. I'm at Smith and Euclid. Smith and Euclid. Down in my beat. I've been hit. I need an ambulance.

NCD: Smith and Euclid, they're on the way.

Officer Maher: The plate is Charles, Boy, 8727. C-Charles, B-Boy, 87-27. He's a male white. Small Toyota. Last seen in the area of Smith and Euclid in Meadows [Rolling Meadows].

NCD: 10-4.
Officer Kirkpatrick: 8144, what's the offender look like?
Officer Maher: Central, description of the offender, is a white male. 25
to 35. Black beret. Tan Jacket. He's armed with an Uzi. Armed with an Uzi.
NCD: 10-4. Male white. 25 to 35. Black beret. Armed with an Uzi.
Officer Maher: Direction of travel is southbound Smith from Euclid.

The confusion that sometimes occurred when Northwest Central Dispatch communicated with officers in those early days of the center's operation was evident in actual transcripts from the shooting event. First, they believed that Maher was at Euclid Avenue and Rand Road, in Mt. Prospect, some five miles from where they were located. However, even Maher got some details incorrect, which is forgivable under dire circumstances. He believed the offender's car was a Toyota and his weapon an Uzi. Neither was the case.

Jim Dunning said, "I remember hearing the screaming engine of the police car of one of his friends as he was arriving. He heard Kevin's radio call and was just blowing his engine to get there as fast as he could. He was actually the first unit on the scene. The officers started putting out a description, and everyone else started showing up. The other officers separated us and made sure we were okay."

Maher said, "The next thing that happened was the paramedics came and threw me on a stretcher. They stripped me from the waist up as they looked for any other injuries I may have suffered. Where I was shot in the shoulder burned, but I never felt excruciating pain. They put me in the back of the ambulance, and the adrenaline and everything was taking their effects, and I was freezing my ass off in that ambulance. So an Arlington Heights officer, Chuck Tiedje, who I was friends with, opened the back of that ambulance door to check on me. I told him I was freezing, and he gave me his leather jacket. The paramedics took me to Northwest Community Hospital. One of those paramedics was Scott Anderson, who is now the fire chief in Palatine."

Dunning added, "Neither one of us knew right away that Kevin had been shot. It was after the police had separated us that I learned Kevin had been shot in the shoulder. Together we had seen where the shots went, and that had he been sitting up, it would've been a totally different outcome. They checked me over and then took me to the Palatine Police station. That's when they found the [suspect's] car a block or so away and just around the corner. Throughout the process of debriefing, the police discovered that we had interrupted the robber as he was on the way to hit a bank around the corner from where we stopped him. It was one of those wrong place at the wrong time, or rather, right place at the right time sort of things. Depending on how you want to look at it."

Neither Maher nor Dunning realized that there was another eyewitness to the entire event. "It was a sunny, cool day," said Frances Cieslek, a Smith Street resident. "I had my two children at home, and they were watching *Nanny and the Professor* on TV." That was the moment Mrs. Cieslek heard a noise outside her home. "It didn't sound like a gunshot. I didn't know what it was. So when I looked out the window, I saw a golden-colored car parked in front of my house, and a police car, and a man standing with a gun and pointing it at the police car." The gunman took several methodical yet aggressive steps forward as he fired, taking vigilant aim as he advanced on the patrol car. Cieslek said, "He was standing straight up, almost like a military stance. He was advancing, and he took careful aim. He was firing very carefully."

Cieslek could see that 24-year-old Palatine Police patrolman Kevin Maher was at the wheel of the police car and that he had a male passenger. "I could tell that he [Bearded Bandit] was skilled in gunmanship," said Mrs. Cieslek, a woman also quite familiar with firearms and their usage. But the entire scenario playing out fewer than 100 feet away from her home had put Francis Cieslek entirely off balance. She said, "I actually thought they must be filming a movie. It's 11 in the morning, and it's a bright sunny day, and we usually have a nice quiet neighborhood. I was looking around, though, and there were no cameras or anything else around. I wasn't worried about us at all because he was focused on the police car. I don't think he [Bearded Bandit] looked around at all. He was very calm, though, and I think that's why I couldn't believe that this was real. I thought that he must be an actor. He just did everything slowly like he wasn't in a big hurry. He was very smooth and took careful aim, and then calmly walked back to his car."

Reality soon took hold of Francis Cieslek. She said, "So then I got a little frightened, but I thought should I open the door and harass him? I never thought he was a bank robber. I thought he was some sort of drug dealer or something. But I had the children inside, so I didn't do anything."

When Maher's retreating patrol car cleared her point of view, part of the fake beard worn by the offender fell away from his face. Mrs. Cieslek added, "So that's why I was able to identify him later [at trial]." The Bearded Bandit calmly turned and walked back to his gold-colored car and got inside. "As if nothing extraordinary had just happened. He pulled away, turned left, and went out of sight."

As the multiple police cars and an ambulance arrived at the other end of her block, the Palatine Police were also in Frances Cieslek's home, attempting to get as much information from her as they possibly could. But, she said, "When the police interviewed my son later, all he could describe was the smoke coming from the police car's tires as he drove away."

The Cieslek family had another close call an hour after the shooting took place. Cieslek continued, "My husband worked for Motorola at the time, and he would come home for lunch every day. I called him at work and told him that we had a bit of excitement here this morning. And he said, 'What, did your mother call twice?'" Mr. Cieslek promptly left his office once the situation was explained to him, anxious to get home so he could be with his frightened wife and children. But as the tan trench coat-wearing Mr. Cieslek stepped from his car in the driveway, a police helicopter swooped down, and several police officers began to encircle the homeowner. Frances Cieslek said, "[The Bearded Bandit] was wearing a tan coat, and the police were scouring the neighborhood looking for him." Frances Cieslek quickly, thankfully, identified her husband for police, and the tense situation dissipated. But, Cieslek continued, "My husband didn't go back to work that day."

Now at the hospital, Kevin Maher was finally feeling the physical effects of the attack he had just endured. He said, "At the hospital, they took x-rays and all of that. The doctor came into the room and told me that there's not much he could do about the injury. The bullet that went through my shoulder didn't cause any real internal damage to the bone. He said that the bullet did fragment a little bit. He said that the chunks of fragments would stay in me." Maher's wound wouldn't require stitches. He was bandaged on the front and the back shoulder and sent home. The through-and-through wound would eventually heal without any more complicated treatments.

Maher was only 24 years old and still living at his parent's home in Mount Prospect. Once released from the hospital later that same day, he went home to rest. "Commander Fleischhauer of the Palatine Police drove me home from the hospital," he recalled, "and as we were driving, he said, 'The FBI and some detectives are going to come to your house. They want you to look at some photos.' The FBI came to the house as well as Pat Dalton, a Palatine PD detective, and they sat at my kitchen and showed me pictures of the Bearded Bandit. They told me their theory that [the Bearded Bandit] was on his way to rob the bank two blocks from where I stopped him and all of that. They talked about how he would steal a car and put cardboard over the steering wheel column to hide that the car had been hotwired."

Maher went to the Palatine Police Department parking lot to see his damaged patrol car only days after the shooting. He said, "I didn't know how accurate of a shot it would've been if I hadn't ducked, until a few days later when I went to the police department and sat in the car. If I didn't duck, the bullet would've hit me right in the head. So one shot went through the windshield, and as I backed up over the hill, he put some shots into the top of the hood of the car. Three rounds hit the car. One round went through the hood, the firewall, the center of the car, between the two front seats, and into the trunk." Because of Maher's quick actions, he and Dunning had miraculously escaped the most severe violence of that November day without losing their lives or the lives of anyone in the neighborhood where the shooting occurred.

Maher's horror story was just getting underway, though. In the days after the shooting, his mind was reeling with swirling thoughts about his near-death experience. Maher said, "I didn't sleep for nearly a week after I was shot. It was bizarre because, at the time, I thought that the Bearded Bandit was trying to kill me, Kevin Maher, not a police officer. My mind was racing. Every time I closed my eyes, a thousand things would go through my mind. I would think about how I could've done things differently. Why did it happen? You know, x, y, z."

Maher was specifically fearful that the Bearded Bandit could try to attack him once again at his parent's home. "I didn't have a gun because the department stripped me of everything I was wearing when I got hurt. So because I couldn't sleep, I called the station a couple of times, and the commanders or the sergeants would talk to me on the phone. The other officers from my shift were awesome, too. Guys like Larry Canada, Joe Semro, and Keith Kirkpatrick. They'd come to the house to visit and see how I was doing. The city of Mount Prospect did a great job. They parked a police car in front of my house."

Maher would finally find some relaxation and comfort through an unlikely source. "I literally stayed up for six days, and then the guys from my shift came over, and we were watching the film *Silence of the Lambs* on video when I fell asleep. I ended up sleeping for almost twenty hours. I was off of work for six weeks while my shoulder healed," he said.

In one of the films produced about the Bearded Bandit, there was a significant sticking point for Jim Dunning, his family, and friends. As depicted in the movie, the shooting scene had a male officer at the wheel of the Palatine patrol car, but there was one sharp difference between the fictional scene and reality. Dunning said, "I want to point out that I am a man, not a woman like they showed in the movie."

Maher would soon be itching to get back into his patrol car. He said, "When I went back to work, I was on midnights. We got on shift at about 11 PM. And I immediately wanted to find a speeder to stop because I needed to get back into the swing of things. I called out a traffic stop on Northwest Highway, in the middle of town, and four of the other officers were there in about ten seconds. I'm sure that the guy I stopped got the crap scared out of him with the massive police response. The guys on my shift were great. They were looking out for me. Those guys carried me through that whole time." Maher added, "It was a weird confluence of events that I stopped him [Bearded Bandit] a few blocks before he could pull off his next robbery."

Within hours of Kevin Maher's shooting, the Palatine Police and the Chicago office of the FBI had put together a multi-jurisdictional task force to help in the speedy apprehension of the Bearded Bandit. The Bearded Bandit's bank-robbing crime spree would soon be at its end.

20

UNDER THE guidance of Chief John Koziol of the Palatine Police Department and the Chicago office of the FBI, the newly formed task force had figured out that the Bearded Bandit was using two stolen cars for each of his bank robberies. One stolen vehicle, always a Japanese or Korean brand, would be utilized to take down the bank in the initial robbery. That first stolen car would then be driven a block or two away to the location of the stashed second stolen vehicle.

The second stolen vehicle would take the robber to his personal car parked nearby, thus confusing any tailing witnesses or police. He'd rob a bank, switch cars twice, and be gone in a few minutes time. The task force members also determined through many victim interviews that it was likely the Bearded Bandit changed disguises when switching cars. This would prove to throw the police further off his trail. If he wore coveralls to the actual robbery, with padding around his midsection, that coverall/padding getup would be stripped off, and he'd be wearing possibly a flannel shirt, or something similar, underneath. The robber's beard would be gone from his face and tucked into a duffel bag along with his gun and police scanner by the time he drove the second stolen vehicle away. There was an evil brilliance to the way the man operated. He was crafty, dangerous, and soon enough, deadly.

On Monday, November 18, 1991, at 10:15 AM, two fake-beard-wearing men robbed the First Chicago Bank branch at 450 E. Higgins Road in Elk Grove Village. One man was described as being larger than the other. Both were described as six feet tall and taller. At first, the authorities didn't believe that this was a bank job by the Bearded Bandit because he always worked alone, but they were later proved to be incorrect. It was possible that the Bearded Bandit always had an accomplice who was there to aid in the robber's getaway, and it wasn't another male subject—she may have been the Bearded Bandit's wife, Jill Erickson. It was later revealed that the Bearded Bandit's wife was nearly six feet tall. The robbery at First Chicago Bank in Elk Grove Village would be the last of the successful robberies for the Bearded Bandit.

Weeks later, a local suburban police department had located a parked stolen Japanese-made vehicle in their jurisdiction with a towel draped over the steering column. A steering column obscured by a piece of cardboard or a towel is a telltale sign that a car thief had hotwired the car, and they were coming back for the vehicle. A good car thief, at that time, could use a flathead screwdriver to crack a vehicle's steering column and get the car running in just seconds. The Bearded Bandit, who also did some vehicle maintenance in the Marine Corps, seemed to be an expert at this process. The parked vehicle located by the suburban officer had been stolen from Randhurst Mall in Mount Prospect a few days prior. The officer who discovered the stolen vehicle promptly left the area where the car was parked and contacted the FBI by phone, making sure not to broadcast his find on a police band radio for anyone to hear.

The FBI staked out the stolen car to see if anyone would come back for the vehicle. And in the meantime, they had come up with an ingenious plan. They located another identical-looking vehicle and temporarily switched it with the original parked stolen vehicle. Once they got the original stolen car into the FBI garage, technicians placed a tracking device and an engine "kill switch" into the actual stolen vehicle before replacing it. So now, all the FBI had to do was watch and wait to see if the Bearded Bandit would return.

Two days later, an old gray van pulled up near the stolen vehicle, and a tall, clean-shaven Caucasian man got out of the passenger side of the van. The man moved to the stolen vehicle, got inside, started the engine, and the gray van and the stolen car left the scene. The FBI followed both the van and the stolen vehicle to a hardware store parking lot in the southern part of Schaumburg, where the man parked the stolen car, got out, and entered the van once more. Finally, the van drove away and was followed by the FBI to a townhome in nearby Hanover Park, Illinois.

Hours later, the police had determined the identity of the homeowners of the tidy little townhome in Hanover Park. They had the suspect's name, but they needed to catch the Bearded Bandit with the stolen car parked in the Schaumburg hardware store parking lot. The FBI needed to see the criminal in the act of using the stolen car to seal a solid court case against the offender. Their chance to arrest the Bearded Bandit would happen on a Monday morning, of course, the day that the Best Used Books store in Roselle would be closed.

It was Monday, December 16, 1991, to be exact.

An FBI SWAT team, all armed with automatic weapons and an engine kill switch transmitter, staked out the stolen car in the hardware store lot from various parked vehicles of their own. Suddenly, a tall clean-shaven Caucasian male carrying a duffel bag stepped into their view and entered the stolen vehicle. The suspect immediately went to work on starting the car. Once started, an FBI agent waiting in a parked vehicle nearby pushed a button on the kill switch transmitter, stopping the stolen car's engine. The suspect in the stolen car tried to start the vehicle once more, and the FBI agent killed the engine once again. As the man in the stolen car placed all his attention on getting the stolen car's engine to spark to life, the SWAT team exited their vehicles and formed a semi-circle around the stolen car and the suspect within. They had their automatic weapons pointed at the suspect, and when he finally noticed them, he raised his hands. The commander of the SWAT team ordered the Bearded Bandit from the vehicle, but he had another idea. The suspect leaned to his right and reached toward the duffel bag now sitting on the passenger seat. In the successive few heartbeats, the suspect would either comply with the shouted commands of the swat team or be shot and killed. The suspect leaned right one more time, but the swat team members quickly advanced and tugged the tall man from the driver's seat of the stolen car. They shoved him to the ground, chest first, and handcuffed and searched him.

One of the swat team members inspected the duffel bag and saw a cache of pistols and fake beards inside. The suspect himself was wearing four different colored layers of clothing and a bulletproof vest.

That's when an old gray-colored Ford Econoline van squealed its tires as it sped away from the scene. The FBI agents hadn't even noticed the van. All they witnessed was the suspect walking from near the hardware store building and entering the stolen car. The van was the same one that had picked up the suspect from where the suburban police officer initially saw the stolen car a few days prior.

As FBI agents stayed with the cuffed suspect, other members of the swat team pursued the van away from the hardware store parking lot in Schaumburg. They were heading southbound.

Will Seelye, a Roselle Police officer, working his regular beat that Monday morning, had very little idea what lay ahead for his usually routine workday. Seelye and I spoke by phone for this book—me calling from the Chicago area, Seelye speaking from a hotel room along the Appalachian Trail somewhere in Pennsylvania. He had just retired from the Roselle Police Department a few weeks before. He said that he was treating himself to some alone time hiking along the entirety of the Appalachian Trail.

Seelye said, "I was fairly new on the job. I'd been on the job for about two years. I was on routine patrol westbound on Lake Street, Illinois Route 20, in Roselle. Dispatch came on the radio and said that the FBI was looking for assistance in stopping a vehicle and that they were on Roselle Road, southbound and heading towards Bloomingdale. No one piped up on the radio right away."

Seelye knew that if the FBI and the suspect vehicle were south on Roselle Road, he would intersect with them in a mile or so if he pulled a quick U-turn. Seelye continued, "So I piped up and told dispatch I would turn around and head towards Lake Street and Bloomingdale Road, and maybe I'd intercept them there. It was all pretty routine radio traffic."

That's when Seelye's shift became a bit more terrifying. He said, "And then a moment later dispatch said that the FBI was in a rolling gun battle with the vehicle that they were trying to stop. I was now going pretty darned quick on Lake Street, trying to get to Bloomingdale Road. As I was passing Rosedale Street and still about a half-mile from Bloomingdale Road, the first thing I noticed were puffs of smoke up ahead. It was sort of surreal, I couldn't exactly figure out what was going on, but then I realized that there was an FBI agent hanging off the passenger side of their vehicle, shooting at the van in front of them. I was going really fast, probably over 100 MPH, trying to get to Bloomingdale Road when I saw them. Dispatch had not indicated that they turned onto Lake Street. I slammed on the brakes, made a U-turn, and came up behind the FBI vehicle. The FBI agents waved me past them, and at this point, the person in the van had maybe fired a couple of shots backwards towards us. I just remember the puffs of smoke."

Seelye knew that more backup officers were needed for the rolling shootout. He said, "I switched radio frequencies to ISPERN, the emergency frequency, and indicated that I was in pursuit and that shots were being fired. At this point, I really didn't know who I was after. We continued west on Lake Street. The FBI was successful in shooting out the left rear tire of the van. It looked as if the FBI agent was 'skip firing,' shooting the pavement and allowing the fragments to hit the tire of the vehicle. I'm assuming that, but they did take out the tire, which was fortuitous."

In Roselle, Lake Street is a bustling thoroughfare, complete with blocks and blocks of strip malls, small businesses, and apartment complexes. Traffic is usually relatively heavy and brisk, especially on a weekday morning during the Christmas shopping season. Hundreds, if not thousands, of people's lives were in jeopardy from the rolling shootout. Seelye said, "We continued down Lake Street, and a couple of times we would go around the stopped traffic on the left. Traffic would be stopped at a red light, and the driver would go around to the left, but with no left rear tire, they would lose control and start to spin. The van would regain control and continue west on Lake Street. So then we were leaving Roselle and entering the town of Hanover Park, and we'd run into one of those scenarios, again, where we were going to the left of traffic for the cars that are stopped at a red light. But this time, the van spun completely out and was facing a side street. The vehicle took off down that side street."

The side street was Bear Flag Drive in Hanover Park. Once a vehicle turned onto Bear Flag Drive, it would be in a small subdivision, with no other way out. Seelye continued, "I can't recall how many police cars were behind me, but I believe a couple of Roselle cars were with me at that point. But I can't remember where the FBI car was at that point. I followed down the side street and saw a 'no outlet' sign, so I called on the radio, 'Block the entrance. Block the entrance. There's no way out of this neighborhood.' Some of the squad cars behind me stopped, and I called for at least one squad to stay with me. Officer Paul Rogner stayed with me."

Now that Seelye and Rogner were the only cars pursuing the gray van within the subdivision, the stakes were raised even higher. There was no easy way out of the situation for any of the occupants of the two patrol cars or the speeding gray van. One looping street encircled the entire subdivision, and seven cross streets intersected the looping street at two different points each. Even with a shredded rear tire, the van driver did their best to shake the trailing police officers.

Seelye said, "We went through that neighborhood, and every time the van would turn left, the driver would shoot towards us, but we were back a little ways. I remember that a Hanover Park officer was out of his car in the neighborhood, and the van driver shot at that officer. We came through the entire neighborhood and right back out to the entrance, and it looked like something out of the Clint Eastwood movie *The Gauntlet.* There were squad cars everywhere at that neighborhood entrance. I remember there were unmarked cars, and I assumed that they were FBI cars, and later that was confirmed. There was no way to get back out of that neighborhood. I slowed down, and there were shots being exchanged between the police and the van's driver. The van then went up on the grass in an effort to go around everybody. I was thinking, 'Uh, oh, they're going to escape.' So I stayed with the van and went up on the grass and ended up being way closer than I should've been, but I was thinking that the driver was going to escape back onto Lake Street. But the van had hit a raised flower bed, which 'high centered' the vehicle, and the van came to a stop. It couldn't go any further. At this point I was way too close. I was right behind the van, and I was basically caught in the crossfire."

Luckily for Seelye and Rogner, they were able to stay low and get safely to cover. Seelye added, "I bailed out the passenger side of my car and was on my hands and knees and crawled to the rear of my squad car. There was another officer there, and the two of us crawled in back of the line of police officers who were involved in the shootout. The shooting went on for a little bit, and then everything fell silent. There was a stand-off until some officers approached the vehicle with shields to determine if the driver was down. I was standing right there when they opened up the van's sliding door and saw that there were all these books in the van. And I thought the driver was a dude. I didn't realize that it was a woman driving that van until the next day. So they got the driver out, and they were hauled away in an ambulance. The other thing I remember about the driver was that they had really big feet. That's all I really remember about the suspect because I thought it was a guy."

The deceased driver of the van was the Bearded Bandit's wife, Jill.

✳

AFTER THE van driver was taken away by ambulance, Seelye and the other officers took stock of the situation once all was safe and secure. Approximately 40 police vehicles were involved in the chase and shootout. Seelye said, "In the end, all the guys from my shift, we checked our cars, and there were no bullet holes, and no one from our department fired any rounds. I was never in a position to fire. We all scooted out of there pretty quick after it was over. The FBI didn't have ISPERN radio frequencies in their vehicles, so that's why they waved me around them at the start of the chase. I could communicate and let all the other departments know where we were. They couldn't. I remember that units from Palatine showed up because one of their officers had previously been shot by one of the bank robbers in the van." Seelye's courageous actions that day had alerted many other departments about the rolling shootout. He said, "Farther west on Lake Street, other officers got road construction trucks to put up a roadblock near Barrington Road. The roadblock wasn't required because things ended before we got there."

Even now, 30 years after the shootout, Seelye still vividly remembers the dangerous pursuit details. He said, "As the lead car, I had to look at the street signs to make sure where we were and give that information in real time so that other officers could position themselves. But it was almost as if everything was in slow motion, and like I was looking at a movie screen at what was going on in front of me. I was new on the job. We had a really good chief at that time. He showed up on the scene and got us all together. We all talked and kind of debriefed about what had happened. In the long run, other than calling the chase, we really hadn't done much. But everyone did a good job of staying off the radio and knowing where to be. It worked out just fine. It was later when we found out exactly who we were dealing with."

The Bearded Bandit's bookstore was also in Roselle, only a few miles from the spot where the bank robber's wife would lose her life by her own hand. Seelye settled as a final thought came to mind about the Bearded Bandit. He said, "We had an officer who would go into the book store and talk to the guy. He [the officer] was there with me the day of the chase. But not until they put everything together did he realize that it was the same guy, the book store owner."

Unbeknownst to the officers at the scene of the gray van and the dead female suspect, was that the Bearded Bandit, handcuffed and in the back of an FBI car on his way to the Dirksen Federal Building in downtown Chicago, would be listening to the entire pursuit on the agent's radios. The Bearded Bandit heard it all, including that his wife was now dead.

Roselle Police officer Pat Dempsey accompanied the FBI when they later entered the used bookstore owned by the Bearded Bandit and his wife to search the premises. Dempsey said, "It looked like crap inside that store. Like it really wasn't a business at all."

A few days after the Bearded Bandit's arrest and his wife's death in the shootout, Frances Cieslek, from Palatine, would be able to see the bank robber in a lineup. Cieslek said, "The FBI called and said on this date and time we'll pick you up so you can come for a lineup. There was actually a large group of us because of all the bank tellers, because of all the banks he had robbed. We were taken in individually for the lineup. For the tellers, they would have the men in the lineup say something like "This is a stickup," or whatever. But in my case, they had the men in the lineup walk. As soon as he stepped forward and walked, I knew it was him right away. The FBI offered to partially remove his beard, but as soon as I saw him move, I knew it was him. I knew it immediately."

Kevin Maher recalled, "After [the Bearded Bandit] was arrested by the FBI, the witness to my shooting, Frances Cieslek, and I went downtown in separate cars to view a lineup. The FBI didn't want us talking to one another. I can't remember if I went into the room first or if she did. The FBI does very authentic lineups. They brought guys in from the FBI that fit the Bearded Bandit's physical description. All the men in the lineup had a beret on, the sunglasses, the beard, and the [same] jacket. I did not pick out the right person, but Frances did. She picked [the Bearded Bandit] out right away." Maher smiled as he added to his last comment, "And to this day, I still get a Christmas card from Frances."

An FBI search of the Bearded Bandit's townhome uncovered a large gun safe in the attached garage. Inside the safe, agents found several weapons. One was a rifle that fired .223 rounds. After examining the shell casings from the shooting scene in Palatine, it was determined to be the same rifle used to shoot Officer Kevin Maher.

In Park Ridge, officer Dick Paul and his co-workers were shocked after hearing the news of the Bearded Bandit's arrest. Paul said, "I remember the day in roll call when they finally put that broadcast message out saying to watch the banks, look in the area for Toyotas and other Japanese cars. The bank robber was stealing those cars, and he was keeping them in the areas where he was going to rob a bank. We were all like, 'Okay, we got it.' Then we'd go over to that 7-Eleven and get a coffee." Dick Paul took a moment to compose his following words. "It was weird when we found out about it when they announced that they caught the guy. All of a sudden, we were all looking at one another saying, 'We know that guy!' It's still strange to me. Kind of surreal when you find out that you knew the guy."

21

Ruth Belluomini, Harry's mother, died in 1991, and with the bit of money she had left behind, and with the end-of-the-year holiday season approaching, Harry wanted to do some communal good with some of the proceeds. "Harry called Father Fagan at St. Juliana's Church to see if there was a needy family in our area," Milly said. "Every year the kids would buy things for a needy family." Father Fagan knew who the Belluominis could assist. It was a large family from the parish whose mother had had a nervous breakdown and was struggling to take care of her children. Milly continued, "So Annie and I went to the family's home. It was a mess. We cleaned, folded clothes, and tried to help the little ones in the family. Harry used some of his mother's money to buy the family a clothes dryer. We actually needed a new one, but...."

Harry Belluomini would constantly give of himself outside of police duties. "Harry always called retired policemen just to say hello. He never missed funerals for friends or their family members and always visited sick friends who were in the hospital," Milly added. Harry's A-B blood type was quite rare, and whenever he was called upon to donate to a sick individual, he'd not hesitate.

Harry and Milly's children would practice their giving ways, too. Anne said, "Karen and I used to go to the Post Office at Christmas and pick out letters from needy kids that wrote to Santa... We would pick out letters, purchase gifts, and drive all over the city." They would usually wind up in the city's poorest and most crime-ridden areas as they delivered the gifts. Anne added, "When my dad found out, he was so angry and would start driving us to the locations, but he wasn't happy about it." As Harry drove the young women from address to address, he'd say, "God damn it. Where the hell are you going now?" Anne continued, "Sometimes we would pick four or five kids. We didn't understand why he was so angry. Finally, he said, 'I'm so proud of you girls for doing this, but you're going to the worst areas in the city, and I'm worried about you. Can you please pick someone closer to home, so I know you're safe?'"

The Belluominis had no problem with assisting those in need. An older Croatian man from their neighborhood was left alone, and without means, so Harry and Milly took the man into their home until he passed away. And then they held a proper funeral for him.

On the afternoon of Monday, December 16, 1991, Milly was making the family dinner. The television was on with a breaking local news story—the Bearded Bandit had been captured, and his wife killed, in the suburbs. Milly said, "I thought, 'how awful, these two people were so crazy to rob banks.'"

When Harry arrived home from working his part-time Court Security Officer's job at the Dirksen Federal Building, Milly told him about the capture of the bank robber. "Harry said, 'Good, the bank robbery spree is over,'" Milly recalled.

It was Christmas time. The Belluomini family was getting ready for holiday parties and a trip to Wisconsin after Christmas Day to celebrate New Year's Eve. Heading north meant spending quality time with their friends, Jim and Jeanette Lalowski, who also had a vacation property nearby. Jim "Whitey" Lalowski was a sergeant with the CPD, and the families shared many happy times.

At their cabin in Wisconsin, the Belluominis looked forward to winter sports, snowmobiling, and cross-country skiing. Milly said, "We celebrated New Year's Eve at Gateway Lodge with friends and had a wonderful time," referring to a small tavern that was tucked into the woods. "As midnight approached, Harry and I toasted one another. We prayed 1992 would be a better year than 1991." Unfortunately, 1991 had been a tough year for Milly and Harry. Besides Harry's mother passing away, one of Milly's brothers and Harry's close police department friend, Frank Gremo, had died. Altogether, more than a dozen of their friends and family members had passed away in 1991. It had proven to be a year of sorrows.

May of 1992 bought some spring-cleaning, garden planting, and a trip to their Wisconsin cabin to get their pontoon boat and canoe into the water during the Memorial Day weekend. There was a bit of happy family news dropped into their laps during that time, as well. Milly said, "Our Annie got engaged, and we were so happy." Milly and Harry tried to have a lunch date every week to get away from the house and enjoy one another's company. During one of those lunch dates, Milly told Harry that she and their daughter Annie were shopping for bridal gowns soon. Milly recalled, "Harry said, 'Good, I'm coming along,' which surprised me. I didn't think he would enjoy the time-consuming ordeal." Happily, on that particular shopping day, Annie found the gown of her dreams—and Harry was able to see his youngest child modeling her entire bridal ensemble. Annie's wedding date would be October 10, 1992, two days after Harry's 59th birthday.

Memorial Day 1992 arrived, and the Belluomini family was enjoying the north woods of Wisconsin yet again. Milly said, "Harry went into town for the *Chicago Tribune*. We missed having the daily Chicago paper there, and we enjoyed doing the Sunday crossword puzzle together." This particular Sunday edition of the *Tribune* had a magazine section featuring an in-depth article about the Bearded Bandit, his deceased wife, and their life story "How awful to write that story," Mill thought. "Two bank robbers, and they're getting a write-up about their love story. Disgusting."

Milly, of course, never realized how close to home the story would strike in the weeks to come.

June 1992 brought four weddings to attend, and Harry's cousins in Tacoma were celebrating a milestone anniversary—which meant a

plane ride across the country and back. Milly said, "Harry hated flying. We had a good time with his relatives in Tacoma, but on the way
back home, he was a nervous wreck. A flight attendant was so nice
to him. She calmed him down. It turned out that the flight attendant's dad was Italian and her mother was Croatian, like me." The
flight attendant got Harry laughing a few times during the flight,
and before the nervous flyer knew it, the plane was on final approach
to O'Hare Airport. While attending the last of the four weddings
that June, Harry was the life of the party, Milly noted. "We never
laughed so much."

The July 4 holiday found the Belluomini family back at their cabin
in Mercer, Wisconsin, where their social calendar was packed with
get-togethers. Their plans included the Independence Day parade
in Mercer, a barbeque at the Lalowski's place, and another at their
friend Bud Wahl's house, in addition to other family parties and
fireworks.

On July 7, 1992, Milly and Harry celebrated their 30th wedding
anniversary while still visiting their cabin. The anniversary celebra-
tion that day had a less-than-romantic start, Milly said. "We started
the day by getting the oil changed in our car at a dinky gas station
in Butternut, Wisconsin," a quaint North Woods town of only 375.
"It was 11 AM, and I said, 'Harry, who would think that 30 years later
we'd be at a gas station.'" Harry got a good laugh and replied, "I love
you more today than ever."

The couple's next stop was in Bayfield, Wisconsin, for a casual
lunch with an ice cream chaser. "We got home to our cabin at 6:30
PM, and Harry said he had to run to town," Milly remembered. He
returned with a heart-shaped pizza for their dinner.

Milly continued, "We always had fun at the cabin. I loved to fish,
and Harry loved to cook. We played a lot of cribbage. We'd play after
breakfast, lunch, and dinner. Harry would look at me and say, 'Fast
game?' I always beat him, but the very last time we played, he took
me to the cleaners.

"Harry would cook while I would be fishing off our little pier, and then he'd ring a little bell that meant dinner was ready. He loved to golf, too, and the two of us would go many times. We were both lousy golfers."

In July, 1992, Harry and Milly were beginning to cement their plans to build their permanent home in northern Wisconsin. They would utilize the same waterfront piece of property where their cabin stood to create a larger ranch-style home. Their overall plan was to move north for good once their daughter Anne was married in October.

When the July festivities had concluded in Wisconsin, it was time for the Belluominis to head back to Chicago. Harry had to get back to his part-time job working as a CSO at the Dirksen Federal Building. Milly said, "Harry hated the thought of going back as he was so relaxed and happy at our cabin. I told him, just call and say you can't be there, but he said, 'Milly, I can't do that. I said I'd be there, and I will.'"

Belluomini had to be back at the Dirksen Federal Building because he was filling in for another CSO who was going on a vacation of his own. Harry made a promise to the other officer, and he'd keep his promise.

"Usually, I was the one always saying 'I hate leaving Mercer.' But this time, it was Harry. I told him we'd be back in two weeks. He said that it wouldn't be soon enough," said Milly.

When they arrived back in Chicago, Milly received some heartbreaking news from Sudbury, Ontario. Her cousin Tom called to say that his wife had suddenly passed away. At that point, Harry actually did try to change his working hours so that he could be there for Milly. When he retrieved his copy of the US Marshals telephone directory for Dirksen Federal Building employees, he dialed what he thought was the correct number for his supervisor. Milly said, "He called the home of US Marshal Roy L. 'Bill' Frakes by accident. Harry never made mistakes when calling people from work. I found that to be a very strange coincidence." Harry didn't personally know Frakes, and Milly would learn of the calling error a few weeks later after meeting Wendy Frakes for the first time. She recounted the brief conversation between Harry and Frakes—both of whom would be gone in a matter of days.

For the next few days, Milly had sadness wash over her. There were so many moving parts to her life at that moment—her cousin's wife died, leaving three young children behind, Harry and Milly were planning the construction of a larger home in Wisconsin, and their daughter Anne would be married soon. Milly also had to attend a wedding shower for a friend. One day, Harry said to her, "What's your problem?" Milly couldn't articulate her emotions, though. Her sadness ran deep.

Milly said, "In the meantime, my cousin Tom called and asked if he could come to visit. He wanted to get away from their house and take his three young children on a trip. We were always close, and I thought I could cheer them all up."

That night, Milly had a terrifying dream. "I dreamt black smoke was pouring from our chimney. In the dream, I asked Harry, why is black smoke coming from our chimney?" When Milly awoke, she remembered something her mother had told her many years earlier, that if someone dreams of black smoke, that it was an ominous sign of dreadful things to come.

The July heat and humidity had settled into Chicago by the 19th, the day Milly went to the wedding shower. Milly said, "At the shower, my friend noticed how sad I was. I'm always usually upbeat and happy." Her friend asked Milly if she and Harry were having problems at home. "I told her no and that I didn't know why I was so blue."

Milly's cousin Tom arrived with his three kids the same night. Harry took them all for a ride downtown to see Buckingham Fountain and the Chicago skyline. Milly said, "Then he drove by the Federal Building, and I asked him, 'Why are you driving by that place?' He said that he wanted to show her cousin and his kids where he was going to be tomorrow."

After their drive downtown, Harry took them to the old Buffalo Ice Cream shop on the north side for a treat. Milly's cousin stayed in a hotel, so she and Harry invited them to their home the next night for dinner.

The morning of July 20, 1992, was a hectic one for Milly and Harry. Harry drove to the south side to retrieve a part needed for their car, and Milly went to a department store to pick up some gifts for her cousin's children. When she got home, Milly got to prepping for their dinner that night. She said, "I was cooking like crazy. I was making some of Harry's favorites. Breaded chicken, breaded zucchini, ham, potato salad, and fresh fruit."

Harry got ready to head downtown for his short shift at the Dirksen Federal Building, and he told Milly to cheer up. Milly said, "I told him I would. He said that he had called Karen to ask her to pick up bread at Atlas Bakery because he was making his good garlic bread." Harry kissed Milly goodbye and went to work.

Milly added, "It's not an easy thing to bring all these memories back up again, really and truly. But all of this is still vivid to me."

Seven months had passed since the Bearded Bandit's arrest and his wife was killed in the shootout with the FBI. Unfortunately, Monday, July 20, 1992, would become the final day of the Federal criminal trial for the violent bank robbery suspect.

22

THE BASEMENT garage of the Dirksen Federal Building, located at 219 S. Dearborn Street in downtown Chicago, is very utilitarian. It's what you'd expect from a federal government structure. The ceilings are just high enough to allow small garbage trucks and delivery vehicles access, and it's a bit dark but well maintained. Cement floors and ceilings, with cables, wires, and pipes neatly crisscrossing throughout. Banks of ceiling-mounted fluorescent lights struggle to illuminate the space.

The vehicular access to the garage itself is from a ramp at 18 W. Jackson Boulevard, which is around the corner from the front doors of the building. A small standalone guard shack is down that ramp and just inside the building, a few feet to the left. The tiny shack features a door and window openings on the other three sides. It's barely large enough to comfortably seat a Court Security Officer inside at a small desk. Nevertheless, there's enough space in front of the guard shack to allow slow-moving two-way vehicle traffic to enter and exit the Dirksen Building. Several feet in front of and to the left of the guard shack are the loading/unloading areas, where garbage trucks come and go, and office supply and food commissary companies drop off goods for the everyday occupants of the busy 30-story building.

There are well-marked lanes for the slow-moving car traffic to safely navigate to and from parking spots farther inside the garage. Several feet beyond the loading dock is an opening to a long cement pedestrian hallway. That eight-feet-wide cement hallway, located 50 feet from the guard shack, is where US Marshals drop off and pick up detainees appearing in one of the courtrooms several floors above. The hallway leads another 75 feet beneath the building and dead-ends at a bank of secure elevators.

The elevators have large cars equipped with cages inside where prisoners are detained while riding up and down from the higher floors to the basement garage. Because of the viewing angle from the guard shack, the CSO sitting inside or standing nearby the ramp does not have a line of sight on more than the first few feet of the hallway opening. A guard is unable to see individuals getting on or off the elevators at the far end of the passageway. As the US Marshals employees corralled the prisoners, all the CSO would see each day would be the transport van blocking nearly their entire view of the hallway opening. The garage's layout hasn't changed much since the events of 1992. Security measures have been upgraded some.

The weather that July day had cooled a bit from the heat of the previous weekend. The temperatures were hovering in the 70s downtown. It was a beautiful, warm, sunny evening. The area around the Dirksen Federal Building was jammed with thousands of Chicagoans, on foot and in their vehicles, leaving their offices for the day and heading home through the busy streets. A garbage truck was noisily dropping off an empty dumpster and picking up a full one in the garage itself.

It was 5:29 PM.

Harry Belluomini was dressed in his US Marshals CSO uniform —white uniform shirt over gray colored pants, gun belt, holstered .38 revolver, and black uniform shoes. He watched as the courthouse employees, judges, lawyers, and clerks all slowly rolled past him in their cars, driving up the ramp to Jackson Boulevard as they headed home for the day. Harry could also see and hear the garbage truck driver and his helper as they did their work 50 feet away at the loading dock. Harry was a relatively trim and fit 58-year-old man who had recently stopped smoking. He kept in shape by jumping rope and taking long daily walks.

The service patches on the sleeves of Harry's uniform shirt read "General Security Services Corporation," but Harry was working at the direction of the US Marshals Service. Officials at the US Marshals had formally deputized him in 1988 before he started work at the building.

It was just another Monday evening as far as the goings-on at the Federal Courthouse were concerned. Harry had an hour or so left on his shift before he would head home to have dinner with his family and Milly's cousin Tom and his children.

At the secure garage elevator, down the long cement hallway, one of the lift's doors slid open. US Deputy Marshal Roy L. "Bill" Frakes, a muscular, 30-year-old amateur bodybuilder, stepped into the hallway and walked to where he had parked a transport van hours earlier, out in the open space of the garage. Frakes was new to the job and the Chicago area, having just relocated to the city with his wife, Wendy, from the western Illinois town of Avon.

A diminutive 23-year-old Chicago woman, Terry Pinta, was a part-time "intermittent" US Marshals employee, hired primarily to do prisoner transports to and from the nearby Metropolitan Correctional Center (MCC) and the Dirksen Federal Building. First, Pinta pressed the button that kept the automatic doors open and locked the elevator in place. Next, she waited for Frakes to move the transport van. Once the Marshal's white transport van was in place, Pinta would be given the go-ahead by Frakes. She would then unlock the cage and allow the prisoners to leave the elevator, single file, and walk the 75 feet to where they would enter the transport vehicle for their departure back to the MCC and their jail cells.

There were nine prisoners in the elevator's cage that early evening. Eight were dressed in orange prisoner jumpsuits. One of the prisoners was in a blue pin-stripe suit and wearing a white shirt, a blue tie, and black dress shoes. All the prisoners had a waist chain around their midsection and were handcuffed—in front—through their chains. None of the prisoners wore ankle chains.

The Bearded Bandit was the prisoner wearing the suit that day while he stood in the elevator's cage. He had had a long day while on federal trial for eight of his alleged bank robberies, which included listening to and watching as prosecution witnesses described how his wife had died in the December, 1991 police shootout. The other prisoners noticed that as the elevator descended from the 24th floor, where their journey began, that the man in the suit turned away from the US Marshals and bobbed and weaved his way into the back corner of the elevator cage. It seemed odd to the other prisoners, but they gave it little thought after a few seconds.

Frakes, wearing a windbreaker with "US Marshal" emblazoned front and back and armed with a .357 caliber Ruger revolver on his hip, moved the transport van into position. He got out of the vehicle and waved down the hallway for Pinta to send the prisoners his way. Pinta was also wearing a jacket that identified her as a US Marshal. She was armed with a .357 caliber Smith & Wesson revolver in her right waist holster. She unlocked the interior elevator cage door, motioned for the prisoners to leave in single file, and ordered them to walk down the long hallway toward the transport van. The noise bouncing off the cement walls from the garbage truck dropping off and picking up, along with the large truck's idling engine, would have been loud.

As the last orange jumpsuit-wearing prisoner moved past Pinta, the Bearded Bandit, his hands inexplicably free of his handcuffs and held chest high, attacked the US Marshal. The 6'4", 240-pound man grabbed Pinta by the throat and rammed her backward into the sidewall of the cement hallway. He then slammed his knee into her chest. Pinta crumpled to the floor and tried to get into a fetal position so that she could cover and protect her holstered weapon. That's when the Bearded Bandit drew back his fist and punched her hard, square in the mouth. The prisoners moving down the hallway heard the commotion in the back of them, and one of them saw the

Bearded Bandit fight to yank Pinta's weapon free from her holster. The Bearded Bandit aimed the large-caliber revolver at the prone Pinta for a second before he began sprinting down the cement hallway toward the transport van.

One prisoner who saw this action, who had been in court with his brother that day and was standing near him in the hallway, called out that the Bearded Bandit had a gun and to run. Pinta later stated that she, too, yelled out to Frakes that the Bearded Bandit had her weapon. It's quite possible that Frakes initially couldn't hear her because of the loud garbage truck, or possibly that Pinta's voice didn't carry.

At the guard shack, Harry Belluomini stood and waved at the driver of the next car that slowly rolled past him. He knew the driver of the car quite well. He was United States District Court Judge James Alesia. Alesia and Harry had started their law enforcement careers together in the 1950s as patrolmen for the Chicago Police Department. Alesia obtained his law degree, and a federal judgeship was bestowed upon him by President Ronald Reagan in 1987. In the car with Alesia were his twin 21-year-old sons, Brian and Dan. The sons had been in their father's courtroom that day to observe as their father presided over a major, noteworthy bank robbery trial—the trial of the Bearded Bandit. As Alesia's car rolled past, Harry heard a commotion near the cement hallway but couldn't see anything because the US Marshal's transport van blocked his view.

Terry Pinta stated that she called out, again, to her partner that the Bearded Bandit had her gun, but it was too late for Frakes. As the other prisoners scrambled for safety, the Bearded Bandit cast aside his restraints, continued down the hallway, took aim while running at full speed, and fired on Frakes just as the US Marshal peered around the side of the transport van. The round struck Roy L. "Bill" Frakes in the forehead and killed him instantly. Frakes wasn't even able to draw his gun from his holster. The Bearded Bandit was an unflappable Marine Corps and police-trained marksman.

Simultaneously, one of the orange jumpsuit-wearing prisoners sprinted around the US Marshal's white transport van and toward Harry and the guard shack, screaming that someone had a gun. Harry motioned for the prisoner to get inside the guard shack as he drew the .38 caliber Smith & Wesson revolver from his hip holster.

Fifty feet away, the Bearded Bandit moved past the downed Frakes, and he shot the US Deputy Marshal once again, this time in the back. The sound of the gunshot was cannon-like and echoed painfully off the surfaces in the enclosed cement-laden garage. The other orange-jumpsuit-wearing and handcuffed prisoners all tried to find cover —mostly attempting to wedge their bodies under nearby parked vehicles and the white transport van.

Mere seconds had elapsed since the escape began and the first shot was fired.

Harry Belluomini knew the sound of gunfire, even over the din of the garbage truck, but the US Marshals van obscured his view.

As the killer stepped around the van and into the open area of the garage proper, Harry finally laid eyes on the large man in the blue suit.

The Bearded Bandit steadied his pace to a walk and pressed Pinta's .357 caliber revolver—still clutched in his right hand—close to his right leg, in a "boot leg" move. He attempted a bit of misdirection, and he pointed with his free hand back toward the transport van as if alerting Harry that the trouble was inside the cement hallway.

Harry Belluomini was a policeman's policeman. More than thirty years of experience as a Chicago Police officer had taught him a thing or two. He automatically ignored the killer's ruse. He stepped into the open space between the Bearded Bandit and the wide opening to the garage ramp that led to Jackson Boulevard—and then he went right after the gunman. Harry Belluomini charged the murderer head-on.

When Harry and the Bearded Bandit were only four feet apart, each man raised his weapon and fired.

Harry's shot missed.

The Bearded Bandit's first round struck Harry in the chest and partially turned him to his left. As he spun away from the shooter, the Bearded Bandit's second round struck Harry in the upper right side of his back. The three shots occurred in a lightning-fast exchange, so rapidly that several of the witnesses would later state that they thought they had only heard one shot fired. In just a second or two, Harry ended up seated on the cement floor of the garage. The rounds the Bearded Bandit fired had downward trajectories, a consequence of the height difference between the two men—Harry was five inches shorter than his assailant.

Each of Harry Belluomini's wounds was fatal—the first bullet had nicked his heart, the second his thoracic artery. But he still had a few breaths and some fight left. From his seated position, as he was dying, Harry raised his weapon and fired three more times, just as the Bearded Bandit reached the base of the ramp and was edging close to the trunk of Judge Alesia's slowly moving car.

The killer's body seemed to jolt as one of the rounds fired by Harry struck him square in the back. The Bearded Bandit began to slow his pace and stagger, all the while aspirating frothy blood from his nostrils and mouth. Harry's .38 caliber round had sliced through the fleeing man's heart.

Having been trained as a Marine Corps combat soldier, the Bearded Bandit realized that he had been seriously injured and probably only had a few seconds of consciousness remaining before he bled out. He screamed out loud, something to the effect that he was going to "take everyone with him," according to witnesses. The man stumbled to his knees at the left side of the ramp. He was fewer than 50 feet from the street and freedom. He struggled to lift Pinta's gun to the right side of his head and fired a round into his brain, ending the bloodshed for good.

Harry lay back on the cool cement floor as the life slowly ebbed from his body. His last act had successfully stopped a murderer from getting away and most assuredly harming others.

Harry Belluomini was a bulldog.

Harry Belluomini was a protector to the very end.

23

CPD HOMICIDE detectives George Holmes and his partner Tom Argenbright arrived at the Dirksen Federal Building crime scene minutes after the violence had ended. Holmes was a seasoned veteran at this point in his career, but Argenbright was just two years into his new detective job after being promoted from the patrol ranks. The men were assigned to a tactical unit in the 7th District, near Ashland and 63rd Street, in Chicago's tough West Englewood area. They were accustomed to handling scenes where violence had occurred, but they were not usually locations like the Dirksen Federal Building, where two law enforcement officers had died.

I first met Tom Argenbright at a restaurant in Rosemont, Illinois. We discussed the case over lunch. Argenbright is a pleasant man, intelligent, and armed with a quick wit. Unlike most of the former detectives I spoke with, he conversed freely and without hesitation when we met. He said, "It was a confusing mess. The [Bearded Bandit's] body was still there. Harry and Frakes had been removed when I arrived."

Holmes, Argenbright, and other CPD detectives began to gather witnesses for an investigation that would only last a short time once the FBI took over. The Dirksen Federal Building was US Government property, and the FBI would eventually handle any long-term investigation at the location. Argenbright recalled, "When we got there, it was a lot of chaos. There were a lot of prominent people from CPD and the federal government, just because of the location alone. We had a deceased police officer and a deceased US Marshal. Chief of Detectives John Stibich was there, and that's pretty high up the CPD food chain. Likewise, there were a bunch of high-ranking FBI agents and other federal agents with three letters in their titles. Everyone wants to know what's going on. Their main goal is not really to make sure we had the right info. It's to feed information up their chain of command. A US Marshal gets killed, and another gets disarmed. And there's another investigation into the origin of the handcuff key."

When Holmes and Argenbright surveyed the carnage on the ramp, where the Bearded Bandit's body still lay, they saw the bloodied .357 revolver the killer had used to murder Frakes and Harry, as well as a handcuff key laying between the murderer's body and the opening to the garage. How had the Bearded Bandit obtained the handcuff key?

Argenbright added, "There were big problems there between the CPD brass and the big brass of the FBI. Going into these types of things there's always a contentious relationship between the two entities. CPD Chief of Detectives John Stibich, shall I say, was forceful in his opinions on how the investigation should be handled. And so was the FBI. So the two groups went into a room, and they came out with a decision on how things were going to be handled. There were liabilities involved at the scene. Training liabilities involving the female US Marshal who was disarmed. She had told us that she got this job, and the US Marshals didn't give her weapons training, but they gave her a weapon. [The Federal agents] were looking at some...liability here. It's a sad case because of her lack of training, or their policies at the time, allowing a single guard to accompany prisoners on an elevator for a period of time. I mean it's not a good situation."

Thirty years after the Dirksen Building violence, Argenbright is still chilled by how formidable the Bearded Bandit was as a combatant armed with a gun. "He was dangerous," Argenbright emphasized.

"He was beyond proficient with a weapon. He was determined to do what he had to do, and he had a bunch of emotional issues surrounding his wife. He had written on his hand, 'I love Jill.' I saw that when I observed his body on the ramp."

But what honestly stunned and equally frightened Argenbright was the fact that the Bearded Bandit was such an effective and calculated killer. He said, "That cement hallway is maybe twenty-five yards long. He only had a small time frame to shoot when Frakes peered around the bumper of the transport van. Now me, trying to make the shot he did, I'd make that about one out of thirty times." Argenbright mentions this with the knowledge that the Bearded Bandit was running when he fired on US Marshal Frakes.

George Holmes, whom I later spoke with on the phone about the case, said, "The entire event transpired over the course of about 15 seconds as far as we could determine." Holmes also inferred that the Bearded Bandit probably didn't shoot Pinta because he either didn't want to alert Frakes, or possibly because Pinta was a woman, and she may have reminded the alleged bank robber of his deceased wife. However, there was one thing George Homes knew for sure. He said, with heartfelt reverence, "Harry did his job."

Argenbright said, "If [the Bearded Bandit] had recognized Judge Alesia driving in the car, he would have shot him—for sport. And I'm surprised he didn't try to get to the judge's car regardless of who was driving because now he has a means of escape if he's not shot. I don't think [the Bearded Bandit], who did all this plotting and planning for his robberies, down to minute details, knew what he was going to do if he successfully ran up the ramp to Jackson Boulevard. I mean downtown is loaded with police, particularly at the Federal Building where this occurred. There's myriad law enforcement and quasi-law enforcement that work in that Federal Building. I mean, [the Bearded Bandit] is not a track star. So what is he planning on doing? He's going to run through downtown? That's probably going to be futile. And he saw that judge's car going through the garage, but he didn't avail himself of that escape vehicle."

Argenbright knows one thing for sure, "Imagine if [the Bearded Bandit] didn't get shot and he does hit that ramp running. Now you have the issue of him going into the downtown area. You have an issue with him going into the city, right? What if he makes good on his escape? Or he ends up shooting other people? So Harry is a hero in the true sense of the word."

The Deputy Superintendent of the CPD, the third in command of the entire department, arrived at the scene soon after the incident. He was George Ruckrich, Harry Belluomini's only true partner when he was a burglary detective, working the "safe car," with the CPD in the 1960s.

"On July 20, 1992, I had been in my new Deputy Superintendent job for about six days when I heard about the shooting at the Dirksen Building." Ruckrich recalled. "I immediately made my way from CPD headquarters to the scene of the shooting. As I walked down the ramp, someone stopped me and told me that Harry had been killed. I stepped away from everyone else and had a good cry...and then I got to work."

The news cameras were on the scene almost immediately, broadcasting the breaking news live to Chicago-area viewers.

Harry Belluomini and Roy L. "Bill" Frakes were transported by Chicago Fire Department paramedics to Northwestern Memorial Hospital on East Huron Street, tucked between Michigan Avenue and the lakefront, where a Dr. Adams pronounced them dead at about 6 PM. The Bearded Bandit's body would be picked up from the Dirksen Federal Building ramp sometime later by the Cook County Medical Examiner's office.

24

ON PRATT Avenue in Edison Park, Milly Belluomini was preparing dinner for her cousin and his children when the breaking news of the Dirksen Federal Building violence erupted on her TV set. Milly watched as paramedics rushed a man on a stretcher away. The man's shoes caught her attention. She said, "It looked like Harry's shoes. I called the Federal Building and asked for Harry, but the person who answered hung up on me. I called again, and the person on the line said they couldn't get to Harry."

Milly's cousin Tom arrived with his kids a few minutes later. Her son Michael had just arrived at home, and a bit later, Karen came with the bread from Atlas Bakery. Unfortunately, Anne couldn't be reached because she was at a baseball game with her fiancé.

Karen said, "When I got off work, the guys wanted to go and get a drink at the bar. I told them that I couldn't go because we were having company over. I went to my apartment to change and check on my little dog. I remember that my dad called me from his work while I was at the apartment to ask if I had gotten the bread. It was right before it all happened. I was the last one to talk to him. He asked if I got the bread, and I told him I forgot. I was just trying to aggravate him. He was like, 'What?' And I told him, 'I got it, I got it. I'll see you in a little while.' We both said 'I love you' when we ended the call, which was something we always did. That was the last time I talked to him."

Karen had another errand to run before heading to her parent's home for dinner. She said, "I had to go to the gun store at Touhy and Milwaukee. I needed a new holster. I happened to drive past my brother Michael on Harlem Avenue. He waved, and I waved, and that's the exact moment the news broke on the car radio about what was happening at the Federal Building. Michael was also on his way to our parent's home. So I went to the gun store and quickly got back to my parent's house."

Karen continued, "My mom had the TV on, and me and Michael stepped into the room to watch the coverage. My mom said, "You know, your dad hasn't called yet." And the thing was, my dad would always call. He would've called to tell us he was okay. I told my mom that if something were to happen, they don't call you; they come to the door."

Karen's worst-case scenario for the situation came to pass. She said, "After a few minutes...the doorbell rang. None of us moved. My stomach dropped. A fellow detective and our neighbor, Richard Stevens was standing there. My dad had trained Mr. Stevens when he became a detective. I looked at him and said, 'Yeah. We're kind of busy right now.' I knew what he was going to say. I just didn't want to hear him say it. If he didn't say the words, it wouldn't be real. I did start to ask him over and over if my father was okay. He said, 'Karen, we have to go. Get your mom, brother, and sister.' I can't remember if I left him on the porch. All I remember is saying, 'Mom, Mike, we have to go.' Annie wasn't home at that time, and we couldn't get a hold of her. They got us in a car, and I remember it being the longest car ride." Stevens drove, and a woman Karen recognized as working with her dad was in the passenger seat. The police vehicle had to utilize the shoulder of the Kennedy Expressway because traffic was so heavy during that Monday rush hour.

Karen continued, "I kept asking Mr. Stevens if my dad was okay, but he wouldn't say anything. We all just kept praying on the way downtown, 'Please let him be okay. Please, God.' When we got to the hospital, there were so many officers and US Marshals all over that place. I remember seeing Wendy Frakes, US Marshal Roy Frakes's wife, in the corner of the room. She was screaming and hysterical. I thought, 'Oh, my God, that poor woman.' I didn't understand at that point that her husband had also been killed."

Milly said, "As we were driving to Northwestern Memorial Hospital, I just thought it was a minor injury for Harry. When we got out of the car at the hospital, there was a battery of news cameras and photographers. The chaplain was waiting, and I said to him that I wanted to see Harry. They took us to a room and told me that Harry died in the shooting. My mind went blank. I couldn't believe it. Not my Harry."

Karen said, "When my dad was killed, Michael and I saw his body. I had nightmares about that forever. I still have nightmares. After it happened, I had this fantasy that he was still alive. I just didn't believe he was dead. I wish sometimes that I never saw him like that. Right after all of that happened, I went back to work, and I probably should've waited because I would go to crime scenes, and some of these jobs had dead bodies. I'd go home from work, and I'd have these nightmares where I would go to a scene and turn a dead body over, and it would be my dad. I would wake up just crying and crying. I still cry thinking about all of that because it affected me. We didn't want my mom to see my dad like that, but she would say that she wished she'd gone into that room and saw my dad. We're glad that she didn't."

Karen, herself, almost didn't make it into the room to see her father. She said, "There were a couple of US Marshals at the hospital, and when I walked in, I told them I'd like to see my father. They said, 'No, you don't want to do that.' I said, 'Don't tell me that. Get the fuck out of my way. I want to see my father.' Michael and I went in... It was difficult. We just couldn't believe it was really him. Before we went in to see him, I was thinking, 'This could be a mistake. Our dad wasn't killed. It can't be our dad. It can't be.' We were both in shock to see him. We both kissed him. We stumbled out of that room, saw our mom, and just started crying. It was just hard. It just was really hard to see the man that raised you, that did everything in the world for your family, was no longer alive. It was the most painful experience. My heart just burst. My heart literally hurt, and I felt so helpless. I didn't know what to do or what to say. I didn't know how to handle any of that. It was awful. And I'm not kidding...I wanted to kill myself. It was all just so painful. How do you deal with that pain? I didn't know. We all dealt with it in each of our own different ways."

"In the waiting room was another woman crying. She said, 'Who's that?' Meaning me," said Milly. The woman was Wendy Frakes. "And my kids didn't want me to see Harry. They said, 'No, Mom, it'd be too much to see.' So we stayed in that waiting room—I can't remember how long—then we went home."

Karen continued, "Our family friend, Cindy Pontierero, drove me to my apartment to get my little dog because I was going back to stay with my family at our mom's house."

Milly added, "I felt terrible that my Annie had to find out in a sad way and wasn't with Karen, Michael, and me. When we got back to our house, there were TV news trucks and a lot of law enforcement there. People were just coming and going. Our priest, Father Fagan, who Harry and I loved, came to the house and talked to us. Henry E. Hudson [Director of the US Marshals Service at the time] happened to be in town that day. He said to me that he'd find out what and how it all happened. He gave me his direct phone number and said that I could call him anytime. And as we sat there, he tried calling his own office number, but the call wouldn't go through. I said to him, 'You want me to call you, and you can't even get through to your own number?'" Once things initially settled down that evening, Milly said, "The four of us locked ourselves in my bedroom and just cried. We were all stunned and in shock."

That night, a thirsty Milly awoke at 2 AM. She said, "I got up to go get water in the kitchen. I saw Harry standing against the stove with his bloody clothes in his hands. He told me, 'They fucked up. They fucked up.' And then he disappeared. He never used that swear word with me. But it was so real." The string of nightmarish events was just beginning for Milly, unfortunately. In the coming years, even more, heartache would cascade into the woman's life.

"We made plans for Harry's funeral," Milly remembered. "My son Michael and my brother John were my pillars of strength during that time. Michael and John went with me to Smith-Corcoran Funeral home, and Michael took me to Park Ridge to buy a dress for the funeral."

Karen said, "I don't remember a lot about planning my father's funeral. All I can really remember was working out the details on his headstone. And we all didn't really think about arrangements for a day or so. We were just numb." Harry Belluomini's headstone has a unique design, complete with an engraving of God's extended hands holding a Chicago Police star and the inscription: "In God's hands."

Milly added, "I wasn't prepared to see what the next few days would be like. It was amazing. There was an outpouring of love and prayers for our family from across the nation. We received so many cards and letters. President George H.W. Bush and first lady Barbara Bush, Cardinal Bernardin, senators, law enforcement, coworkers and friends, neighbors, and strangers all sent us notes. It was unbelievable. The day of the funeral, all the federal judges from the Dirksen Building lined up as my family and I came to the funeral home. Harry would have never imagined this all would be for him. Harry's pallbearers were his fellow Chicago Policemen, plus my brother John. I came home afterward broken-hearted and still stunned. Harry's cousins from Tacoma stayed for a while to console me. It was just so hard for me to believe Harry was gone from our lives."

Karen said, "I felt like I lost 40 pounds over the days following my dad's death. It was awful. You don't want to eat. You don't want to sleep. I couldn't sleep. Every time I closed my eyes, I saw my dad. And it was worse for me watching my mom and my brother and sister going through all of that. It was painful. My heart...my heart just hurt. I felt like I couldn't breathe. It was the worst pain in the world, the worst pain. I always argue with people who say that suicide is so selfish. It's not. When people are in that type of excruciating pain, and there's nothing that will help them, who am I to judge them and to say that they're wrong for what they do? I'm telling you...I thought about it. I hate saying that, but I'm being honest. I thought about it. I was having such a horrible time, and I remember my mom called our family priest from Saint Juliana's Church over to the house. Talking to the priest helped. His name was Father Fagan, who my dad loved, and he loved my dad. Father Fagan wound up marrying my husband Curt [Blanc] and me. He helped me to get through the grief. He said, 'If something happened to you, do you think you'd like to put your mom through that pain?' and I said, no, of course not. That's what snapped me out of it."

Karen did find a healthier outlet to try to ease her spiraling emotions. "I also had to go to the local batting cages just so I could hit something. It was unbearable. And he wasn't even supposed to work that day. He wasn't supposed to be there. He filled in for somebody else. My dad wasn't afraid of anything. He was fearless. That's how he was."

The outpouring of love and respect for their father was overwhelming and very much appreciated. Karen said, "We had my dad's wake over two nights. The funeral home was packed. People were lined up to get into the building. And the funeral itself, my gosh, there were people lined up all along the streets everywhere you looked. It made us cry watching as the people stood there with their hands on their hearts, or holding American flags, or saluting as we drove past."

Anne added, "We had the news media outside our house all week, which was horrible. I mean, you'd walk outside the house to just sit on the porch, and the news media would be there... It was just a bad week. I specifically remember one incident where my sister and I... were sitting on the porch just to get out of the house. A reporter walked up from CBS Chicago. And I'll never forget his name, Jon Duncanson. He said, 'I'm not going to ask questions or film. I just want to express my condolences to the family.' And then he walked away. He was the one class act. I remember when he started walking up to the porch, we were like, 'You've got to be kidding.' His news truck was parked down the street near Harlem Avenue. They didn't even park it in front. He walked up, and we were like, is this guy serious? Is he really going to come up to us and—but that's what he said. He said, 'I'm Jon Duncanson from CBS, and I'm not going to ask you anything or film, you guys. I just want to extend my condolences.' And then he walked away. I remember that, specifically."

But there would be one final emotional wound endured by the family during the funeral process. Karen added, "And the worst part of the day was that we had the funeral luncheon at a banquet hall on Milwaukee Avenue. Guess who else was having a funeral luncheon at the same time in the hall?" It was the Bearded Bandit's family and friends. She continued, "It happened, and we didn't have a clue it was going to happen. The other family didn't have a clue that that was going to happen. I don't think it was intentional. It was just strange. I don't know if the banquet hall didn't know that the Bearded Bandit's luncheon was going to be in their building the same day as our dad's. I just don't know. I really don't have a clue. We didn't mix with the people from their banquet room. I think that they were just as much in shock as we were. And we actually didn't really know what was going on until we got inside and were sitting down, and then we were all like, 'What?' We were angry and thinking, 'How in the hell did this happen?' There were no problems with the Bearded Bandit's family or with us, though. And on top of everything else, we were just in shock. We were kind of walking around like we were in a daze, too. It was surreal, and we couldn't believe that my dad was dead. We just could not believe it. If you look at some of our family photos from that time, we not only had that look on our faces of sadness and sorrow, but we also had that look of disbelief in our eyes, like deer in headlights. Just walking around like zombies. We had that thousand-yard-stare. We were absolutely numb. We could only take in so much. I don't know if us not remembering some of the details from that time was our bodies putting up some sort of defense or not. But we had that thousand-yard-stare."

"It was sickening," Milly added. "I could not believe that had happened. It was awful of the funeral director who handled the Bearded Bandit's funeral to do that. Maybe he didn't even realize what they had done. But they would've known that the funerals were on the same day. I didn't find out that that had happened until afterward. But I had looked into the room where the Bearded Bandit's luncheon was being held, and I got a strange feeling when seeing the people. There were not that many people in the room. Our luncheon was gigantic. I couldn't tell you how many people were there."

Michael Belluomini had this to say about the luncheon fiasco, "I really wasn't aware of it right away. Someone in our group ran into someone from their group, and that's how we found out about it. It was really awkward. We couldn't believe that the banquet hall would do that, for one. It's a huge place. But maybe they didn't even know, who knows? His family probably didn't know what was happening, either. But at some point, they had to see all the policemen and police vehicles there. It's a weird irony. It's a twisted thing, you know. Their paths crossed, to begin with, and who would've thought their families would end up in the same place. It's just crazy."

"We were all like, 'Are you kidding?' It was just crazy," Anne agreed. "We were all in shock and had a brutal week. You would think that the management of the banquet hall would know who my dad was, and you'd think they'd know the story. And you'd think that they'd probably put two and two together, but you know, sometimes people don't care. It was very odd. I know that it was very odd."

And even George Ruckrich echoed the Belluomini family's luncheon thoughts. "When I went to the luncheon after Harry's funeral, I found out that [the Bearded Bandit's] family were having the funeral luncheon for him right down the hall in the same banquet facility, at the same time. It was so strange."

Harry was laid to rest at St. Adalbert Catholic Cemetery, directly across Harlem Avenue from their Edison Park neighborhood.

25

CPD HOMICIDE detectives Tom Argenbright and George Holmes wrapped up their initial murder investigation as the FBI took control of the overall case. Next, it would be up to the Feds to determine how the Bearded Bandit obtained the handcuff key that provided him freedom from his restraints so that he could undertake his murderous rampage.

Once the Medical Examiner reports were filed and officially verified the Bearded Bandit's actual cause of death, a murder investigation was launched—targeting Harry Belluomini. The CPD's overall investigation of the Dirksen Building shooting, which began on July 20, 1992, was completed on July 24, 1992.

The Medical Examiner determined that Harry's .38 caliber bullet had, indeed, caused the Bearded Bandit's death. The bullet that the Bearded Bandit fired into his head was simply a formality. Harry's round caused a fatal wound, and if the Bearded Bandit hadn't pressed the .357 against his temple and squeezed the trigger, it would not have mattered because he would've died anyway.

The CPDs homicide investigation report for Belluomini concluded with the following heading and accompanying findings: *Exceptionally Clear and Closed, Homicide-Justifiable Case Report. The above listed subject, Harry A. Belluomini, while employed as a Court Security Officer for the Federal Government, shot and killed the above subject, Jeffrey E. Erickson. Erickson had shot and killed Deputy Roy L. Frakes and was attempting to escape from Federal custody. Erickson then shot and killed the above listed subject, Harry A. Belluomini, in an exchange of gunfire.*

A simple yet bold x marked the status box on the written report. The x signified that the homicide case against Harry Belluomini was a "closed non-crime."

26

HARRY'S FRIENDS and former detectives on the CPD, as well as Milly's former Motorola coworkers, were so very shocked to learn of his death but also not surprised by how he had aggressively dealt with the Bearded Bandit during their violent altercation. Additionally, in the thirty years since the bloody clash in the basement of the Dirksen Federal Building, the raw emotions of that July 1992 moment still linger. Each of the former CPD detectives who had worked alongside Belluomini grew emotional when discussing Harry and his final actions.

Stan Golucki said, "When that guy came down in that elevator and disarmed that first US Marshal, Harry could've hid behind a pillar, or he could've done a lot of things. He could've looked the other way, but he didn't. That was Harry. He decided to do the right thing, and that's the type of individual Harry was. He saved lives. He was so unique." Golucki took a moment to collect his thoughts and gather his emotions, and then he continued, "Like I said, Harry could've hid from that shooter. He could've hid behind his desk, he could've went the other way, but he chose to... Harry wouldn't back down from anybody. And it cost him dearly. I wish he would've shown a different side in that moment. Hid. But that's who Harry was."

After hearing about Golucki's words, Karen Belluomini Blanc said, "He pretty much says what we all thought. I think about that all the time, and I know I could live with that choice had my dad made it, but I know my dad could not have lived with it himself if he backed down or hid, because that's not who he was."

Jack Lorre said, "Harry retires, and he takes that job just before he and his wife, Milly, were planning to move to Wisconsin. It wasn't supposed to be a dangerous job. It just wasn't. Harry had already lived through the danger. But Harry was always alert. That's probably why he...." As Lorre's thought trailed off, he became quite emotional. Once he settled, he continued, "A week before he was killed, my wife and I saw Harry out walking down the street where he lived. And then, a week later, he was gone because of this...incident. You should've seen his funeral. It was unbelievable, the people who were there—blocks and blocks of people. Well...he had a lot of friends. He spoke loudly, but he didn't really have enemies. Well, I guess he may have had a couple, but he had many, many more friends."

Ken Berris said, "There was a judge who was driving right past [the Bearded Bandit] and Harry just as they were about to shoot it out. That judge said that if Harry hadn't done what he did, [the Bearded Bandit] would've taken him hostage or worse." The late James Alesia was quoted in the *Chicago Tribune* the day of Harry's funeral, echoing Berris' exact sentiment.

Former CPD detective Brian DuFour said, "Working down there at the Federal Building, you'd think the government would have the resources to give the guys a front [bullet-proof] panel that would go under their shirts. But that's 20/20 hindsight. It's one of those things. What happened at the Federal Building was heroic. I wasn't shocked that he did that [go after the Bearded Bandit in the shootout]. It was something that Harry would do. Harry was a bulldog. He was a guy who once he grabbed you by the butt, he wouldn't let go because that's what kind of a copper he was. He was a good copper. He had his heart in the right place. It was so unfortunate what happened. He was just a very nice man. He was really a nice man... I was stunned the day I heard that he got killed. It really knocked the wind out of me. We were at his retirement party, and he was having such a good time, and Milly was there. He was talking about getting a part-time job with the US Marshals at the Federal Building. He was looking forward to a lot of nice things. Unfortunately, that all got cut short. I miss Harry. He was a character, and a true policeman, a great detective. He was an asset to the department. He really was."

Harry's neighbor and former fellow detective Luis Alviso said, "It was exactly like Harry to do what he did in the end. He went right after that guy. He was retired and working that part-time job. And what didn't happen on the police department happens on some bullshit side job. It was a shame. But he never turned away from danger. He was an aggressive police officer. God takes all the good people, like Harry, and leaves all the shitheads behind for us to deal with. He had just retired..."

Former CPD detective Ed Pyrcioch said, "When that guy [the Bearded Bandit] tried to escape, and Harry engaged him, and they got into that shootout and basically killed one another? That was Harry. That's the kind of guy Harry was. He wasn't being dumb and blindly charging the escapee. He was a policeman in the true sense of the word. If [the Bearded Bandit] got away, he would've killed someone else on the street."

Milly's work friend from Motorola, Maureen Kowalski, said, "I was at Harry's funeral, and that was very emotional. I saw the news unfold on TV, and I tried to call Milly, and I couldn't get a hold of her. I finally got through later that night, but she had a house full of people, and she was in shock. We just cried on the phone together. I didn't see her until the wake, and that was huge. All the policemen and firemen were there. The funeral at St. Juliana's was beautiful."

Kathy Paddock, another Motorola employee, said, "Harry had finally officially retired from the police department and was working at the Federal Building for a little longer to fund the building of a new home. I came home from work one night in 1992 and turned on the news. I saw a story about a bank robber at the Federal Building escaping custody while being transported and shooting two officers before being killed. My stomach sank, and I had such a bad feeling about Harry. Mo [Maureen Kowalski] and I talked about it and waited to hear. It was such an awful thing when we heard that it was Harry and another young officer, Roy Frakes. I know that it was a whirlwind for Milly after that. We saw her and kept in touch. I believe that she felt hounded by people asking her about what happened and decided that she needed to get away from the city. She went through with the plans for the house up there and built a beautiful home. Mo and I visited there, and our visit coincided with a visit by Wendy Frakes, the widow of the other officer. Milly tried so hard to help Wendy move on. Milly is a really special person to a lot of people."

Milly said, "Dennis Farina knew Harry, and our sons went to Weber High School at the same time. When Harry died, Dennis sent the most beautiful bouquet of roses with a beautiful note. The note read: 'To Harry, my hero. Love, Dennis Farina.'" Milly added, "Dennis Farina was a very nice man. They knew each other from being on the job together, but they never worked directly with one another. Farina was in a different unit. When there were police functions, they'd see each other."

Out of all the hundreds of mourners who had paid their respects at Harry's funeral, one visitor was very memorable for Milly Belluomini. The flight attendant from Harry's fearful June of 1992 flight from Tacoma to Chicago came to the funeral home to pay her respects to the Belluomini family. Milly said, "She couldn't believe what a heroic thing Harry did, and yet he was afraid of flying."

27

THE WEEKS and months that followed their father's death were a period of deep depression and despair for the Belluomini family. Karen said, "I went back to work a week or so after my dad's funeral. It was too soon to go back. We didn't have any counseling. We didn't have anything like that. We were all just going along, bumping into life, always thinking, 'now what?' We were all numb. Other than Father Fagan talking to me for an hour, that was about it. Annie was in denial. She acted like none of it ever happened. Michael was more quiet. We all handled the situation differently. Despite the situation, I had no regrets. I was the last one to talk to our dad before he died. And I look at it this way: we were so lucky to have our dad in our lives as long as we did. There are kids who won't even know their dads. I look at these poor kids whose dads are killed in the military...it's horrible. Am I mad that my dad was taken from me? Yes, I am, but at least I had him for 29 years of my life."

As Karen stated, she had probably gone back to work sooner than she should have. But she tried to make the best of it. She said, "It was weird when I went back to work. Most people didn't know what to say to me. Some people would just express how sorry they were. The 13th District was a small district. Everybody knew everyone else. We all got along, and after this all happened, everyone was very nice. They really were. I thought going back to work would take my mind off of things, but it didn't. I just did the best I could."

Former Chicago Police patrol officer Tammie Pena Arroyo was Karen's partner on most shifts during that time. Tammie said, "I remember the day her dad died. I was working with another partner that day, and we heard about the shooting on the news. We got to a television, and I saw on the news other police officers walking with Karen and her mom and other family members. I just freaked out. I had my partner take me to the station, and there I told my sergeant that I had to go. I had to go find Karen. I didn't know what to do. Karen was living in an apartment on Forest Preserve Drive at the time, but I went to their house. I didn't know what to do. I sort of knew that she wasn't going to be there, but I had to do something. We didn't have cell phones at the time, and I couldn't get a hold of her. It was just horrible. Her dad and my dad did not know one another personally, but they were like...the same guy. They had the same personality. They had the same mentality. We'd always laugh because our dads always had to have a shirt on with a pocket in it to keep their cigarettes. I felt such a connection to the whole thing because if that was my father... It all took a big piece of me, too. One morning after we worked a shift, Karen and I went to the morgue to collect her father's personal items. That was brutal. I didn't say anything; I was just there. Karen didn't want me to go, but I didn't want her to go by herself. It was heart-wrenching."

As Tammie considered how the tragedy had affected her partner, she said, "I know her demeanor changed a little bit. A big piece of her heart was taken, so that affects a person. She was always a rebel type, but afterwards, she seemed even more anti-rules, anti-policies, anti-supervisors telling her what to do, what not to do. Not where she totally went off the page and did her own thing. But her opinion and her way were her way."

Michael Belluomini's life became very insular after his father's death. He said, "I still lived with my parents when my dad was killed, and I didn't really leave the house, other than to go to work and back, for about five months. It was terrible. I felt bad for my mom. She was 52 years old when my dad was killed. I had to be strong for her. When I went back to work a week after he was killed, the people there didn't know how to handle interacting with me. They weren't sure if they should talk to me or not, stuff like that. I was at the natural gas company still at that time, and I happened to be on a job in Evanston right next to Ryan Field, where Northwestern University plays their football games. On my lunch break, I ended up getting into the stadium, and I sat in the stands at the 50-yard line, all by myself in that stadium, and thinking, 'did this all really happen?' I sat there by myself and cried. I felt so empty, just like that stadium."

Harry's daughter Anne said, "I was engaged when my dad was killed. I was happy about the engagement initially, but then I started having doubts and anxiety about the engagement and wedding. We set the date for October, 1992."

As the spring weather warmed, Anne's anxiety was growing. She said, "About a month and a half before my dad was killed, I was very stressed and upset about the wedding. Everyone told me it was typical jitters, but it didn't feel that way to me. I was crying a lot and very upset. The Thursday before my dad was killed, he sat me down to talk to me about the wedding and life. He had asked me what was wrong and why I was feeling the way I did. I am the youngest child, but I had always been a homebody and didn't really want to leave home. He had said that he thought I was afraid to take a chance and told me there were no guarantees in life. During our conversation, he said, 'I can walk out the door tomorrow and never come back.' Little did both of us know that that would happen just a few days later. It was a beautiful conversation, but difficult since a few days later, he was killed."

Anne said, "When I was dating my ex-husband, we had broken up for a few months prior to getting engaged. We belonged to the same gym. It was a racquetball gym. My family and I played there together, too. Anyway, I remember after the breakup, I was nervous about going back there because my ex would be there with all his friends. My dad said, 'You go there, and you walk in with your head held up high, and don't let that stop you from going there.' As strict and as hard-ass as he was, he was always supportive and showed us how to be strong."

She added, "The last full weekend that I spent with my dad was the 4th of July weekend when my then-fiancé and I spent a long weekend in Wisconsin with my parents. It really was a wonderful weekend with my parents as we went to dinner and played a bean bag toss game and watched fireworks. Little did we know a few weeks later what would happen."

What would typically be joyful moments for most families had now soured for Anne. "I hate the 4th of July. It always reminds me of that last weekend. To be honest, I hate Christmas and Thanksgiving, too. They're just a reminder of who is missing at the table. I'm sure many families whose loved ones are gone feel that way." But there's one Christmas memory that Anne still holds dear. She said, "Once when we were older, we decided we would stop exchanging Christmas presents with each other and focus on being together." Harry Belluomini decided to go against his wishes that Christmas. "My dad had gone out and bought us some gifts because he said it was Christmas and he wanted to give us presents. He bought me a sweatshirt. I still have that sweatshirt. I don't wear it. I just keep it along with one of his old sweatshirts."

"I'm glad that the offender is dead," Anne concluded. "If he were in prison, I would wish he was dead every day, and I think that would be hard to deal with, knowing he was alive while my dad was dead. At least my dad killed him. There's no forgiving what that person did that day to my dad or to my family. I'm okay with myself for thinking that way. I don't talk about that day too much, but sometimes when I go to bed or wake up even still, I stare at the ceiling and think back, and I still can't believe it happened. My mind starts to wander, and I think if only he was five minutes late or working in another area. But that doesn't change anything. Reality is reality."

Michael said that slowly, life started to churn along for their family. He fondly recalled some of Harry's unique habits and ways. He said, "He was like a packrat. He'd buy all this shit here and then haul it up to his cabin in Wisconsin. I remember after he died and I was up in Wisconsin helping my mom go through all the stuff in the garage, I was by myself, and I just started crying. I was thinking about all the stuff he did and what he did to get to this point and... You don't take any of that stuff with you. Material things don't really mean anything to me, you know. There are some things I hold onto for sentimental reasons, but you know."

28

UNFORTUNATELY, THE years following Harry's death brought even more tumult and heartache to Milly and her children. The caravan of life defeats would be nearly too much for the family to tolerate. For one thing, the violent episode at the Dirksen Federal Building was not simply a local Chicago-area event. It had far-reaching national ramifications and revealed apparent cracks in the security protocols followed by the Federal Government, specifically the US Marshals Service, and their prisoner transport procedures.

On July 24, 1992, US Senator Paul Simon from Illinois stood on the Senate floor in Washington, DC, and read aloud a proclamation recognizing Harry Belluomini and Roy L. "Bill" Frakes for their sacrifice the Monday prior. In part, the proclamation read: *Monday's catastrophe underscores the dangers and risks that our federal law enforcement officers face daily. We must study this fatal incident and learn from it so that in the future, we can better protect our officers, our Marshals, our judges, and citizens.*

One month later, in August of 1992, three US Marshals superiors based in Chicago, were disciplined by the Justice Department for the apparent security breaches that resulted in the violence that took the three lives at the Federal facility. The US Marshals Service in Chicago had been without a permanent leader since 1986. Some believed this contributed to the Bearded Bandit obtaining the handcuff key and causing so much death and sorrow.

Also in August of 1992, attorney Todd Smith of the law firm Corboy & Demetrio, at the direction of Milly Belluomini, filed a motion in court that she intended to sue the US Marshals Service for a wrongful death action. Milly sought $7 million in damages in the death of her husband. Due to the legal technicality that Harry was working with the government at the time of his death, though, the case was dismissed. However, after the suit was publicized in the media, a man from her neighborhood visited Milly. He stated that he was seeking friendship from the widow, but she soon learned that the man wrongfully believed that Milly had already been awarded millions of dollars from the lawsuit. The opportunist's visit would be the first of many such misunderstandings that Milly would have to endure.

Nearly one year after her husband's death, Milly Belluomini was contacted by a chief judge at the Dirksen Federal Building about an upcoming ceremony that would honor her husband and US Marshal Frakes. She said, "They all got together and decided that they should put up a plaque at the Dirksen Building in honor of Harry and Bill Frakes. The US Marshals were involved also." The unveiling ceremony for the black plaque with gold lettering was held on April 7, 1993. "It was really something. All of the Federal Judges were there, and Wendy Frakes and I were there with our families. We were sad but honored to unveil the plaque. I believe that Judge Alesia had a lot to do with the plaque," Milly continued. "We went to the Italian Village restaurant afterwards. That's where Harry's father had been a waiter. Before we went to lunch, Judge Abraham Lincoln Marovitz, a wonderful judge, took us into his chambers before the event. He felt so bad over what happened. And then, every time we went to the Federal Building afterwards, he made it a point to talk with my family. I sent thank-you notes after the plaque unveiling, and Judge Marovitz wrote the nicest letter to me. He told me that he had never received such a nice thank you letter in his lifetime."

The black plaque with gold lettering unveiled at the Dirksen Federal Building reads: *In Memoriam. The Judges of the United States*

*District Court for the Northern District of Illinois dedicate this plaque
in memory of Deputy United States Marshal Roy L. "Bill" Frakes and
Court Security Officer Harry Belluomini, who gave their lives in the line
of duty while preventing the escape of a federal prisoner from the Everett
McKinley Dirksen Building on July 20, 1992. This Court recognizes the
dedication of these men in preserving the integrity of the Court and pro-
tecting those who come to this Court to seek justice. Their sacrifice will not
be forgotten.*

In 1994 Milly sold the family's Edison Park home to her son Michael. With the proceeds from the home sale, she moved forward
with their plan for heading north and building a new home. She
had the small cabin on their property in Wisconsin torn down and
built the permanent residence on that same site. It was a beautiful
ranch-style home, wrapped in natural wood, ringed with decks, and
complete with a few hundred feet of water frontage. The impeccable
views of the natural beauty of the north woods were all around.

Michael said, "I purchased my parent's home from my mom, and
she moved to Wisconsin. She had family and friends there. I lived
in that house for a while. After my daughter was born, I bought
the house right across the street. It's kitty-corner. When the movers
came, they didn't even use the truck. They just loaded everything
on dollies and rolled it all across the street."

In the summer of 1995, filmmakers were in the Chicago area to
produce a multi-million dollar theatrical feature film titled *Normal
Life* that was based on the Bearded Bandit and his wife's violent criminal exploits. The late Luke Perry and Ashley Judd starred in the
movie. It was released in 1996, but during the filming *Chicago Tribune* columnist Bob Greene interviewed Harry Belluomini's daughter Anne. The July 19, 1995 article was titled "A Life They Won't Make
a Movie About." In the piece, Anne revealed how she and her family
felt about the cinematic glorification of the killer Bearded Bandit
and his life. One of Anne's quotes in the article would hit home for
Greene's readers. She said, "You know, my Father was a very good
man. He lived his life by the rules. My sister and my brother and I

loved him, and he and my mother loved each other so much, and I pick up the paper, and I have to read about this movie they're making about the man who murdered him."

Anne recently said, "I do remember feeling lost during the '90s after my dad was killed. At the time he was killed, I was engaged and was having doubts about getting married. After my dad was killed I did eventually call the wedding off two weeks before the day, but somehow the date was set again for the following April. I went through with the wedding knowing it was a mistake, but deep down, I thought everyone needed a happy occasion after the tragedy, and I felt a huge internal and external pressure.

"In 1995, two years after the wedding, I was in an unhappy and abusive marriage. Part of the reason I did make the decision to get divorced is because of the strength my dad instilled in my sister and me when we were growing up. He told us if we ever got married and we were yelled at, hit, or abused, to get out no matter what, even if we had kids. He always told us that men should never treat women badly, and we should never put up with that kind of behavior. He taught all three of us to defend ourselves."

After Belluomini's death, Anne's life was spinning out to a degree, and she needed to make a change. She said, "I felt that the family had been ripped apart and changed forever. I think everyone was dealing with the tragedy and grief. Part of the reason I moved away was to get away from everything, the city, and seeing people in the area who would bring the tragedy up. Just everyday reminders. Though you eventually realize it's with you wherever you go. It took me a long time before I could visit my dad's graveside without crying or being unable to catch my breath when I approached. That day is still hard to talk about to this day."

When the film *Normal Life* was finally released, it depicted Harry Belluomini as a slovenly man. Milly said, "Harry was not a dumpy 58-year-old man. He was trim and physically fit. Harry always kept in shape. He played handball, walked, and jumped rope. Our kids used to laugh at him when he jumped rope, but Harry said it was a great exercise for strengthening his knees and that if he had to chase someone on the job, he was ready for it."

Anne said, "I think my dad was such an extraordinary human being. There are not too many people you come across like that in your life. I realize that everyone says that about people they love, but he truly was. He believed in right and wrong. Doing the right thing even when no one was looking. Speak up for yourself. Speak up for other people. Women were just as capable as men. Always be able to look yourself in the mirror. We were taught to treat the maintenance person the same as you would treat the president of the company."

After Harry Belluomini died in the shootout, Milly received a monthly death benefit payment from the US Labor Department for her husband's sacrifice to his country. But nearly four years later, in 1996, the government cut off those payments. The US Labor Department determined that Harry worked for General Security Services Corporation (GSSC) at the time of his death and not the US Marshals Service. GSSC is a private company contracted by the US Government to provide security services at federal buildings throughout the United States. Therefore, they determined that Harry was not actually in the government's employ, even though the US Marshals Service deputized him in 1988. The US Labor Department stated that being deputized was not the same as being employed by a US agency. As a result, Milly, living in her new home in Wisconsin, was forced to get a series of seasonal part-time waitress jobs to make ends meet.

In 1997, the US Justice Department notified Milly and Frakes's widow Wendy that the agency could not bring charges against two suspects they believed gave, or sold, a handcuff key to the Bearded Bandit. The statute of limitations had run out on what would've possibly become an aiding and abetting charge. The Justice Department representatives explained to Milly and Wendy that their evidence had been retrieved through jailhouse snitches. Therefore, it was circumstantial evidence that would most likely not bring a conviction.

The FBI believed that the handcuff key used by the Bearded

Bandit was most likely stored each night in a hollowed-out portion of a book in the murderer's jail cell. The Bearded Bandit allegedly brought the key with him every day of his trial, either wrapped in some paper tissues and tucked into a pocket of his suit coat or stowed away inside his mouth. Neither of these theories would ever be proven.

Also, in 1997, actors Bruce Campbell and Lori Laughlin starred in a television movie about the Bearded Bandit and his wife, Jill. It was titled *In the Line of Duty: Blaze of Glory.* The second movie about Erickson also glorifies the criminals. It's just another painful reminder for the Belluomini family of what they've lost.

29

In the early morning hours of Tuesday, March 3, 1998, Milly awoke in her new Wisconsin home to the smell of smoke. She was barely able to get out of the house, wearing only her pajamas and robe, before the structure quite literally burned to the ground. Nearly all of her family mementos, including the American flag that was draped over her husband's casket, were lost. She said, "Two weeks before the fire, a piece of metal flashing came down inside my fireplace. I called my builder and told him what had happened, and he came and checked it out. He called the fireplace manufacturer, which was in Canada, and then told me that everything was fine. The night before the fire, it was bitter cold, and I had a fire going in the fireplace. I closed the fireplace glass doors and went to bed, and apparently, the burning embers went up the chimney somehow. When it was about 6:30 in the morning, I thought, my God, it smells like someone's making popcorn. So I opened the door and stuck my head out of the bedroom, and said, 'Holy shit, my house is on fire.' Had I walked out of my bedroom and into the hallway, I would have fallen right through the floor and into the basement. I would've been burned to death. I still have nightmares about the fire. The phones were dead, the fire alarm was dead, and I couldn't leave my bedroom because the hallway was engulfed. The pine paneling on the inside of the house was popping like crazy. Thank God I had patio doors in my bedroom. I opened those doors, and I threw out a couple of pictures I had on the wall. I just threw them into the snow. I had a jewelry box on the dresser, and I threw that into the snow. I grabbed the blanket off my bed, and I just ran out barefoot. None of the other neighbors were up there at that time of year because it was early March. They usually didn't come up in the snow. The neighbors all went south when the snow came."

The flames from the burning house dramatically altered the landscape all around her beautiful home. "The trees were even scorched as I ran to this little tavern called the Gateway Lodge. The owners were just getting up in the morning and getting their kids ready for school. And I said, 'Please help me. My house is on fire.' Luckily, the fire chief lived a short distance away, and he had seen the smoke. He quickly came over and turned off the LP gas tank right away. The fire trucks responded immediately. I couldn't believe how fast they got there. The firemen kept saying, 'Is Milly in there? Is Milly in there?' Someone told them that I was in an ambulance. They wanted to take me to the hospital, but I told them that I didn't want to go. I was in total shock. Thank God I wasn't hurt. I was just cold."

Her only available shelter remaining at that moment had four wheels on it. She added, "Luckily, my SUV was in the garage, and there was a firewall between the garage and the house, so the car was not damaged. The firemen were going to move the car, but everything had burned, my purse, my keys, my IDs. Everything was gone. One of the firemen went to a car dealer and got replacement keys for my car right away. They took my car out of the garage, cleaned it up for me, and checked everything to make sure it was okay. The car wasn't damaged, but some of the other stuff in my garage got singed."

And soon, the community began to rally as they helped Milly get back on her feet. She said, "I was in shock for the whole week. The neighbors who were in the area were just wonderful. My one brother Mike lived right down the road from me, so I stayed with him. And then, the people in town had a fundraiser for me. Everyone turned out, and they raised money for me. The outpouring of love was unbelievable."

Milly had to rework her living arrangements as her house was re-built. She said, "I stayed with my brother for a short time. Then my neighbor, who was in Florida at the time, told me to stay in her house, which was right next door. I stayed at her house for a little while, but then I went back to my brother's house and stayed with him until November. I had the house rebuilt in that time. I had gotten ahold of a new builder. I didn't want to use the one who built the original home because I wasn't happy with him. I think he did wrong, and I think he knew it. But I couldn't prove it.

"When the house was completed, the neighbors had a house-warming shower for me. It was a surprise party, but I didn't want to go out. It was cold that night, and my brother said, 'Let's go to the Hideout.' And I said, 'Oh, Mike, I don't want to go out tonight.' He said, 'Come on, I have the taste for a beer.'" And I said, 'No, I don't want to go.' Of course, he knew about the surprise. When we got to the little resort, I said, 'Oh, I don't want to go in. Look at all these cars. It looks like they're having a meeting here or something.' And my brother said, 'Wait, there's a parking spot right here.' They had left a parking spot at the door available for him. He made me go in first, and of course, everyone yelled, 'Surprise!' The bar was just loaded with friends and neighbors. And there was a table just load-ed with presents for the new house."

Milly added, "I still have the cards that were given to me after the fire. I can't part with them because the words that were written were just unreal. The words made me feel good. Someone at the party said, 'Milly if you'd run for mayor, you'd win.'"

The Dennis Farina note from Harry's funeral was lost in the house fire, along with many of Harry's keepsakes. Even though more than twenty years have passed since the fire, the loss of the precious mementos still stings. "Harry was a great writer. He wanted to write a book about his career when he retired. He was a great storyteller. He said to me once, 'I'm going to have to put my experiences into words when we move up north,' but.... Harry could write. He wrote little stories. He wrote a wonderful poem for our daughter Annie.

All of Harry's mementos burned in the house fire. The day Harry died and the house fire, you never forget. Those two horrible things."

Anne said, "I was at work when I got the call. Thank God she was okay. You just can't believe it. I didn't go up right away because I was in Dallas at the time. I know that she lost all the photos of the family, but we were just happy that she was able to wake up. We just knew that it was a close call."

Mike added, "Me and Karen were up there the next day. We were just happy that my mom was alive because, man, when you saw what that fire had done to that house. It was an all-wood home with cedar siding... The fire was so hot that there was really nothing left of the house, just the foundation. I was looking through the debris a couple of days later after the insurance company had done their thing. I was able to put a ladder down into the basement and go through what was there. I just wanted to look through stuff, and there was nothing left. I was looking for a little snub-nosed gun that my dad used to have. My mom had it in the basement, and I couldn't find it. It melted. I couldn't even find the remnants of toilets or sinks, all the fittings in the bathrooms, the faucets, all of that. It all melted. Nothing was left, just ash and rubble."

Michael echoed Milly's thoughts on the lost mementos. He said, "We lost a lot of things, the hardest being the flag that was draped over my dad's casket. We lost some of the awards that he received posthumously. I had some of my stuff up there, all my snowmobiling clothing and fishing gear in the basement. But that stuff could be replaced. So my mom lost her husband, and then everything else got wiped out."

Michael was appreciative of Milly's Wisconsin friends and neighbors. He continued, "I'll say this, for all the stuff my mom had to go through, that little town of Mercer, Wisconsin, where she lived, that little town had a benefit for her and got her whatever she needed after the fire. There were always people to help her."

Michael and his sisters visited their mother often as the home rebuilding process got underway. Michael said, "So she rebuilt the house on the same footprint. The builder took down the garage and was able to clean up that foundation and rebuild using the existing foundation. The original foundation wasn't damaged. The second house was nicer than the first, but it didn't have a fireplace. It was a beautiful house. My mom went with a different builder the second time. She had to move a few years later, though, because her real estate taxes about tripled. She was on the water, and if you live on the water in that county, you're going to pay a lot of taxes. She was on a fixed income, so she had to move."

Karen said, "I couldn't believe it. I was working when I heard. Michael and I took off the next day and drove up there. We first went to see the burned house before we went to see our mom, and I just cried when I saw it. I was overwhelmed. You know, when you see house fires, you'll see that part of the house burned, but this was leveled. You could see all the charred rubble down in the basement... I couldn't believe that my mom got out of there and how severe that fire was."

Karen continued, "My mom had nothing, so I was helping her out the best I could. I was working a couple of jobs and trying to help her with all her stuff. My Auntie Anne and I drove back up there, and then the three of us drove to Minnesota to the Mall of America for a clothes shopping trip. We got her clothes, and we went to the casino, and we forgot about everything. We just had so much fun. We really had a good time."

Her fellow CPD officers helped as much as they could. Karen said, "My bosses were nice. They said to take as much time as you need. When I got back, my partner Tammie and a bunch of the guys took up a collection. So we got a couple of thousand dollars for my mom, which was so nice. I will never, ever forget that."

Before the tragic fire at Milly's home, whenever Karen would visit, her mother would try to give away family mementos to her children for safekeeping. Karen said, "She was always saying, 'You can have this, and you can have this.' And I told her to stop giving stuff away. She gave me my dad's mother's pink 'Depression-glass' cordial glasses. I always loved them, even when I was a kid. I remember that my grandmother would set them out for drinks. And my mom kept saying, 'Take them, take them.' I'm so glad that I did. I still have them. The glasses are something that I treasure. They would've been gone if I hadn't taken them."

Milly's Motorola friend, Kathy Paddock, said, "Milly is the most positive person that I have ever met in my life. She never complains or has a bad day. Despite all that she has been through, she always has a smile and a positive word. We enjoyed spending time up there with her and Wendy Frakes. She showed us some beautiful commemorative items, including a flag and his badge that she received from the Police Department. Sadly when there was a fire in the home, she lost all of those memories of Harry. She basically lost everything she had. She did rebuild, and the home was really nice, but I don't think it was ever the same for her. Everything was new and didn't hold the memories."

Despite her loss, Milly has consistently moved forward with her life. Paddock continued, "Whenever we are able to get together, it seems like no time has passed. Milly is such a special person. She never forgets a birthday or special occasion... She's amazing."

30

IN SEPTEMBER of 1999, Milly finally experienced a victory of sorts. She was able to employ attorney Thomas Pleines at Lodge 7 of the Fraternal Order of Police in Chicago to bring a case against the US Labor Department so that she could have Harry's death benefits reinstated. She argued that no matter if Harry worked for GSSC or the US Marshals Service, he engaged in sanctioned police activity when he died in the shootout with the Bearded Bandit. Word of the hearing made it to the media in Chicago. Even Judge James Alesia, the man who had emphatically stated that Harry had saved his life during the shootout, stepped forward to become a witness for the Belluomini family.

The day before the hearing was to take place, attorney Pleines received a phone call from the US Labor Department—Harry's death benefits would be reinstated immediately. The US Labor Department would eventually deem their earlier action to deny benefits "incorrect." The media also reported that US Attorney General Janet Reno wrote a letter to the US Labor Department asking for the denied benefits to be reinstated.

Also around this same time, the FBI finally, solidly, zeroed in on a single person of interest responsible for getting the handcuff key to the Bearded Bandit. The US Justice Department had a new game plan to bring some justice for the Belluomini and Frakes families. Robert Burke, an Irish national housed in the MCC with the Bearded

Bandit at the time of the escape attempt at the Dirksen Federal Building, is that suspect. Burke was recently released from the Federal Penal system after serving a sentence for a bank fraud conviction. Once freed from prison, Burke failed to stay at a halfway house as ordered by a judge. Unfortunately, no one knew the whereabouts of the convicted felon. He was in the wind.

31

LIKE THAT of his mother and sisters, Michael Belluomini's life had been turned on its head. He had tried to make a change a few years earlier, but it didn't work out the way he thought it would. Michael said, "I applied to the Chicago Police Department in 1987 or '88. There was a test you had to take, and I took it at Lane Technical High School. There were probably 20,000 people there. I went to take that test with a couple of friends of mine, and we had to park several blocks away. I remember us saying we had to be crazy applying for this job with this many people. We never had a chance."

Part of the testing process involved solving a problem scenario and working with other applicants in a small group of six to figure out a solution to the scenario. "You were supposed to wear business attire, and I was the only one wearing a suit. We had to do a team exercise where we had to interact with one another, and then one of the candidates had to act as a presenter to explain what we were doing as a team, and that was me." Michael's efforts on the testing day would not be enough to get him on the department, though. "I didn't get hired at that time," he said. "When I came out of that room that day, one of my dad's friends was coming out of another room. He sees me and says, 'Hey, how did you do?' I told him I wasn't so sure about anything. He said that he wished I was in his room, and so did I. [But] I also found out that they were disqualifying anyone related to another police officer. So that's why I got knocked out of that round."

Michael tried again with the CPD a few years later. "So I took the test again in 1991." This time, Michael's efforts got the department's attention. He had successfully made it through the testing process and was awaiting a spot in the police academy. He said, "But when they called me to come in, I was going to be out of town. I was going up to Wisconsin to go snowmobiling at our place in Mercer. They called me on a Thursday and told me to report to the academy on Monday, and I said, 'That ain't going to happen. I had this vacation planned.' I let it all go. I really didn't care if I got the job at that point."

Michael's mind was not in a suitable space yet for the CPD job, but he kept his options open. He said, "Then I got called in 1994 twice, but I turned it down again because I wasn't sure the job was for me. I finally did take the job in 1995 because the gas company wasn't promoting people like they should've been. I thought, 'you know what? I'll try this police thing and see what happens.' And the other reason I took the job was that I already lived in the city limits. I had bought my mom's house in Edison Park. I took a big pay cut becoming a cop. My pay was cut nearly in half. My dad knew that I took the tests, but he said, 'Stick with the gas company, dummy, don't get on this department. You have a good job.' And, in hindsight, I think, yeah, my dad was probably right in a lot of ways. I've been fortunate to do a lot of different things on this job, and I've met some great people, but there are a lot of politics and some BS you have to put up with. There's a lot of upper-echelon people on this job who think they're really smart, but if they were that smart, they'd be running Fortune 500 companies and not working on the CPD."

Michael continued, "My dad never knew that I got on the job. He was killed in 1992, and I got on the job in 1995. At the academy, a couple of people knew my sister Karen, and they knew my last name. A couple of the instructors came up to me and said stuff like, 'I knew your dad, and what a guy he was.' It's nice to hear those things."

After speaking with Michael on several occasions, one could conclude that he downplays the personal dedication and the 'willingness to selflessly serve his fellow citizens' part of taking on one of the most dangerous jobs in society. Yet, like his father, mother, and sister, he is the sort of person who always seems to be on call to help their fellow man, and humbly so. That noble quality that the Belluomini family members exhibit is something they can't seem to escape, nor should they. It's ingrained in their familial DNA.

Michael said, "I remember while I was at the academy, an officer was killed in the line of duty. His name was Daniel Doffyn, and he was killed in the 15th District. I remember that all the academy recruits had to go to the funeral service. That was something. It brought everything right back. I had to hold back the tears, and my instructor asked if I was okay, and I said, 'Yeah, I'm fine.' But I was thinking about that officer's family because they were going through the same thing that we just went through a few years before."

A few decades after becoming a Chicago police officer, Michael Belluomini is on the Marine Unit, patrolling Lake Michigan and the Chicago River. His office is either a 27- or 44-foot SAFE Boats International vessel. Michael has received several awards for assisting boaters in distress and participating in numerous dive operations with his partners. Michael and his CPD partners have recovered bodies, weapons, and vehicles in Lake Michigan, the Chicago River, and the many lagoons that dot the Chicago lakefront. Michael's sense of humor was on full display when he said, "I like being in the Marine Unit and being on a boat. At this point in my life, I wouldn't own a boat. I remember when I got on the Marine Unit, my wife said that maybe we should get a boat. I told her that I'm on a boat about six days a week. Why would I want to own one for my days off?"

Milly Belluomini is very proud of her son. She said, "Michael is a good man, a good son, and a good police officer."

His sister Karen, when thinking back to when her brother first joined the CPD, before he was on the Marine Unit, said, "Mike worked in the district right next to mine, and we both picked midnights to work our shifts. We would always meet up at some point on the border of our districts. He was in the 11th, and I was in the

13th. We'd hang out at this gas station for a little while. I always worried about my brother. He's such a nice guy. I worried that the job would change him. Annie and I are very much alike. We have the same type of attitude, but Michael? He was the nice one. I just didn't want him to deal with the crap we had to deal with."

Michael added, "My friends tell me that I'm not 'like a cop.' Some people change when they become policemen." And when the topic of police brass comes up, Michael doesn't hold back, just like his father before him. He said, "A lot of those guys who become supervisors on the police force, they got their clout, and they have to get involved in the politics of the job. My dad was never like that. He wouldn't play those games."

Michael Belluomini's father is never far from his thoughts, especially when he's on a CPD Marine Unit boat out in Lake Michigan. He said, "Now when I'm out on the boat, and I see Castaways on North Avenue beach, I think about those times with my dad." Castaways is a large, red, white, and blue painted structure situated directly on the beach at North Avenue. The Castaways building seen today is a recently rebuilt replica of the original, boat-shaped building constructed decades ago. It houses a seasonal beach club and eatery. Michael recalled his family's many outings to North Avenue Beach when he was a kid. Michael said of Harry, "He'd say, 'Do you want to go down to the big boat today and fly a kite?' Stuff like that."

32

CONVICTED CONMAN Robert Burke, at the time a 50-year-old Irish national living in the US, was released from federal custody in July of 1994 and had to report to a Salvation Army facility to serve out the supervised release portion of his total prison sentence. He was last seen at the Salvation Army facility in Chicago in August of 1994. The court presiding over his case issued a warrant for his arrest for breaking the conditions of his supervised parole. The US Justice Department and FBI also believed that Burke was responsible for providing the handcuff key to the Bearded Bandit in July of 1992.

Federal authorities learned that Burke was residing in London, England, and Interpol was contacted so that the convicted conman could be detained for extradition back to the States. Burke eluded the police in the UK for nearly four years but was finally arrested in London in 1998. It would take two more years of legal wrangling to finally extradite Burke to Chicago on December 22, 2000.

Karen Belluomini had a close encounter with the wanted felon upon his arrival back in Chicago. It was an encounter that Burke probably was not even aware of at that time. She said, "I met Burke at the airport when I was working there. I was on duty. I found out that he was flying in, and I thought I had to go to the gate. I had to go. I wanted to see him. Leading up to that day, all I was thinking about was, 'What would I do if I saw him?' And I'm not kidding. I thought about killing him. I know that he didn't cause everything, but he helped. It was just so emotional when I saw him. And I thought how ironic it would be if I pulled out my gun and shot him right between the eyes and killed him with the gun that my father gave me when I first came on the job? At the time, I thought, wow, that would be great. And my hands were so sweaty, and I thought, 'Here he is. Here he is.' But I remember seeing John O'Malley, who was one of the US Marshals, and who was very good friends with Bill Frakes. O'Malley was bringing Burke in. And man, when O'Malley saw me, he was livid. I thought, screw you, I have every right to be here." Karen noticed, at that moment, that O'Malley was shocked and then angry, but neither said anything to the other. "I was seething, but I was glad that they brought him back to the US." Karen kept her gun in its holster.

Once back in the MCC in downtown Chicago, the US Justice Department had questions for Burke regarding how the Bearded Bandit obtained the handcuff key back in 1992. As a result, Burke was seated in front of a Federal Grand Jury and given immunity if he truthfully testified in the inquest into how the Bearded Bandit obtained the handcuff key.

The US Attorneys then determined that Burke lied to the Grand Jury, and he was indicted on six counts of perjury and immediately taken back into custody.

Burke's perjury trial began October 28, 2002, in a Dirksen Federal Building courtroom—the very same courtroom where the Bearded Bandit had been tried years earlier. The prosecutors would argue that Burke's mother allegedly smuggled the handcuff key to Burke during a jailhouse visit, and then Burke either gave or sold the key to the Bearded Bandit.

During the trial, Milly and Karen, and her fiancé Curt Blanc, attended nearly every day, except for Milly missing two days due to illness. Michael Belluomini would attend when he could. Anne lived in Dallas, Texas, at the time and did not attend. Michael said,

"I was working a lot when the trial happened, but I was able to go to a couple of the trial days. I know that Karen was at the trial all of those days. She didn't miss anything."

Milly said, "It was very emotional. Karen, Curt, and I went to that trial almost every day. It was very emotional, very hard to do that every day, to go through that trial and hear all the nonsense. But sometimes, I don't even remember half of it. Most of the trial is a blank in my mind now. It could be that I just don't want to remember. The US Attorney was Patrick Fitzgerald. He was wonderful. He was determined to solve the mystery of the handcuff key. We sat right in the front row so we could see Burke, and we could see the jury."

Karen would not miss a single day of the Burke trial. She said, "I had time on the books, and I went to my commander, and I asked to take a couple of weeks off to go to the trial, and the commander said no." The particular commander in question had an unfortunate if highly descriptive nickname: "The Screaming Skull." Karen added, "I was shocked, and I asked, 'Excuse me?' And he said no again. So I said, 'Listen, I really need to go to this trial,' and he said no. I was pissed off all day. I couldn't believe that asshole wouldn't let me take the time off. So I went above his head. Frank Radke [her old neighbor] was commander of special functions, which meant he was in charge of the entire airport. I called him, and he allowed me to take the time off to go to the trial. I did not want my mom to go alone. I didn't want her to be sitting there by herself. And more importantly, I had to go on behalf of my dad. I wanted to be there for my father."

Karen continued, "We sat pretty much upfront during the trial. I know that I didn't miss a day. My mom got sick and missed a couple of days, but I was there every day. And Curt was with me. He was still on the job and not retired yet. We were getting married at about the time the trial was taking place. It was stressful... We had a lot going on."

As Karen sat in that courtroom, only ten feet away from Burke, she had one consuming thought. "Hate," said Karen. "That's what I was thinking. It made me sick to look at him. And especially sick to look at his lawyers. We called one 'The Rooster,' and the other was some asshole. He was such an arrogant defense attorney. They tried to make Burke look like a saint. And they argued that he shouldn't be tried for what he was accused of. But I had to be there at the trial every day. I'd go if I had my legs cut off. It was just a long trial and long days, just going down to the Federal Building every day. But I had to be there. I had to be there to represent my father."

Michael added, "I was more angry at the Bearded Bandit than Burke, and probably even more mad about the negligence of the US Marshals Service, to be honest with you, for letting it all happen. Burke had a major part in it, but my anger was more toward the Bearded Bandit. He was hell-bent to get out of that building, and then he killed Frakes and my dad. And I was angry at the US Marshals. I mean, how do you have a high-risk prisoner with the other inmates, and you just have two people guarding them all? One was inexperienced, and the other a rookie Marshal. In my book, the inexperienced female dropped the ball. Frakes was a big guy, but what could he do by himself? There should've been another properly trained officer instead of the untrained part-time Marshal, in my opinion. With a high-risk prisoner like the Bearded Bandit, the whole scenario, it just didn't make sense. You want the US Marshals to learn from what happened so that it never happens again. I remember when the preacher Jim Bakker was arrested for embezzling money, my dad saw it on the news and said, 'They got him all shackled up like he was a big-time prisoner. He didn't kill anyone. He's just an embezzler.' The government made an example out of him by the way he was chained up. Why wasn't the Bearded Bandit handled the same way? He wasn't even shackled at his legs. And he's wearing a suit."

Former CPD detective Tedy Nadile summed up what most of Harry's old buddies thinks these days about how the US Marshals Service brass dealt with the Bearded Bandit. In their minds, the US Marshals Service supervisors let their collective guards down and endangered not only their officers but the public too, and botched the entire prisoner transport process at the Dirksen Building in July of 1992, which allowed three lives to be lost. Nadile said, "Harry was a policeman to his last breath. To not have that prick [the Bearded Bandit] completely surrounded when they took him in and out of that Federal Building was wrong."

Michael Belluomini added, "And they had caught the Bearded Bandit with a key before when he was being transported from the MCC to the courthouse." This previously unreported bit of information was provided to the Belluomini family by an unnamed Federal Government source.

Michael continued, "[The Bearded Bandit] had fashioned a key from the pop-top of a juice can. So the US Marshals knew that the guy was trying something. He was at least trying, you know? If he was my prisoner, and I had known he was found with a key on him before, I'd have four guys on him. He was dangerous, and he should've been treated like Hannibal Lecter. They should've cuffed the Bearded Bandit behind his back with his thumbs facing up and the keyhole of the cuffs facing away from the prisoner's fingers."

During the court proceedings, though, Michael thought he knew why government officials were so pleased with themselves that they had Burke in custody and on trial. He said, "The US Marshals were trying to deflect, saying things like, 'Yeah, we got the guy who gave the Bearded Bandit the cuff key,' and things like that. That was them deflecting from their blame, in my opinion. And also, in my opinion, they were 100 percent negligent. That's the way that I look at it. [The Bearded Bandit] was in custody, so this should have never happened. His own mom tried to warn the officials about him, that he was acting strangely, and that he may try something."

On November 2, 2002, a jury of eight men and four women deliberated for only five hours. Burke was found guilty on five of the six counts that he was facing for making false statements. It was determined that Burke lied when he told the Federal Grand Jury that he did not provide or make the handcuff key available to any person at the Metropolitan Corrections Center in Chicago. His sentencing was initially set for August 2003, but it was later delayed to September 2003.

Milly added, "I was very happy when he was convicted. And Burke was sentenced to about 20 years in prison, and he was released last year, I think. I wasn't notified of his release. The last day of the trial, when Burke was convicted, we went out afterwards for martinis. All of the US Attorneys and my family got along so well, and they thanked us for being there every day. The presiding judge was Rebecca Pallmeyer, who today is the chief judge at the Federal Building."

On September 12, 2003, Robert Burke was sentenced to 20 years in a federal penitentiary for his perjury convictions. The sentence was steep because underlying offenses occurred due to the key being offered to the Bearded Bandit—mainly, and quite obviously, leading to the murders of Frakes and Harry Belluomini.

For that initial decade following her husband's death, Milly Belluomini never truly understood what had occurred, in detail, in the Dirksen Federal Building garage in July of 1992. She said, "While we were there for Burke's trial, an FBI agent named John Larsen took us through a tour of the Federal Building and showed us exactly what happened when Harry was killed. How [the Bearded Bandit] escaped, and he walked us right through where the shooting occurred. It was very, very sad to take that tour. And to see just how close Harry and [the Bearded Bandit] were to one another when the shooting started. They were about four feet apart. Most people would've probably run for cover. But to be face-to-face and realize that [the Bearded Bandit] was not a good guy. Like I've said, Harry's intuition was so good, he knew [the Bearded Bandit] was bad, and Harry did what he had to do. He ultimately lost his life doing that, but he saved other lives. If [the Bearded Bandit] got up that ramp and out onto Jackson Boulevard, he would've killed people. He would've shot anyone he could have because he didn't care. Harry put a stop to all of that. Some days I ask 'why did it happen,' and other days, I think, 'things happen for a reason.' I don't know."

As part of Robert Burke's sentencing, Milly and Karen were allowed to read aloud victim impact statements for the court record. The following is Milly Belluomini's statement:

"I choose not to tell publicly what the last long eleven years were like for me since the death of my late husband, Harry. But, I'd like to say a few words if I may.

Our parents were Italian and Croatian immigrants who came to this country for a better life and to raise their families the best they could. They were not educated but taught us much common sense—such as being good Americans and to try and do the best with our lives.

We were told there were two roads to take as we grew older—The right road and the wrong road, and that we had choices to make. We both knew where the wrong road would take us. So we did work very hard and raised our children the best we could. Harry worked so many side jobs so I could stay at home and raise the children. Some days he only slept three hours, and off he would go to another side job just to make sure things were better for me, Karen, Michael, and Annie. We set our goals and tried to make the right choices. We both felt we were on the right road.

Harry was the smartest man I ever knew. He could read a person like no one I ever knew. He was always happy, funny, witty, could remember things like the score of a Bears game 20 years ago or who won the Kentucky Derby, Shakespeare quotes, operas, movies, and do the crossword puzzle in no time flat. He loved to write poems, short stories, and he won every Monopoly game or Trivial Pursuit game we played together as a family. When we planned to retire, he wanted to write a book on his career as a Chicago Police detective. He had so many stories to tell, but that all ended on July 20, 1992, when a man on trial, in this very courtroom, in this building, made a very bad choice. He decided to try an escape, and we all know the outcome of that fateful day. And today, another man is sentenced because he, too, made some bad choices. They both took the wrong road that put an end to our right road.

I never wish anyone any harm or evil, but I certainly do not wish this man here today well.

Again, I would like to thank the US Attorney Patrick Fitzgerald, Assistant US Attorneys Diane MacArthur and Bill Hogan, FBI Agent John

Larsen, the US Marshals, the CSO's, the jury who found this man guilty on five counts, and to the press for their coverage. And to all who sat with my family and me during this trying time once again."

(signed) Milly Belluomini

Karen Belluomini Blanc's impact statement follows:

"Someone in this courtroom stated that 'this was a fun trail.' I have to disagree—it was anything but fun. It was very long, aggravating, and emotionally draining. It was also very painful

I would like to begin by thanking Diane MacArthur and Bill Hogan for all their hard work that they put into this trial; for their professionalism, dedication, heart, and soul. My family and I can't thank you enough —also, thanks to John Larsen, who was also just as dedicated in bringing Burke to trial.

A lot of people have told me that once this is all over, we should have closure. Well, I know I will never have that. My dad is gone, and nothing will ever take away that empty feeling that I will have for the rest of my life.

What makes it even harder is to have seen what my mom has gone through, and still watching her struggle with the pain from this horrible tragedy is very difficult.

The same person who commented on this trial being 'fun' has also stated that Burke had no idea this tragedy would of occurred. I disagree. He just didn't care.

Had Burke not given Erickson the handcuff key: My dad would be enjoying his retirement up in Wisconsin with my mom, fishing, doing his crossword puzzles, drinking his Manhattans on the deck, and just enjoying life.

Had Burke not given Erickson the handcuff key: My dad would be enjoying his grandson, Mikie.

Had Burke not given Erickson the handcuff key: My dad would have seen all three of his children follow in his footsteps to become Chicago Police officers.

Had Burke not given Erickson the handcuff key: My dad would have been able to walk me down the aisle at my wedding last November.

Had Burke not given Erickson the handcuff key: I would not be standing here today.

My dad died a hero on July 20, 1992, but he didn't become my hero because of that terrible incident—he was always my hero, as is my mom. What my parents have done for our family, provided for us, and taught us, is the best gift they could have given us, and I will be forever grateful. My dad always put his family first and was so devoted to my mom. I'm lucky to have such wonderful memories of him, but that's all I'm left with, and not a day goes by that I don't think about him. I miss him more than anything and feel like a part of me has also died.

Lastly, I'm hopeful that Burke will receive the maximum sentence possible—hopefully, Burke will die in the custody of the Bureau of Prisons and will realize what he stole from my family and me."

(signed) Karen Belluomini Blanc

33

IN HER victim impact statement at Burke's sentencing, Karen mentioned that her younger sister, Anne, had recently joined the family business. However, like her siblings before her, Anne's route to the CPD was not a straight-line pathway.

Anne explained, "I moved with Duo-Fast to Dallas and worked there for four years. I spread my wings in Dallas, and I think I kind of needed that at that time. It was shortly after my dad was killed. By that point, both my brother and sister were on the Chicago Police Department, and I was not. It just got to be a bit too much for me. And people were always bringing my dad up, and I wanted to go someplace where no one knew about it. I just needed to leave."

Her time away from Chicago allowed Anne to take a 360-degree view of her world and where she might belong in it. She said, "I wound up moving back to Chicago for family, and then to take the police department test. I had been talking to my sister about taking the test. When I lived in Chicago before Dallas, I had signed up to take the test many times but just blew it off when it came time to take the test. I just never showed up. I was getting sick of the business world. It was very cutthroat. And you had to play politics. I did not play politics well. I'm kind of a very blunt person. If you ask me a question and you want the honest answer, but you really don't want the honest answer, then you shouldn't ask me. I also didn't like some of the things I saw at work, and I wanted to leave the business world."

CPD officer Mike Simmi was one of Anne Belluomini's instructors at the Chicago Police Academy. In a strange stroke of fate, he was also personally familiar with the Bearded Bandit. Simmi said, "I knew [the Bearded Bandit] from Triton College, where we went to school. And then he was an auxiliary officer in Rosemont, for a short time, when I was in Rosemont. He got hired as a police officer in Hoffman Estates after that. He was a student in the criminal justice class with us, but he wasn't a friend that went out drinking with us."

Simmi also knew Anne Belluomini's father. "I had met Harry Belluomini on the job, but it was just in passing. When I got down to the training academy as a range officer on '01 or '02, here comes all these recruits, and there was this young lady with the last name Belluomini. Of course, everyone's butchering her last name. So I walked up to Anne and said, 'Your last name's Belluomini (bell-Wah-mini), right?' She said, 'Yes, it is, sir.' And I said, 'Are you related to Harry Belluomini?' And she goes, 'That was my father.' So Annie and I became friends, and I pinned her star on her at her graduation. Annie is just a wonderful, caring human being. Her sister Karen worked at the airport with me when I got out to O'Hare. She was on midnights when I got out there. But Annie is so different from Karen because their personalities are so different. It's not that Karen's a mean person, or bad or anything like that. It was just that Annie was such a caring person. A very caring individual."

Simmi was impressed with Anne's capabilities while at the academy. He said, "I was her range officer, and I had her as a recruit. She was ahead of the game. Smart, funny, but very respectful. She had her A-game on from the day she walked into the academy. She knew what to do and what to say. She was just sharp. It's just so strange, this circle, and how things all came back around. Here I am sitting at Triton College as a student next to this kid in class. And then working as an auxiliary officer with him at Rosemont, and then he ends up becoming this rogue individual, kills this retired copper who I had met on the job in Chicago. And I wind up having his daughter as a student in the police academy."

Retired CPD detective Ken Berris, a neighbor of the Belluominis in Edison Park, said of Anne, "What a wonderful lady and a good police officer. A very good police officer."

Once Anne had graduated from the police academy, she was patrolling the streets on the northwest side. She said, "I was placed in the 25th District. It's at Grand and Central, where my dad used to work upstairs as a detective. I worked there for nearly 14 years before I moved to the 16th District. I requested the move. I just wanted a change. I'd been in the 25th District for a long time."

Anne added, "About eight years ago, some friends and I went to the theater, and I made dinner reservations at Italian Village under my name." Upon the group's arrival at the restaurant, the maître d' told Anne that there used to be a waiter that worked at the establishment with her same last name. Anne was pleasantly surprised that anyone at the restaurant would remember her family's name. She said, "I told him that that was my grandfather. He told me he knew and worked with my grandfather." When the man walked away from their table, Anne jokingly said to her friends, "Jesus Christ, is this guy a vampire? My grandfather would be well over 100 years old right now." After their dinner was over, Anne spoke again with the maître d', and he proceeded to show her where her grandfather waited tables. She said, "He remembered that his son, my dad, had become a police officer. I told him what happened to my dad. I know the man had to have been in his 80s at least, but he walked around that room like he was way younger, and he had a great memory."

Anne is still on the job at the CPD. And like her father and her siblings, Anne has held many side jobs during her law enforcement career. But, she added, "I think my dad would be shocked today that I work so much."

34

KAREN BELLUOMINI Blanc had transferred to work at the CPD's O'Hare Airport division after many years patrolling the west side of Chicago. She said, "I was working at O'Hare when 9-11-01 happened. I was just doing my rounds, and Annie called me. She said, 'Get to a TV. A plane just crashed into a building in New York.' We went to one of the bars, which had TVs on all the time, and we saw the second plane crash. We didn't really know what was going on. We were like everyone else. But then people started freaking out, wondering if O'Hare was next. But we didn't know what to do. What do you do? We weren't trained for something like that. We had to just wait for our supervisor to tell us what to do."

Karen's supervisor was a commander. A man named Tom Argenbright, the one-time homicide detective, who had initially investigated the aftermath of the Bearded Bandit's escape attempt and her father's death.

Karen continued, "That was when the US Marshals started showing up with automatic weapons. Before that day, anyone could just walk into any part of the airport as long as they didn't set off a metal detector, but then all the protocols changed, obviously."

Even after her transfer to the airport, thoughts of her father were constantly on her mind. She said, "There was a priest I'd see when I worked at O'Hare, and he told me, 'If you think you have a problem, write that problem down and put it in a hat with everyone else that has problems, and you'll want to pick your own problem back out of the hat once you read everyone else's.' That's so true. I always think that I'm lucky. I'm blessed, and other people have it worse than me."

Nearly a decade removed from the 9-11-01 terror attacks, Karen retired from the CPD after garnering numerous honorable mentions for her work. She said, "I retired August 2, 2011. I wanted to retire on my dad's retirement date. When I retired, I gave my star to my brother Michael."

Karen and her husband, former Homicide Sergeant with the CPD's Detective Division, Curt Blanc, soon moved from Chicago to a rural area near Paducah, Kentucky. There, they took care of 23 acres of land and animals, including rescue horses and dogs. Sadly, in early 2020, Curt passed away. Karen still lives in the Paducah area.

35

MICHAEL BELLUOMINI is nearing retirement from the CPD and his much-loved Marine Unit. His complimentary history with the department runs deep. He'll leave his post after receiving dozens of commendations, honorable mentions, and other awards for his work. He'll watch as his son Michael makes his way into the world and as his daughter, Ava, graduates from high school. On tap for his retirement is a possible relocation for himself and his wife, Deanna, to the western United States. His father's CPD star, which was first handed down from Harry to Karen, and then from Karen to Michael when he became a police officer, will soon be pinned to his sister Anne Belluomini's uniform.

36

MILLY BELLUOMINI, now entering her 80s and still physically active as ever, resides in the same area of northern Wisconsin where she and Harry owned their cabins. It's also the location where many of her siblings, nieces, and nephews currently live. Her caring ways remain legendary among her family, friends and neighbors. Milly's civic-mindedness carries on as she volunteers weekly for the Meals-on-Wheels program in her area.

The City of Chicago renamed the street corner outside the Dirksen Federal Building at Dearborn Street and Jackson Boulevard 'Harry A. Belluomini Way.' Michael said, "The US Marshals Service wanted the plaque to be put up in the Federal Building. It was an honor, and every time you walk past it and see it, or when they had a ceremony on anniversary dates of the event, you can't help but get emotional. I was there for the 25th-anniversary ceremony with my son and daughter, and I gave a little speech. It was hard to keep my composure because there are so many people who still show up for those ceremonies, and they still remember. It's something to see my dad's name up there with Frakes, and even to see his name on the street sign. It's something to be proud of."

Harry Belluomini's name and badge number were added to the Chicago Police Gold Star Families Memorial and Park near Soldier Field on Chicago's lakefront. Harry's name has also been added to the National Law Enforcement Officers Memorial in Washington,

DC, and the American Police Hall of Fame memorial in Florida. And once every calendar year, the US Marshals Service awards one of their Court Security Officers the 'Harry Belluomini Court Security Officer of the Year' award for heroic acts performed while on duty.

Harry may be gone now, but the Belluomini family's dedication to serving their fellow citizens is ongoing.

37

FORMER PALATINE Police officer Kevin Maher, who was shot and injured by the Bearded Bandit in November 1991, is reminded almost daily of the sacrifice Harry Belluomini, "Bill" Frakes, and their families made in July of 1992. His reminder comes in the form of the ornate plaque that graces the first floor of the Dirksen Federal Building in downtown Chicago where Maher has an office. Maher said, "I left the Palatine Police in July of 1996 because I was hired as a Special Agent with the United States Secret Service. I was assigned to the Milwaukee, Wisconsin, Field Office. I'm now an agent with the United States Department of Housing and Urban Development, Office of Inspector General. I'm the regional head trainer for the Midwest region. I am responsible for conducting all the training in the Midwest for Firearms, CPR and First Aid, Active Shooter Response, and Control Tactics. I am also responsible to lead the Firearms Transition Team in the research and implementation from a .40 caliber duty pistol to a 9mm platform."

Although he was injured decades ago, Maher has had regular reminders of the day he nearly lost his life to the rogue cop who fired a high velocity .223 round through his shoulder. But, Maher said, "The bullet fragments are very little. I've had three of them taken out over the past, what is it, nearly 30 years."

When Maher walks past that plaque in the Dirksen Federal Building these days, he thinks, "Who knows how many people Harry Belluomini saved. If the Bearded Bandit gets out of the courthouse, he's on the run."

38

MILLY BELLUOMINI received the following letter in July of 2010 —eighteen years after her husband Harry had given up his life in his final act of courage and heroism.

July 12, 2010

Family of Officer Harry Belluomini
Federal Court
Dirksen Building
219 S. Dearborn Street
Chicago, Illinois 60604

Dear Family of Harry Belluomini,

The other day, I was at the federal courthouse at the Dirksen Building and happened to pass by the plaque commemorating the sacrifices of Security Officer Harry Belluomini and Marshal Roy Frakes by the giving of their lives on July 20, 1992. As I looked at this silent witness to the events of 18 years ago, my mind went to the respective families of each officer.

I am an attorney, and on July 20, 1992, I had just left the federal courthouse after appearing for a bankruptcy case. As I left the Dirksen Building, I began walking up Jackson Boulevard and passed by the ramp that leads down to the garage under the federal courthouse. There, halfway down the ramp, was a man lying motionless on the pavement in a pool of blood. No one else was on the ramp as this man had apparently just fallen after running halfway up the ramp.

Later that night, on the news, I learned that this man was a prisoner who had killed Officers Belluomini and Frakes while trying to escape. Apparently, Officer Belluomini shot the prisoner before he could escape, which led to his dying out on the ramp.

As I listened to the news, I realized how close I had come to possibly having been caught up in this terrifying drama. If this man had not been wounded during his attempted escape, I easily could have found myself amidst flying bullets when the prisoner reached the top of the ramp as I was passing by.

It is impossible to know what would have happened. If not me, some other innocent person could have been hurt or even killed. I just wanted you to know that I, and every other potential victim who was walking by the ramp that fateful day, have been permitted to live out our lives because of what your loved one did. I was given the opportunity to continue raising my son, to hold my wife in my arms, to go to work, and hopefully, through these years, contribute to the well-being of others.

And herein lies the irony and tragedy of my words. The gift given to us of the ordinary pleasures of life has come at the cost of the same being deprived of you. I suspect that the sharp edge of Harry's loss that was felt immediately after his death has been replaced by a numbness that is the result of his absence all these subsequent years.

I just want to make sure that you know that the loss of your loved one, although tragic beyond words, was not meaningless. His sacrifice permitted the rest of us to continue with our lives uninterrupted by the events of that day. In essence, the sacrifice of Officer Belluomini continues to reverberate and impact on the course of my life and all the other possible victims of that day.

So, this coming July 20th, when you look out your living room window and watch the world going about its business, oblivious to your ongoing loss and the significance of this day, I hope that this will not add to your sense of loneliness. It is only because of the sacrifice of Officer Belluomini and his family that the ordinary pleasures we all take for granted are available to the rest of us. That "life goes on" should not be seen as an affront to the sacrifices you have made. It should only affirm how important Officer Belluomini's life was then, and even now, as each of us, who were there that day, continue to live out the course of our lives. That is the quiet living tribute to Harry's sacrifice that no plaque can ever fully explain.

With all my gratitude,
Timothy J. Hufman

APPENDIX

THE EVENTS described here about Milly's life were both gifts, for the friendships she forged while working at Motorola, and tragic, for her missing out on a financial windfall that would have helped to sustain her in later years—and for the ill-at-ease feelings she experienced every time Harry left the house for his job in the Federal Building. This appendix material also goes the extra step in illustrating the resiliency Milly Belluomini exhibits for the world, and more importantly, for her children and grandchildren to witness. She is a master of showing, and not telling others how to live, and thrive, with humor and humility, even in the face of daunting adversity.

In the late 1970s, the Belluomini kids grew, came into their own, and began to take care of themselves. Milly wanted to dive back into the working world, not only for the extra money but for the social setting work environments tend to offer. She and Harry were confident that their children would be able to look out for themselves. Sure, there would be minor hiccups along the way, like with any family. But Milly and Harry were confident that their kids would make the right decisions as they went about navigating their worlds.

Milly said, "One time, another detective's wife and I put our applications in to become Chicago police officers. Harry said, 'Are you crazy?' I told him I was going to take the test, and he told me I was nuts. So this woman and I went and took the test. I didn't care if I passed or not. We were just doing it for fun. I missed passing by two points, and I thought, 'thank God, I could never do that job.' When they made some women detectives that was a big deal in Chicago. Harry had to break in this one female detective. And that woman and I were friends. She was married to a detective, also. That first day when they stopped for lunch, the woman asked if Harry would buy her lunch. Harry told her, 'No, I'm not. You're making the same salary I'm making.'"

Milly went back to work for Motorola. Instead of pursuing a police career, she knew that returning to Motorola would afford her the chance to qualify for a pension when she retired. However, complications would stop her second tour of duty at the company. Milly said, "When I went back to work in 1977, the office was in Park Ridge. It was so close to our home I could go home for lunch if I wanted to. I had so much fun going back to work. I was in inside sales. Karen had just started high school when I went back to work at Motorola in 1977. After my first day, I came home, and my daughter Karen had made me dinner. I'll never forget it. It was a recipe that she had seen in *Seventeen* magazine. She made me these stuffed pasta shells, a salad, and she baked me a cake. She had the table set so beautifully when I came home from work. I couldn't believe it. I told her, 'I could never do what you just did at age 14. I'll never forget this.' I thought it was so neat."

During an "all hands" meeting at the Motorola Schaumburg main offices, Milly was reintroduced to a special person from her past, a person she'd not seen since she was a 20-year-old Motorola Sweetheart. Milly said, "There was a meeting, and Khaki Bhote was the main speaker. I was sitting in the front row, and when he started speaking, he talked about how great and dedicated Motorola employees were. And then he said, 'I see right there in the front row is Milly Cutich. She worked for me when she was right out of high school.' I was so honored that he said that. I didn't think that he'd ever remember me, but that was a thrill."

After a few years at the Park Ridge Motorola facility, Milly's offices moved to Schaumburg. Unfortunately, after that office relocation, her mother became ill, and Milly had to give up her job, once again, to care for her ailing parent. Milly's mother passed away in 1982.

But Motorola was not finished with Milly just yet, and they re-acquainted themselves with a bit of panache. Milly continued, "In 1983, Motorola called me and asked if I could come back to work in the semiconductor division, and I thought, 'boy, I think I will just because it would be good therapy for me since my mom had passed away.' It was wonderful. It was in March of 1983 that I went back to Motorola, and I was getting ready to leave the house for my first day back when this limousine pulled up in front of the house. The chauffeur knocked on the door, and I told him that he had the wrong address. The chauffeur said, 'Is your name Milly?' I said it was, and he said, 'I'm taking you to work today.' Motorola had sent a limousine for me. In the car, there was a bouquet of roses and a bottle of champagne. I thought, 'I can't drink the champagne before work. I'd be bombed!' When I got to the office, they were all so happy that I had come back. I worked there until 1988, when Harry said he was retiring. I remember telling him that I wanted to work a couple more years at Motorola to get a pension. Harry said, 'You don't need no pension, Honey. We're going to be fine. We're going up north to Wisconsin.'" Not staying on with Motorola for two more years, and being awarded enough time on the books to qualify for a pension, would be a decision that would haunt Milly and the Belluomini family in the years to come.

But there was a personal upside to going back to Motorola that would prove to be even more valuable than a paycheck. Milly met two women at work who would become a lifeline in the future. She said, "There were two friends I worked with at Motorola that could've been my daughters, Maureen Gallagher Kowalski and Kathy Paddock. We all worked together except that they were younger than me. We got along so well. These girls still send me gifts for my birthday, Christmas, and Mother's Day. They still call me and come up here to Wisconsin to visit me. I find that amazing."

I spoke with Kathy Paddock and Maureen Gallagher Kowalski separately by phone. Maureen said, "My first impression of Milly was that she reminded me a lot of my mom. Milly was beautiful, and she had big blue eyes like my mom had. Milly was so welcoming and outgoing. She kind of adopted me as her daughter. So Kathy, Milly, and I became fast friends. We worked together in the distribution quote center. We gelled together at work, and we gelled together outside of work. We just built a great friendship."

Maureen enjoyed her time visiting with Harry Belluomini, too. She said, "Harry had us over for dinner a couple of times. We'd have a big Italian dinner at Milly's house. Harry was probably a typical Italian Chicago Policeman. He was in his early 50s then and had jet-black hair. Harry and Milly gelled together. She would say that when she got home from work, he'd have a martini made for her, he'd have dinner on the table. He just adored her. And I thought what a great relationship they had. Harry was the perfect husband. I don't think that she ever talked about them fighting. It was a good family, and they passed down good values and morals to the kids."

Kathy Paddock said, "We all had such a good chemistry. She would talk about Harry all the time. In the beginning, he was at the Police Department and did some security on the side. I remember that he would sometimes be working security at Carson Pierre Scott, and the ladies in cosmetics would give him freebies for Milly. He was very sweet to her. She had us over to their house, and he cooked for us ladies a nice Italian feast. They had their cottage up in Mercer, Wisconsin, and had a plan to move up there when he retired."

Maureen added, "We laughed so much at work. We had a great time together. We'd go out to lunch together. When we could, we'd go out to dinner together."

Kathy added, "You had to be a people person to do the job, and Milly was amazing. She could talk to anyone and make it into something fun with her way of joking around. It was probably the best time I ever had at work with those two, and we became lifelong friends. We talked about family a lot, and she had three kids that she talked about a lot. I was just getting married, and [Maureen] was dating her eventual husband."

Kathy and Maureen still recall a bit of sage advice Milly would dole out every so often. Kathy said, "Mil always had this funny expression: 'You're three times seven,' meaning you're 21 and an adult, and you should know better. Sometimes [her expression] still pops into my head, and I chuckle."

There was a spot a little west of their office for work lunches where the women loved to eat. "We enjoyed our lunches together at The Assembly in Hoffman Estates, where we indulged on Bionic Burgers," added Kathy.

Maureen Kowalski said, "Milly draws people in. She doesn't try to. She doesn't have to try. That's how she is. That's the best part of who she is. And she's just so appreciative. Like when we do talk now, it's like I was just with her a few days ago. We've been friends for over 35 years, and she is still so appreciative that I reach out to her. I just recently mailed her a bunch of family pictures of my girls because she doesn't get photos on her phone or do email. I called her after she got the pictures, and she was practically crying and said, 'Thank you so much for sending me the pictures. The girls look beautiful, and you and Kathy look great.' I try to stay in contact with her. That's a trait Milly helped me with, too. I'm the oldest of the group of women at my work now, and I've kind of become a 'Milly.' I have a friend at work who is almost twenty years younger than me, and she calls me 'mom.' She has red hair, and I have red hair, and we kind of clicked. She came to the office about seven years ago, and I became her 'Milly.' I love the fact that Milly, Kathy, and I are still connected. It's very heart-warming. She's a wonderful person, and they had a great marriage. She was lost when Harry passed. Kathy and I made it a point to go up to Wisconsin and visit her a lot. That was a five-hour drive, and I had a couple of little kids at home at the time, so it was not always easy to tell my husband, hey, Kathy and I are going to be gone for four or five days. You stay here with the kids." Maureen and Kathy have made countless trips to the north woods to see their friend Milly.

While working at Motorola in the 1980s, Milly Belluomini was called to jury duty. But this wasn't Cook County jury duty—the Feds came calling. Milly said, "I was on a grand jury at the Dirksen Federal Building for eighteen months. It was the mid-'80s, and I was working at Motorola again at that time. I said to [the court], 'Listen, I can't do this. I have a job.' They told me, 'That's too bad. You're going to be on a jury.' And Motorola had a policy in place that if any of their employees were called to be on a jury, that they'd do just that. I had to appear every Thursday. The chief judge at the Federal Building told me that the grand jury duty was more important than my work at Motorola."

Milly made the best of her situation and took a leadership role among her fellow jurors. She continued, "I ended up being the secretary for the grand jury. We were a diverse group of people, and we had to be there every Thursday, so we had to get along. And we did. But the type of people going in and out of that Federal Building were scary. And then Harry wound up taking the part-time US Marshal's Court Security Officer job there a few years later... That job Harry took was actually through a private company that managed the Court Security Officers, and it was out of Minneapolis. I never knew how or why the government would hire these outfits to manage a government building. Anyway, he got paid from that security company and not the Federal Government. That security company hired former police officers because they had some police powers. They knew how to handle weapons, and they could legally carry them at that time. So I was very uneasy when Harry took that job at the Federal Building."

While on Federal jury duty, Milly was confronted with a familiar face, someone Harry had worked with at the CPD. She said, "During one grand jury session, there were some Chicago policemen involved, and I knew one of them, so I had to excuse myself. I had to leave the jury room. And I couldn't tell Harry about any of that."

Milly and her co-jurors were doing such a great job, and the Feds wanted her to extend her stay. Milly said, "When my eighteen months

244 * MATT HADER

on the grand jury were up, the court asked us if we wanted to go another eighteen months. I told them no, that I had served enough time on the jury already. When I left, all of the jurors went to lunch at The Berghoff. The other jurors presented me with a wristwatch to thank me for my service and being the secretary for those eighteen months. I had to record everything, and there was a log I had to keep of all the people that came before the jury. Some of us became very good friends. We had to become a team because we had to be there once a week whether we liked it or not."

Soon after Harry Belluomini put in for his retirement from the Chicago Police Department, Milly did the same at Motorola. Maureen Kowalski said, "Our boss Neal Westenberger got Milly a limo to pick her up on her last day on the job. He and Milly had worked together for quite a few years before I got there. He just thought the world of her. The idea that someone thought that much of her to do that was just wonderful."

Milly was sent off in style. She said, "Oh, I loved my job. It was so much fun. I gave my notice, and they had a big party for me at Walter Payton's Studebaker's restaurant in Schaumburg. And again, they sent another limousine for me on that last day."

Milly added, "All the salespeople I worked with were there. Probably 50 or 60 people. It was a wonderful sendoff. It was unbelievable. We had a ball. We were dancing up a storm and just having fun."

Milly's not qualifying for her Motorola pension was a sharp financial blow, especially after Harry's death. But, of course, that defeat was tempered by her longtime friendships with Kathy Paddock and Maureen Gallagher Kowalski.

ACKNOWLEDGMENTS

THE AUTHOR would like to acknowledge the following individuals for their generosity of time and spirit and sincerity in providing vital information for this book. Thank you to Curt Blanc, Joe Vuich, Anne Vuich, Bill Broderick, Neena Pellegrini, Tom Minasola, Larry Coffey, Ed Wodnicki, Frank Radke, Tedy Nadile, George Ruckrich, Jack Lorre, Stan Golucki, Luis Alviso, Bob Mette, Brian DuFour, Ed Pyrcioch, Ken Berris, Maureen Kowalski, Kathy Paddock, Joe Greco, Joe Marchetti, Tammie Pena Arroyo, Betsy Weiss-VanDie, Dick Paul, Kevin Maher, Jim Dunning, Frances Cieslek, Will Seelye, Pat Dempsey, Scott Phillips, George Holmes, Tom Argenbright, Michael Simmi, Gary Feltman and family, Dennis Farina Jr., Sandy Shaughnessey, Saul Boscan, David Greising, Sarah Koz, Jay Amberg, John K. Manos, Timothy J. Hufman, Ralph Reporto, and to those who wished to remain unidentified. Finally, I want to extend my heartfelt thanks to the Belluomini family: Milly, Karen, Michael, Annie, and Harry. May your wonderfully giving nature and selflessness live on for generations to come.

MATT HADER'S circuitous route to becoming a professional writer followed an unlikely path through post-collegiate classes at The Second City, on-air shifts in Chicago-area radio station studios, and work as a 9-1-1 communications officer. Matt served for a time on the board of directors of the nonprofit American Screenwriters Association, and he's a current member of the International Association of Crime Writers (North American branch). He and his wife make their home in Brentwood, Tennessee.

Made in the USA
Monee, IL
30 June 2022

4ea214b8-0068-4d95-bd3e-4d63fbf55c98R01